SCARE TACTICS

Syracuse Studies on Peace and Conflict Resolution
Louis Kriesberg, *Series Editor*

MICHAEL P. COLARESI

SCARE TACTICS

THE POLITICS OF INTERNATIONAL RIVALRY

SYRACUSE UNIVERSITY PRESS

Library of Congress Cataloging-in-Publication Data

Colaresi, Michael.
Scare tactics : the politics of international rivalry / Michael P. Colaresi.
p. cm.—(Syracuse studies on peace and conflict resolution)
Includes bibliographical references and index.
ISBN 0–8156–3066–2 (alk. paper)
1. International relations. 2. Competition, International. 3. World politics—1989–
4. War. I. Title. II. Series.
JZ5595.C646 2005
327.1'01—dc22   2005020288

Manufactured in the United States of America

For Chandra Colaresi

Michael P. Colaresi is an assistant professor in the Political Science Department at Michigan State University.

Contents

Figures

Tables

Acknowledgments

MOST OF THE IDEAS in the book were conceived while at Indiana University. I would like to thank the Political Science Department for funding my graduate studies and for taking a chance on a kid straight out of a small rural undergraduate institution. Many other programs were not willing to run that risk. In Bloomington I accumulated large debts to graduate students and faculty alike. Specifically, I owe thanks to Raphael Reuveny, Michael McGinnis, and Karen Rasler for taking the time to read an early version of the manuscript and provide extensive criticisms. William R. Thompson was the most professional and effective advisor I can imagine. I consistently left each meeting more excited and more informed than I entered it. Whatever forward progress I have been able to maintain in my career began in these meetings and has been spurred on by our communications since.

A substantial amount of polishing and rewriting was done while I was at the Mershon Center at the Ohio State University in 2002 and Oxford University in 2003. At Columbus, Rick Herrmann, Brian Rathbun, Jacques Hymans, Brian Pollins, and Janet Box-Steffensmeier poked, prodded, and challenged each and every argument I made. In Oxford, Chris Wlezien, Geoff Evans, Ian McLean, Sean Carey, Mark Kayser, Luke Keele, Steve Fisher, Berthold Rittenberger, Natalia Letki, Emelie Hafner-Burton, and Richard Caplan showed me that a great deal of work can be done over a cup of tea. I would also like to thank Mark Philip for helping to make my time in Oxford productive.

The book's finishing touches were applied while I was at my first tenure track job in East Lansing, Michigan. The faculty in the Department of Political Science at Michigan State University has been a model of why departments are important units for developing sound arguments. I continue to benefit from the structured and unstructured opportunities to bounce ideas off other faculty. Between moves, the manuscript benefited from my discussions at conferences and invited talks with Norrin Ripsman, Harvey Starr, James Lee Ray, Katherine Barbieri, John Vasquez, Paul Diehl, Charles Kegley, Donald Puchala, Christopher Kam, Steve Saideman, T. V. Paul, Mark Brawly, and Douglas Gibler. I would also like to thank Michael O'Connor and Mary Selden Evans at Syracuse University Press for believing in the project and seeing it through to publication.

This book has taken shape at four universities spread over two continents. There were only two constants through out this process: my wife, Chandra Colaresi, who has been an unwavering source of support and inspiration, and me, to whom all mistakes herein are directly attributable.

Introduction

Sheep, Snow, and Bear Diplomacy

INTERNATIONAL CONFLICT can emerge from seemingly benign situations. In 1955, some 480 sheep straying into Jordan from Israel led Israeli defense minister Moshe Dayan to call for immediate military action against Jordan (Burns 1969, 41–44). The Soviet Union and China, previously allies, intermittently volleyed heavy artillery at each other to capture uninhabited snowdrifts in Manchuria for several months in 1969 (Chang 1990, 277; Tyler 2000, 48–60). In 1962, when a bear climbed a fence at a military installation in the United States, the world's preeminent superpower prepared nuclear-armed jets for launch (Sagan 1993, 3–4, 92–102).

Incidents like these bring to mind Keystone Kop routines. But unlike the humorous silent movies, international crises involve thunderous fighting and real casualties. How are we to understand the causes and consequences of international conflict? Under what circumstances would governments use multimillion-dollar military equipment to retrieve sheep, cordon off snow, or prepare a nuclear attack in response to a climbing bear? International wars and conflicts take many unfortunate shapes and sizes, but few are as bizarre or, at first glance, irrational as the crisis situations that emerge between states that identify each other as enemies. However, there is an identifiable method even in this deadly madness.

Such rivalry interactions only become comprehensible when placed in the context of enduring competition. For example, Israel and Jordan, China and the USSR, and the United States and the USSR each had many good reasons to feel threatened by the other side. Just before the Bo-Peep crisis, Israel was plagued by a series of border incursions from Jordan. The USSR and China were competing for control of the world communist movement, not just snow. Most dramatic, the bear alert occurred during the Cuban missile crisis, a time during which some researchers have hypothesized that the world was as close to nuclear war as it has ever been (Allison and Zelikow 1999).

Because of the bizarre nature of the immediate crisis triggers, it may be tempting to write off these events as errors or peculiarities. Yet sheep, snow, and bear diplomacy is a part of a rivalry process that produces an enormous proportion of international drama, death, and destruction. The disputes between Israel and its neighbors produced four wars in twenty-five years. India and Pakistan have fought three wars in just over fifty years and have come to the brink of war on many other occasions. The United States and the Soviet Union avoided outright war with each other during the cold war but fueled a succession of regional and global crises from the Berlin blockade to conflicts in Korea, Vietnam, Somalia, Angola, and Afghanistan. Today, rivalries involving Syria and Israel, Turkey and Greece, Taiwan and China, North and South Korea, and India and Pakistan, among others, continue to rage under the surface of contemporary world politics.

As I will argue in this book, there is a distinct constellation of domestic and international pressures that ignites rivalry crises. Much of this drama results from seemingly routine and nonthreatening events that in the context of continued international competition rationalize military action. For better or worse, international crises do not occur randomly.

It may also be tempting to explain these dangerous hotspots as overt manifestations of enduring hatred. To refer to a region as a "hotspot" suggests some constant source of friction. However, serial international conflicts are not unswerving or unbending contests of attrition. On the contrary, even the most virulent relations are punctuated with periods of peace and cooperation. For example, although Egyptian leaders had compared Israel to a disease in public speeches (Sachar 1981), a process of accommodation between the adversaries commenced in 1974 and led to a peace treaty in 1979. Politicians in Washington were comparing Mao to Hitler in the 1960s, but in the 1970s, Nixon opened the door to rapprochement with China (Chang 1990, 217–223, 229). By 1991, a representative of the Soviet Union's "evil empire" was being hailed as a "man of peace" (Lebow and Stein 1995). Any attempt to explain surprising situations that result in war must also tackle the equally unexpected overtures of peace.

A Dynamic Two-Level Solution

We are left with a multifaceted puzzle. Previous explanations of international conflict offer unsatisfactory guidance in charting these undulating rivalry courses. While we know that states often answer conflict with conflict and cooperation with cooperation, a process known as reciprocity, most interesting international events are deviations from this pattern. Wars, peace agreements, and threats all originate somewhere. Likewise, other theories deal in general terms that do a fine job of explaining cross-sectional differences between states but do a much poorer job of predicting deviations across time. For example, some researchers suggest that democracies will be less likely to start wars (Russett 1993) and more likely to offer international cooperation (Leeds 1999). Although this research may explain distinct patterns of relations between pairs of states involving democracies or autocracies, it cannot explain the changes in one democracy's (or nondemocracy's) policies. Further, the international record is filled with about-faces and new initiatives from democracies and nondemocracies alike. We are still left to guess the timing of foreign policy changes.

In this book, I introduce the concept of dynamic two-level pressures to explain the violent ebbs and flows of international conflict between enemies. By identifying the domestic and international pressures of rivalry politics, we can predict when even mundane events like sheep straying across a border may boil over into international war. Equally, the ideas in the book help to forecast the political factors that can cool off even the hottest of relations.

The argument is dynamic in the sense that past interactions lead decision makers to form expectations about the future costs and benefits of a conflict. When future costs are expected to be low because resources are relatively unstrained and new external threats are not emerging, a change in rivalry behavior is not expected, ceteris paribus. On the other hand, if the future looks bleak because economic growth is stunted by international conflict and external threats are rising, a state is likely to attempt to alter its rivalry situation. This change can happen in one of two ways, either by de-escalating the conflict and lessening the strain of international competition, or by shifting the grounds of competition by escalating the conflict and altering future cost-benefit calculations.

However, international expectations alone are not enough to predict the direction of policy change. Will leaders choose to escalate or de-escalate their rivalries to avoid a deteriorating status quo? To answer this question, we need to trace the interaction between domestic and international factors. Specifically, under situations of external threat, elites[1] can use international pressures to centralize power, playing toward the need for domestic strength and stability. In fact, as Snyder (1991) notes, elites use information monopolies between themselves and other relevant members of the population to inflate the external threat a state faces and to accelerate the pace of centralization. Threat inflation, if successful, creates a domestic environment of distrust and hostility toward the external adversary. This process makes de-escalation less likely, while simultaneously increasing the probability of escalation. A leader who attempts to de-escalate a rivalry when the domestic audience is mobilized against cooperation faces possible replacement and a loss of political prestige. Therefore, de-escalation may be unlikely even if rivalry costs are high owing to domestic variables.

At the international level, the likely response from a rival is also an important predictor of de-escalation/escalation. If a rival state reneges on an agreement, continued de-escalation becomes less likely, even when continuing the conflict is prohibitively costly. Similarly, an opportunity for escalation that includes having a favorable military capability balance makes escalation more attractive. Therefore, dynamic two-level pressures are high when the future looks bleak and backing down is unattractive. It is specifically under these conditions that bizarre patterns of conflict, death, and destruction emerge.

The Plan of the Book

In the following chapters I explore previous work on international conflict and conjoin various theories into the dynamic two-level explanation of rivalry escalation and de-escalation. After presenting several hypotheses on when rivalries are likely to run hot and cold, I analyze the predictions within case studies of three international rivalries, Somalia-Ethiopia,

---

1. I use the term "elite" to refer to both the national leadership and potential challengers.

Egypt-Israel, and United States–China. Each case breaks down the rivalries into phases of maintenance, escalation, and de-escalation, although not always in that order. The expected costs during each phase are explored as well as their interaction with information asymmetries, elite outbidding[2] for conflict, and the perceptions of the rivals' intentions. Then I test the dynamic two-level pressure theory using a large database of interactions representing fifty-six rivalries. In the final chapter, I discuss the importance of the model and several potential extensions.

2. Outbidding refers to the process whereby elites attempt to convince the public that they are hawkish and their political opponents are dangerously dovish.

SCARE TACTICS

1 Pieces of the Puzzle
Theories of Rivalry Politics

THE STUDY OF WAR AND PEACE has a long pedigree. In this century alone, thousands of scholarly books and articles have attempted to explain the underlying causes of conflict and cooperation in the international realm. Why do some nations fight, while others ally or ignore each other? Definitive answers have proven elusive. A recent review and replication of the literature on war and peace found that surprisingly few answers remained consistent with the historical record (Bennett and Stam 2003). One prominent historian has seized upon the surprising end of the cold war as a failure and indictment of international relations theory (Gaddis 1998). Although much of this criticism is misplaced, it remains true that a reliable model of international escalation and cooperation has not yet been formulated.

Recent research has suggested that we need to rephrase the war-peace question. Instead of looking at international relations as distinct and separable pixels of history, we should focus on the way those pixels align to form a picture. For example, Thompson (1995) has defined a rivalry as a pair of states that view each other as threats and enemies. Many rivalries involve serial conflicts that breed the expectation of future conflict (Vasquez 1993). However, rivalries are only visible when relationships between states are not parsed into separate independent interactions. Rivalry is a process, not an event. Treating international relations as a stream of evolving interactions allows a researcher to ask questions concerning conflict momentum, threat perception, and other dynamic processes that are assumed away when interactions are cross-sectionally isolated.

Rivalry analysis challenges most traditional thinking in international relations. As Goertz and Diehl (1993) and Thompson (1995) note, past research has treated international events as if they were interchangeable. A crisis between Canada and the United States could be treated as functionally identical to a crisis between the United States and China. However, empirical and theoretical findings point to the importance of international dynamics such as momentum and expectations. First, researchers have found that a few states have been responsible for a majority of the militarized disputes over the past two centuries (Goertz and Diehl 1993; Vasquez 1996). More sophisticated methods and research designs show that the probability of international crisis and war increases with the past number of disputes between states (Colaresi and Thompson 2002). Thus, some pairs of states find themselves involved in serial crises. More specifically, apart from the mere presence or absence of previous disputes, the outcomes of past crises affect the behavior of states in future crises (Maoz 1984; Hensel 1994; Colaresi and Thompson 2000).[1]

Theoretically, both social-psychological and rational-choice explanations have come to appreciate the important role past interaction plays in conflict behavior. Jervis (1976) suggests past interactions guide decision makers' expectations about future actions and intentions. In many cases, these expectations can lead to self-fulfilling prophecies, where expectations of violence rationalize more conflictual policies, which in turn trigger a reciprocal spiral (Lebow 1981). From a formal modeling perspective, Kydd (1997) notes that expectations concerning the preferences and motivations of a rival are important predictors of violence. Therefore, perceptions of the "type of player" involved in a game, even if objectively false, can influence international behaviors. Although not directly related to international relations, Peyton Young (1998) goes further by specifying a general model of expectations that directly relies on past interactions. Just as a soccer coach looks at the past form of each player to judge what lineup to field, rivalry analysis suggests that past interactions between states will influence contemporary international relations.

---

1. Diehl and Goertz (2000), Thompson (1995), and Vasquez (1993) identify the analytical gains in studying conflict from a rivalry perspective. Although the rivalry literature has been split between strategic and enduring rivalry measurements, these three works share a focus on dynamics and process. For a summary of measurement issues see Thompson (2001).

Reaching Beyond the On-Off Switch

Most research on interstate rivalry has analyzed the processes of initiation and termination (see Goertz and Diehl 1995; Bennett 1997, 1998; Colaresi 2000). For instance, Goertz and Diehl (1995) argue that international shocks, in the form of wars or territorial shifts, are necessary conditions to both begin and end rivalries. Bennett (1998) uses a bargaining model to explain why external threat and security concerns, along with democracy, lead to rivalry terminations. Although the politics of rivalry initiation and termination are important theoretical constructs, other fundamental problems have remained relatively unexamined.

Rivalry is almost always treated as a dichotomous variable. It is turned on (initiated) and then at some point turned off (terminated). This explanation, of course, fails to incorporate the great variation in rivalry interaction over the course of the relationship. For example, few would doubt that relations between the United States and the Soviet Union were more bellicose in the late 1950s as compared to the late 1960s, or that periodic détentes were struck between Ecuador and Peru during their century-and-a-half dispute. The same can be said of such hot spots as India-Pakistan and Egypt-Israel. Conflict propensity within a rivalry is not static.

However, Azar and Sloan (1975) and McGinnis and Williams (2001) each posit that a rivalry has a baseline level of interaction that represents a stable proportion of cooperation and conflict. While there are deviations from this baseline rivalry level (BRL), they are usually temporary because other domestic factors (McGinnis and Williams 2001) refract higher or lower levels of hostility/cooperation back toward the normal interaction level. From this perspective, variance in rivalry behavior is either random or inconsequential.

Similarly, a host of studies suggest that a majority of international state behavior can best be explained by the actions directed toward it by other states (Ward 1982; Goldstein and Freeman 1990; Leng 1984). If a state receives hostile messages from other countries, it will answer in kind. Similarly, cooperative international initiatives are likely to be met with equal cooperation. This reciprocity norm in international relations can potentially converge to a BRL, as two states repeatedly echoing each other's actions would create a conflict equilibrium.

There are two problems with relying solely on a tit-for-tat or BRL explanation of rivalry behavior. The conflict level within a rivalry is neither a flat line nor is it dyadically symmetrical, as these two theories suggest. There are times when states deviate temporarily from their BRL and reciprocity, for example in an abortive attempt to de-escalate a rivalry, but there are also cases when states shift to a new equilibrium. While Ecuador and Peru continued to compete for territory in the Amazon after 1942, the level of tensions was much lower after the signing of the Protocol at Rio de Janeiro. Alternatively, the hostility level between the United States and the Soviet Union rose in the early 1950s, only to fall in the mid 1960s and then rise again in the late 1970s and early 1980s. Linear interpretations of rivalry behavior smooth over these important deviations.

Analogously, these deviations from the BRL and reciprocity are not always dyadically symmetrical. Both states involved in a rivalry do not de-escalate/escalate at the same time or with the same intensity. Ward (1982) finds that the Soviet Union reacted twice as strongly to U.S. conflict behavior as the United States did to Soviet conflict behavior, and that Israeli responses to United Arab Republic (UAR) competition were also more escalatory than the UAR response. Variance in hostility levels occurs across time as well as cross-sectionally between the two states involved in rivalry. Merely averaging the two states' scores together over the lifetime of the rivalry into a BRL misses who is escalating or de-escalating and why.

For the most part, there is scant research on escalation and de-escalation processes within rivalry settings.[2] Although higher conflict propensities are almost always relied upon to underscore the importance of rivalry research (Goertz and Diehl 1993; Colaresi 2000; Thompson 1995; Vasquez 1996; Bennett 1998), the reasons for this escalatory potential are rarely systematically analyzed. Instead, theorists have assumed that rivalries produce more conflict because of embedded enemy images (Herrmann and Fischerkeller 1995), a zero-sum outlook on issues (Vasquez 1993), or a combination of the two that leads to conflict spirals (Rubin, Pruitt, and Kim 1994). In these spiral models, past conflict between rivals breeds mistrust and insecurity, which in turn leads to more competition, conflict, and, ultimately, war.

---

2. Colaresi and Thompson (2003), Diehl and Goertz (2000), and Maoz and Mor (2002) are exceptions.

In studies that do analyze the dynamics of conflict within rivalries over time, the spiral model's predictions have not been supported. Diehl and Goertz (2000) derive a volcano model from the assumption that states build enemy images of each other that then lead to more conflictual relationships. Yet their empirical evidence does not lend support to that interpretation. Instead, rivalries tend to follow a much more diverse pattern, if there is a pattern at all. Colaresi (2001), using event data, finds that rivalries evince a polytonic trend, whereby conflict rises during the early stages of rivalry and then descends after twenty to thirty years. This interpretation fits with research by Cioffi-Revilla (1998) that also finds rivalries have nonlinear dynamics. Conflict in rivalry is neither constant nor can it be described by a constant factor, as would be produced by increasing enemy images.

This evidence does not suggest that psychological processes are irrelevant to escalation propensities. Colaresi and Thompson (2000) have found that being involved in a rivalry makes conflict situations much more prone to war and violent conflict, even when controlling for myriad material- and system-specific variables. Given the same objective stimuli, a subjective rivalry frame increases the potential for escalation. Further case study evidence from specific rivalries has uncovered an important role for enemy images in conflict escalation (Elbedour and Bastien 1997; Lebow 1981; Jervis, Lebow, and Gross Stein 1985).

In addition, the spiral model does not exhaust the social-psychological processes that can perpetuate conflict. As Jervis (1976) cogently argued, all people, including elites, suffer from misperceptions. One potentially important perceptual bias is cognitive dissonance, whereby the goals perpetuating rivalries become increasingly important as the rivalry endures (Festinger 1957). Rather than critically evaluating the pros and cons of military conflict and then adjusting behavior, leaders may adjust their values to match past behavior. Similarly, Brockner and Rubin (1985) argue that leaders become entrapped by sunk costs. Despite the fact that military dollars and lives have already been spent, regardless of future choices, executives feel increasing pressure to avoid turning back and "wasting" the resources.

However, the psychological drift of cognitive dissonance and entrapment can potentially be refracted toward the ends of de-escalation. Once a cooperative gesture is made, the issue under contention may be devalued to justify the action. Similarly, once a leader has expended resources and political capital attempting to end a conflict, these pacific sunk costs may propel future de-escalation. Because of these multidirectional predictions, social-psychological variables have been shown to work more effectively in tandem with other political and organizational theories (Kriesberg 1992; 1998, 153, 182–85, 339).

Past Research

Past research gives some partial clues to what drives escalation and de-escalation in rivalry situations. However, most previous work fails to leverage theoretically both domestic and international factors into a multilevel model of conflict escalation. A portion of the research on initiation and termination can be applied within rivalry as well. Goertz and Diehl (1995) and Diehl and Goertz (2000) suggest a punctuated equilibrium model of rivalry initiation and termination, whereby two competing states quickly rise to a high level of conflict after a shock. This competition is then constant for a long period of time, until another shock decreases the conflict level. While the theory suggests that conflict within rivalries is constant, as applied to escalation it leads to the possibility that events exogenous to the interstate rivalry are driving the level of threat between states. Thus, Diehl and Goertz suggest that territorial changes, world wars, civil wars, and regime changes each can alter the behavior of rival dyads.

One limitation of the punctuated equilibrium model is that it does not specify the intensity or direction of the shocks/punctuation process. Regime changes or other shocks can either raise or lower the level of conflict between states, presumably depending on other factors. The theory is indeterminate, since a world war can either escalate or de-escalate tensions within a rivalry. For example, the end of World War II eventually led to a de-escalation of tensions between Germany and France but an escalation of tensions between the United States and Russia.

Another problem is that the punctuated equilibrium model conflates domestic and international causes of rivalry change without specifying an interaction between the levels. To Diehl and Goertz (2000) and Goertz and Diehl (1995), both civil wars and regime changes can alter international behavior in the same way as world wars or territorial changes. But it is also probable that rivalries involve multilevel processes, whereby international events alter the importance of domestic concepts, and vice versa. For instance, civil war can make territorial changes more likely, and the combination of both may lead to more escalation given a diffusion of violence and insecurity (Lake and Rothchild 1998). More directly, the exigency of a civil war may knock a state out of an international rivalry, as in Afghanistan, until the domestic violence subsides. Instead of lumping domestic and international factors into a large catchall category like "shocks," a process model (Bremer 1993) that highlights the interactive effects might be helpful. To summarize, more theory is needed to draw directional hypotheses concerning rivalry escalation and de-escalation from punctuated equilibrium models.

One theory that links international behaviors and domestic politics in a tight theoretical framework, is Snyder's logrolling and coalition-building theory of over-expansion (1991). Snyder hypothesizes that cartelized political systems, where elites support each other's policies with little incentive to account for diffuse domestic costs, leads to bellicose and threatening foreign policies. Eventually, these policies lead to "over-expansion." The aggressive state keeps acquiring more weapons and territory than it needs, provoking an encircling coalition of other states bent on stopping them. He uses Japan and Germany during the previous century as exemplars of this process.

Snyder lays out a clear domestic theoretical logic for escalation. States escalate conflicts because of domestic pressures from elites who seek to benefit from conquest and conflict. For instance, manufacturing and agricultural industries could both use an aggressive foreign policy to generate more sales and more demand in Germany prior to World War I. The key to Snyder's theory is the type of institutional constraints placed on elites. In states where elites share power among themselves without accountability to a central dictator or to the masses, logrolling toward aggression is likely. Democratic states, because of their inclusion of the masses in the decision-making process, are able to avoid many (although not all) of these pitfalls.

While the focus on domestic politics is helpful, one major problem with Snyder's argument is the absence of any international concepts.[3] In his theory, domestic politics drive escalation and over-expansionist policies for the aggressive state. Yet he explains that encircling coalitions were

---

3. I am talking specifically about independent variables.

triggered by the threat from these over-expanding nations. Thus, international threat can have an effect on some states; for instance, England was threatened by German naval build-ups prior to World War I, but the German decision to build was domestic in focus, according to Snyder. Unfortunately, this argument leaves out the international context from a discussion of escalation. Why do some states react to the international environment, while others endogenously derive foreign policy goals?

In short, the outside world is missing in Snyder's theory.[4] An international disagreement on colonial borders, as was present between Germany and other states, brings with it a threat of international conflict. Under these external circumstances, domestic hard-liners are more likely to gain power because arguments underlining the need for strength will have more credibility than if no threat was present. Snyder's theory that elites can manipulate and amplify perceptions of an international enemy and threat is well taken, but it is also probable that elites will have a hard time creating threats out of thin air. Instead, they can use existing international rivalries and threats to their own benefit. However, those threats would already have to exist (at least in latent form),[5] and further, the more acute the threat, the more material with which elites have to mobilize. Interestingly, Snyder (1989) argues something similar in relation to the Soviet-U.S. rivalry.

Domestic-centric theories ignore the process by which international threats facilitate the centralization of power by elites (Colaresi and Thompson 2001) and direct policy toward their own benefit. Each state Snyder uses to illustrate his argument was involved in a long-standing international rivalry with at least one member of the resulting encircling coalition.[6] Thus, there was already an international threat present to set off the elite expansionist chain reaction.[7]

Another domestic-level theory that may be particularly applicable to rivalries is the diversionary hypothesis. In its simplest rendering, diversionary theory states that leaders may attempt to start an international conflict to redirect attention from domestic problems. These domestic eco-

---

4. Snyder (1991) does allow for marginal international processes.

5. For a discussion of threat perception, see chapter 3.

6. This calculation utilizes Thompson's (2001) dataset of rivalries.

7. It should be noted that the Germany–Great Britain rivalry was late to start owing to French-British antipathy.

nomic problems, such as unemployment and lack of economic growth, or political problems, such as protests or low public support, can make international escalation more enticing to leaders (Simmel 1955; Levy 1989). In times of international crisis, internal cohesion increases and support for the government is hypothesized to expand, as the "rally-'round-the-flag" effect operates (Mueller 1973). Likewise, rivalries may be more likely to escalate conflict when leaders feel domestic pressure, and so they divert attention toward external enemies.

A number of important questions have been raised concerning the extent to which diversion occurs. First, empirical research has been inconsistent on the subject. While some studies have found important links between domestic upheaval and international escalation, others question this result (Levy 1989). Second, Bennett and Nordstrom (2000) point out that, like Diehl and Goertz's shock theory, diversionary theory is underspecified. Leaders may attempt to divert attention to domestic problems through international conflict, or alternatively, leaders could attempt to de-escalate an international threat to devote more resource to domestic programs, which may facilitate support at home. How capabilities (Bennett and Nordstrom 2000) and regime types (Gelpi 1997) interact with diversionary incentives also needs to be explored in greater depth.

A final limitation deals with the target of diversion. In the context of interstate rivalries, diversion seems like an attractive course. If a leader is suffering domestic trouble, the benefits of diversion are directly related to the intensity of the rally effect. In some rivalries, where the public is intensely mobilized against an enemy, this rally effect will be much stronger than a situation where the populace has little enmity toward a putative adversary. The rally effect should be quite different in Pakistan toward India than it would be in Pakistan toward Turkey. Yet without accounting for the international environment and interstate relations, as well as public opinion, the existence of a likely target remains vague. Again, more information from the international environment (a possible target) is needed in order to specify the probability of diversion.

Although the previous theories give priority to domestic factors in explaining escalation, recent research on great power conflict has suggested that international factors are the most important drivers of bellicosity. Copeland suggests that fear of a future unfavorable capability shift leads to escalation. Expectations about the future of a state's international relations can induce risky behavior and preventative war in order to avoid a more costly war in the future. For example, there is evidence that World War I was caused by Germany's fear of a rising Russian threat (Copeland 2000).[8]

The most appealing part of Copeland's theory is the emphasis placed on expectations. Numerous historians have noted that decision makers project trends into the future. Lebow (1981) argues that expectations about the inevitability of war are a strong predictor of escalation in brinkmanship crises. If a state (or both states) views war as highly probable, the question becomes not if but when, and under these tense circumstances Lebow theorizes that war becomes a "self-fulfilling prophecy" (254).

A weakness of Copeland's theory is the lack of any space for domestic politics. Different decision makers within the same country often have very different expectations regarding the future. For instance, from 1871 until at least 1898 two cadres fought for control of French foreign policy. The first was continentalist in focus and expected Germany to be the greatest threat in the future. The second group was colonialist in orientation and saw British hegemony as the true threat to future French conquests. In post–World War II Egypt, the Wafd party identified Britain as the principal rival, while King Farouk and his advisors in the palace singled out Israel. Similarly, in China, Lin Biao and Mao disagreed over whether the United States or the Soviet Union was a greater threat to China in the late 1960s and early 1970s. The policy chosen by each rival was directly influenced by these diverse expectations and viewpoints (see Lebow 1981, 72–73).

Further, if we are to take logrolling and coalition-building processes seriously, it is through domestic politics that the leaders whose expectations will count are selected. Snyder (1991) notes that different institutional structures select different types of elites, with presumably different types of expectations. In addition, a leader will be more likely to construct expectations about the long-term future of a state and to act on these expectations if the leader could be in power to suffer the consequences of inaction and reap the possible rewards of preventative action. Therefore, the tenure of leadership and the electoral horizons, set domestically, are also likely to influence the type of expectations on which Copeland relies. While diver-

8. See also Doran (2000) for an analysis of how changes in expectations can increase the probability of war.

sionary theory and Snyder's over-expansion explanation ignore important international variables, Copeland's expectations argument supplies no understanding of the domestic sources and selection of elite expectations. Other theories that rely solely on a balance of capabilities or threat are subject to similar criticisms.[9]

There are also two extant theories that deal explicitly with de-escalation that are of note. First, Hensel, Goertz, and Diehl (2000) suggest that democratic states are less likely to become involved in repeated international conflict, drawing on the democratic peace literature (Chan 1997; Russett and Starr 2000). They note that a democratic dyad should be able to de-escalate tensions before overt conflict breaks out because of: (1) norms of peaceful conflict resolution (Dixon 1994); (2) the greater audience costs that democratic leaders face (Fearon 1994); and (3) an in-group feeling that encompasses democracies (Hermann and Kegley 1995).

Democratic institutions allow for debate and disagreement without recourse to violence. Over time leaders learn the value of peaceful conflict management. If those norms are transferred to the international level, de-escalation between states may be less risky because violent outbursts are less likely. For example, Schweller (1992) finds that democracies have never launched a preventative war. Also, the ability of voters to cast elites out of office for ineffective international policies injects an institutional check on risky foreign policy (Fearon 1994). Leaders in democracies are not prone to bluffing, and this allows democracies more credibly to threaten their potential adversaries into backing down. Finally, Hensel, Goertz, and Diehl (2000) note that democracies may view each other as an "in-group," sharing the same values and beliefs about the world. These similarities can also facilitate de-escalation, as overt military conflict may be deemed fratricide (Weart 1998).

While democracy has been shown to be a pacifying force in international relations (Chan 1997; Russett and Starr 2000), Box-Steffensmeier and Zorn (2000) find that the pacifying effect of democracy declines as the number of past conflicts between states increases. And in times of strong external threat, when escalation is most likely, democratic institutions can be retracted through the postponement of elections, centralization of

---

9. Baldwin (1993) and Keohane (1986) summarize the debate concerning theories that rely on international concepts.

power, and the media, and outlawing of opposition parties. Democracy may not be a stable catalyst for de-escalation if its concomitant institutions hibernate when peace is in jeopardy. This democratic decline is much stronger in new democracies as opposed to those that are consolidated (Colaresi and Thompson 2001). A simple rendering of the democratic peace fails to look at dynamics over time, both in repeated conflict and also in how states become democratic. A more satisfying theory of de-escalation must account for how states are able to stay democratic in the face of large external threats, as well the dynamic relationship between escalation, threat, and democratization (Thompson and Tucker 1998; Mansfield and Snyder 1995).

Rock (1989) offers an extension of liberal arguments, such as the democratic peace, to the process of de-escalation between states that have a history of enmity. He hypothesizes that states having similar regime types and cultural heritages avoid economic and political competition and are most likely to de-escalate their rivalries. Having similar regime types and cultures increases the perceived costs of escalation and thus increases the relative attractiveness of de-escalation. Also, a lack of economic and political competition eradicates the reasons underlying the conflict. But even when these de-escalatory factors are in place, Rock stresses that a catalyst is needed to change leaders' perceptions of the situation. He relies on Lebow's (1981) notion of crises as times of crucial learning to provide just such a catalyst for his theory, noting that international crises allow states to divine the intentions and capabilities of their adversaries more clearly than do periods of relative peace. There are also similarities between Goertz and Diehl's idea of shocks and Rock's and Lebow's use of crises as catalysts. In both cases only dramatic events cause leaders to reevaluate their position in a rivalry. When a shock/crisis occurs, there is a chance for policy change as old stereotypes are challenged, myths of security are disproved, and the costs of future conflict are apparent.[10]

Of course, as Goertz and Diehl (1995) point out, all crises do not lead to de-escalation. In fact even the United States and Britain, while scoring quite high on Rock's qualifications for peace during the middle to late nineteenth century, had to endure numerous crises, from the Alabama

---

10. On the other hand, crises can also reinforce stereotypes, security myths, and previously held expectations.

claims controversy to the northern fisheries disputes, before the Venezuela border crisis catalyzed peace talks.[11] Rock notes that the "danger of war" pushed the United Kingdom and the United States toward peace (1989, 26). However, there was a danger of war previously, for instance surrounding the Maine border issues, which did not lead to peace. Theoretically, it seems the "danger of war" can lead either to escalation or to de-escalation. As noted previously, if war is expected in the near future, one response is to launch a preventative war (Copeland 2000), another is to capitulate and lower tensions to change those expectations.

Rock provides some guidance as to which fork in the road a state may take, based on the importance of issues and the cultural similarities between the states. Yet a few pieces still seem to be missing from the theory. The idea that states simply learn to make peace from a crisis situation contradicts a substantial amount of literature on learning and international relations. In his analyses of repeated conflict, Leng (1983 and 2000) finds that it is much easier for states to learn more coercive lessons, as opposed to peaceful lessons. He concludes that states get trapped in an escalatory cycle of crisis brinkmanship because leaders continue to use more coercive strategies, even in the face of high costs and previous policy failure. Similarly, Tetlock (1998) uses a study of international experts to understand how people evaluate past decisions. Instead of admitting failure, people use various defense mechanisms such as denial to avoid having to learn from their mistakes.[12] Empirical research has found that past international crises make future violent conflicts more likely (Colaresi and Thompson 2002). Of course, some states do learn peace, as Rock notes. France and Britain in the early twentieth century de-escalated their rivalry after the Fashoda crisis, and the relations between the United States and Britain became more cordial after the Venezuela border crisis. Despite this example, and in light of the previous works, learning peace does not seem to be so simple a process, and may be the exception rather than the rule.

Also, Rock's theory suggests that states will make peace when the issues under contention become less important, but frequently conflicts take on a life of their own, apart from the objective issues at stake. Even

---

11. For more information on these disputes, see Rock (1989).

12. Janis (1982) presents a theory of inhibited learning at the group level that would lead to similar results.

when states fail to compete for the same markets, issues of little material value remain flash points for conflict. For example, Israel and Jordan can fight over sheep; Greece and Turkey can compete over rocks in the Aegean; the Senkaku/Diaoyu Island dispute can remain a bone of contention between China and Japan; and the Aksai Shin, a tract of uninhabitable borderland, can bring India and China into conflict. Within a rivalry setting, issues are placed in a politically charged atmosphere that may trump objective issue value judgments (Vasquez 1993). In these cases, a choice to de-escalate a rivalry is likely to be seen as weakness or capitulation.

In addition, while Rock suggests cultural similarities make de-escalation more likely, culture is a multifaceted term with many meanings, even for those people ascribing to a particular culture (Esman 1994). When do states accentuate race over language, or a common experience over ideology? Koreans share many cultural traits but find themselves divided, as did the Vietnamese, Germans, and Chinese in the past. Further, empirical studies have found that conflict is more likely within cultural groups than between groups (Ross 1993; Russett, Oneal, and Cox 2000; Huntington 2000). Instead of looking at objective cultural traditions to predict de-escalation, it may be more fruitful to look at the way elites can use culture and history to gain support for their political causes. Instrumentalists in the ethnic conflict literature note that leaders can use whichever cultural dimensions they choose to mobilize public support (Horowitz 1985). In some cases it may be religion, in others language, and in still others common historical experiences. Therefore, while objective ethnic and genetic ties may remain constant throughout a rivalry, elite politics may better explain the variation in rivalry competition. Since Rock does not emphasize domestic processes, except to compare similarities internationally, elite bargaining and incentives are absent from the analysis.

Conclusion

Most theories that aim to explain the variation in rivalry behavior are indeterminate because they cannot predict whether escalation or de-escalation will occur. Shocks and crises can lead to either contingency, and whereas cultural similarity and low salience issues make de-escalation more likely, many cases do not fit this pattern. Further, when there is an expectation of future conflict and a fear of a future incapacitating capability shift (Copeland 2000), a preemptive war may be the result. As an alternative, it is possible that a state will de-escalate a rivalry to avoid conflict with a growing adversary. The case of the British decision to de-escalate its rivalry with a growing United States is a commonly cited example. More important, these theories rarely take advantage of the interaction between domestic and international politics. As Putnam (1988) and Tsebelis (1991) have noted, different domestic situations can change the substance of international relationships. Adding domestic politics to international models, and vice versa, may help to alleviate some of the ambiguity in existing theoretical predictions.

Of course there are many persuasive arguments present in previous research. Snyder's (1991) emphasis on elite motivations for escalation helps to specify some of the needed international and domestic linkages. In addition, Copeland's (2000) dynamic perspective reminds us that leaders not only look at the present costs and benefits of certain actions, but also make projections about the future. The "shadow of the future" is especially salient in a rivalry context because a history of past conflict may lead to an expectation of future confrontations. Although Canada and the United States may not be preparing for future border clashes, India and Pakistan and North and South Korea can not afford to ignore the possibility of future military conflict. In the next chapter, I attempt to use the complementary strengths from these conventional theories to forge a more convincing model of rivalry politics.

2 Building Pressure

Dynamic Two-Level Pressures and Rivalry Politics

IN THIS CHAPTER I synthesize several previous theories of international conflict into an explanation of rivalry conflict and cooperation. My dynamic two-level pressure theory interweaves international threat, future expectations, and domestic politics into predictions of rivalry patterns over time. Following Copeland (2000), I expect leaders to undertake a cost-benefit analysis of future rivalry. They should calculate the probable outcomes of escalation, de-escalation, and inaction, taking into account both the international and domestic context. If inaction is untenable because of high development costs (Colaresi and Thompson 2001) or a rising threat (see Copeland 2000), some change in behavior is likely.

As I have noted in chapter 1, most conventional explanations of rivalry interaction are unable to differentiate between predictions of escalation and de-escalation. A leader can divert attention from a troubling economy by either escalating a dispute or enjoying a possible rally-'round-the-flag effect or can de-escalate a dispute to free up resources to promote domestic development. As an alternative, a leader facing a rising challenger can either launch a preventative war, as Copeland suggests, or de-escalate the conflict through accommodation or compromise.

In order to make directional predictions, I look also at a second decision-making level, where leaders are nested within a competitive domestic political environment. The attractiveness of escalation and maintenance versus de-escalation [1] is directly related to the job security of the elites mak-

---

1. When I discuss de-escalation I refer to a unilateral decision to bargain, negotiate, or compromise with a rival. It does not necessitate a bilateral exchange of good will or cessation of threats. Although this result is possible, and the behavior of the rival has an

ing the decisions, and to what extent their continued tenure involves an external threat. If those who can depose a leader view their international rival as an aggressive state that needs to be dealt with strongly, de-escalation may not be feasible. First, détente may be taken as a signal of weakness in the regime. There are numerous instances of leaders being called traitors and deposed from power because of conciliatory gestures that were made toward an enemy of the state (Colaresi 2004). Ehud Barak's recent electoral defeat in Israel is an example of this process. And even though a leader himself might prefer peace, escalation may result from public and elite pressure. Huth (1998, 96–97) found that public support for confrontational international policies has trumped attempts to de-escalate territorial disputes between Morocco and Algeria, India and China, and many others.

Similarly, if the public is intensely distrustful of an adversary, and a leader attempts to de-escalate the rivalry, even dovish elites have an incentive to criticize the pacific leader. This process is similar to the notion of ethnic outbidding in the ethnic conflict literature, whereby elites compete for the most extreme and confrontational policy positions to take advantage of public mistrust of an enemy (see Rabushka and Shepsle 1972; Horowitz 1985). In a rivalry setting, elites have a motive to inflate external threats to undermine peace and to promote their own interests (Snyder 1991). Threat deflation is comparatively less attractive, given the possibility that the true threat will attack when ignored. Of course, many domestic variables can mitigate the threat-inflation dynamic, including a secure leader who has strong domestic support and an educated and informed populace that is not easily led astray by elites. Yet rivalry outbidding, to the extent that it is present, undercuts de-escalation opportunities.

Finally, the behavior of the external rival is also highly relevant. Just as the actions of another ethnic group can exacerbate or relax ethnic outbidding (Rabushka and Shepsle 1972), the behavior of the international adversary can either support outbidding (by increasing the fear of attack) or

---

impact on the unilateral decision, I believe bilateral cessation of threats comes closer to the notion of rivalry termination (see Goertz and Diehl 1995) than to an attempt to de-escalate the rivalry. I will point out situations where mutual de-escalation is predicted by the theory, but this outcome is not always the case.

help bring more pacific leaders to power (by showing a willingness to negotiate). If peaceful moves are not likely to be reciprocated, for whatever
reason, de-escalation becomes a less attractive option. The worst of all possible worlds for a leader is to attempt to appease an external enemy and
then have the rival take advantage of the situation by escalating a dispute.
Although leaders can never be sure of their adversary's intentions, capabilities, or strategy choices, there are times when uncertainty is reduced.
Lebow (1981) as well as Rock (1989) suggest that times of crisis and change
serve as learning experiences for states. Most important, they allow a state
to learn about its adversary's intentions. Will they escalate? Are they willing to negotiate? More subtly, communication between the groups can
ease tensions by breaking stereotypes (Fiske and Taylor 1991).

Thus, through interaction and crisis, states can update their beliefs
concerning a rival. Lessons from past crises frame future decisions to escalate and de-escalate. Through the Cuban missile crisis, the United States
and the Soviet Union learned both about the costs of future conflict, and
that each was willing to be reasonable, if stern, in attempting to avoid a
nuclear disaster (see May 1993). A similar process was involved in the 1898
Fashoda crisis between France and Britain, the Venezuelan border dispute,
and possibly the most recent border dispute between Ecuador and Peru in
1992. The model is summarized in figure 1.

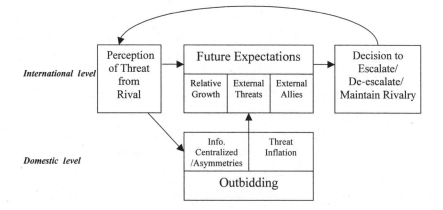

Figure 1. A dynamic two-level pressure model of rivalry interaction.

Building Pressure

Threat

A state competing in international rivalry finds itself by definition faced with some variable level of international threat. For example, Pakistan is threatened by India, while India is comparatively less threatened by Pakistan. Of course this balance of threat can change, as the nuclear tests on the Indian subcontinent illustrate. International threat triggers two processes. Domestically, government coalitions can change with international circumstances, and in the face of external competition, the arguments of hard-liners may be accepted by a greater majority of people (Colaresi 2004; Snyder 1989; Vasquez 1993). For example, calls for greater military budget appropriations may gain momentum when there is a credible international threat, compared to when the international environment is more benign. Although U.S. military spending as a percentage of GDP was still among the highest in the world in the late 1990s, it was 39 percent less than during the last years of the cold war.[2] The greater the external threat, the more leverage hard-liners have to increase governmental centralization and military preparations.

Internationally, external pressure induces more vigilance as the foreign policy elite watches and gathers information about its threat environment. In general, a state's threat environment includes the likely sources of conflict discounted by the probable external aid that it may receive from allies. Therefore, policy makers must form expectations concerning the capability balance with the main rival, with other rivals, and with potential allies. Information on the intentions and capabilities of the adversaries and allies must come from intelligence and past interactions with the rival.[3]

2. Information from the Stockholm International Peace Research Institute (SIPRI) comparing defense spending as a percentage of GDP from 1998 to that same figure in 1990, available at http://projects.sipri.se/milex/mex_database1.html.

3. As Lebow (1981), Rock (1989), and Vasquez (1993) point out, international crises involving rivals are possibly the most intense learning experiences for states. In these interactions, states must mobilize significant resources and face possible losses of credibil-

Outbidding

At home, the public receives select information about an international threat. This information comes from policy elites, the media, and, if available, direct observation. As Page and Shapiro (1992) and Holsti (1996) note, the public in the United States is generally uneducated about foreign affairs, and there are multiple avenues for elites to manipulate public opinion for their own purposes. This information, however biased, then shapes or reshapes the public's attitudes toward the adversary and the policies that they will ratify and support if given the choice. Under threatening situations, fear may be a powerful mobilizing force, leading to outbidding pressure toward escalation and away from cooperation.

The reverse pattern, where a leader correctly perceives a threat is present but the public refuses to support escalation, is theoretically possible. However, in these blind-to-threat circumstances, the executive would have the ability to disseminate information to the relevant public to make the case for war. It seems unlikely that it is in most politicians' or citizens' interest to see the country conquered when a rising threat is ignored. The dynamic two-level pressure model does not assume an ever-mobilized bellicose public. Instead, the theory suggests more modestly that within threatening international circumstances (rivalry), hawks will have an easier time selling their policies as compared to doves.

Great Expectations

At the same time, the information learned about the adversary and the threat environment updates the leadership's expectations about the costs and benefits of future conflict with the rival. The leaders decide whether overt hostility or cooperation is likely because of the putative intentions of

---

ity, prestige, and capability. Because of the higher stakes, moves are less likely to be bluffs, although they still can be, and communication is more likely to be informative rather than just "babbling" (Fearon 1994). Lower-intensity interactions such as negotiations or low-level meetings offer less opportunity for learning because agreements are not binding and there is little cost to committing to a particular action. Thus, external threats and international crises serve as catalysts to update information concerning a state's threat environment.

the rival, and they calculate the likely consequences of war, peace, and in-action. As Copeland (2000) suggests, these expectations form the guiding hand of rivalry interaction. Higher expected costs, such as facing rising debts and a growing rival, may force a change in rivalry behavior. More op-timistic expectations, such as competing with a weak rival, which does not divert resources from domestic development, make the continuation of ri-valry more likely.

Policy Decisions

Expectations and outbidding combine, guiding a leader's hand toward es-calation, de-escalation, or rivalry maintenance. Specifically, international expectations are mediated by the domestic considerations of the policy-making elites. For example, if there are high future expected costs, but the public is mobilized against a rival because of the information they have re-ceived, de-escalation is unlikely. A leader who attempts to accommodate a rival may be replaced if the public, or those who choose the leadership, will not support the decision. On the other hand, if the public, or those empowered to choose a leader,[4] are worried about domestic problems that could be assuaged by a toning down of rivalry hostilities, one barrier to de-escalation is lifted. The institutions that centralize information into the hands of the executive, resulting in large foreign policy information asym-metries between the leadership and public, play a key role in deciding whether this domestic dynamic directs pressure toward cooperation or conflict.

Feedback

Whatever is decided, to maintain, escalate, or de-escalate the rivalry, has a feedback effect on future relations between the rivals. A decision to escalate a dispute increases the probability of future bellicosity. Threats may rico-chet into greater pressure when the hostility is reciprocated, supporting the arguments of hard-liners. The increased conflict can further mobilize the populace against the aggressive rival. In time, this feedback constrains opportunities for de-escalation. Likewise, an attempt to cooperate with a

---

4. Another term for this group is the "selectorate."

rival will echo into the future. The leadership will need to show some tangible reduction in threat to weaken hard-liners and stay in power. Successful cooperation can build momentum toward de-escalation, although the perception of a previous negotiation failure can reinforce outbidding.

Caveats

Of course, there may be instances where the international-domestic interaction does not substantively alter rivalry behavior. For example, if an external rival attacks a state, reciprocation at a high level of hostility is likely regardless of threat inflation domestically. Although each step of the model may occur, whereby the public receives select information and the threat environment is analyzed, the escalatory response was preordained by the international attack. In these cases, dynamic two-level pressures should help to explain why the initial escalation, which triggered the crisis, occurred. Similarly, domestic considerations may heavily influence a leader to escalate or de-escalate tensions to divert attention from some domestic shortfall and thus marginalize the explanatory power of the international level. Here, dynamic two-level pressures should help to explain who was the target of the diversion. It should identify the rivals in the threat environment as well as what distribution of domestic distrust is aligned against each adversary.

What the theory cannot explain are escalations in tensions that are not controlled by a centralized authority. If a general takes it upon himself to begin shooting in the Ecuadorian Amazon or a suicide bomber attacks downtown Tel Aviv, the expected future costs of rivalry to the leadership have little bearing on the situation. Therefore the dynamic two-level pressure model of rivalry interaction is not deterministic. It cannot predict all events of escalation or de-escalation given the immense uncertainties in the real world. Instead, the theory highlights the interaction between domestic and international variables and how expectations about the future, external threats, and rivalry outbidding can increase the probability of escalation and de-escalation.

Concepts and Hypotheses

The following sections probe the dynamic two-level pressure concepts in more depth. Anticipating the discussion, figure 2 presents the general hy-

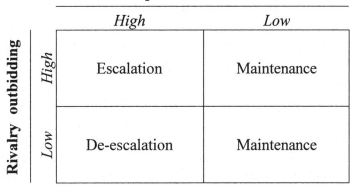

Figure 2. The relationship between rivalry outbidding, expected future costs, and escalation/de-escalation.

potheses drawn from the dynamic two-level pressure theory. If, for the moment, we hold opportunities for de-escalation and escalation constant, then we can capture the theory's expectations in a 2 x 2 matrix. The higher the expected future costs of rivalry (as measured against the benefits), the more likely is a change in rivalry behavior. If expected costs are low, rivalry maintenance is expected without significant escalation or de-escalation, since the benefits of rivalry outweigh the costs. If costs are high, the domestic situation within the country influences the direction of the predicted change in rivalry behavior. A highly skeptical and mobilized domestic constituency makes de-escalation less likely, especially if past rivalry interaction has triggered elites to inflate external threats. Similarly, this suspicion makes escalation more probable as elites attempt to outbid each other for domestic support. Finally, an opportunity to escalate the dispute and change the expected costs of rivalry makes escalation more likely, while an opportunity to de-escalate in the form of confidence in a cooperative response from the rival increases the propensity for de-escalation.

Future Expectations and Rivalry Behavior

This theory first predicts that changes in rivalry behavior will be related to the perceived costs, as balanced against the benefits, of future rivalry. In order to maintain a rivalry and the external threat it entails, states must continue to compete over the issue at stake. This competition consumes resources in the form of material and currency. Of course the strain of competition is relative to the strength of the states running the competition, as the stronger state in a rivalry will have more resources. Thus, Chinese domestic developments have been affected less by Taiwan, as compared to Taiwanese responses to Chinese threats. The costs of rivalry are difficult to measure because they involve unobservable counterfactuals, but Colaresi and Thompson (2001) find that the higher the external threat a state faces, the lower the domestic development and economic growth of that country. Also, states tend to have lower standards of living and investment when faced with external rivals (Colaresi 2002).

Another cost associated with continued rivalry is the drain of resources away from other external threats. Just as resources are diverted from domestic production to military production in conflict, they are also diverted from deterring other external threats. The greater the number of rivalries a state is involved in, the greater the resources it will need to expend to compete, all else being equal. Therefore, the optimal policy may be to de-escalate one rivalry, or alternatively to knock one enemy out quickly, in order to deal with a more pressing threat (Walt 1987). For example, some historians hypothesize that Hitler tried to do both in balancing Russian and Western threats to German interests (see Copeland 2000). Also, a special case of the external threat process occurs when both states in rivalry are also competing against a third state. In this case, one duo within the triad may find it compelling to de-escalate their disagreements to deal with the third power. Historical examples of this process involve Anglo-French and Anglo-American détente in partial response to rising German threats (Campbell 1980).

Counterbalancing these external threats are external alliances and arms transfers to lower the costs of rivalry. A strong ally, China, has helped Pakistan continue to compete with India. Likewise, alliances between the United States or the Soviet Union and multiple states in the Middle East and the Horn of Africa have allowed the comparatively weak to continue to compete with stronger rivals. U.S. and European aid to Israel has been instrumental in supporting that country's continued sovereignty from multiple external threats over the last half-century. Similar aid from the Soviet Union to Somalia helped Mogadishu perpetuate claims against a stronger Ethiopia until the Ogaden war. Therefore, changes in third-party alliances and new rivalries serve as exogenous shocks, raising or lowering the costs of future rivalry.

In addition, future costs cannot be known a priori. Instead, leaders must guess what actions will be prudent in the future, and what means must be mobilized to continue the competition. If two states are involved in a border dispute, each has to make a guess as to what mix of rhetoric and military might will deter attack and credibly threaten the adversary. This calculation revolves around what the adversary is producing and positioning along the border. Thus, both the capabilities and the intentions of the adversary must be predicted to gauge future costs. Should a state equip itself with enough weapons to deter limited excursions or full-scale war? The answers depend on the expectations decision makers hold about the rival's likely behavior. As in the previous section on reciprocating peaceful initiatives, these expectations change with new information from crises and interactions with the adversary. Through crisis situations and other interactions, rivals must come face-to-face with escalation and its potential for destruction (Lebow 1981). If future conflict is expected to be costly, either in terms of what will be lost or what it will take to win, a change in rivalry behavior becomes more probable.

The costs of continued threat need to be balanced against the benefits of continued rivalry to the leaders making the decisions. The first and most obvious benefit that leaders get from continued conflict is the probability of winning what is at stake in the rivalry. In a territorial dispute, this reward might be either a symbolic or a resource-rich parcel of land, which would increase domestic support and decrease external insecurity. Issue importance can range from the survival of the state to symbolic conflict over unpopulated land (Brecher and Wilkenfeld 1997). The more important the issue at stake, the greater the pressure to maintain the rivalry. However, the domestic constituency that supports a leader's rule will be one integral component in determining the value of the international issue.

Information Asymmetries and Threat Inflation

There are also contingent political incentives to continue maintaining a rivalry. Berend (1998) finds that elites in Eastern Europe in the postcommunist and interwar periods were able to use external threats as a justification for banning opposition parties, eschewing general elections, and centralizing governmental power. In the face of external threats, policies that strengthen the state and, with it, those in power are more popular because the uncertainties of democratization and liberalization entail serious international risks (Przeworski 1991; Colaresi and Thompson 2003). International security concerns, real or imagined, justify the creation of information centralization mechanisms. Specifically, institutions that create the direct classification of information, penalties for treason, executive privilege, and press censorship aggregate foreign policy information into the hands of the executive. In many cases, foreign policy secrets are important for effective policy (Colaresi 2005). However, the nonporous information border between the public and the executive creates an informational imbalance and asymmetry.

Snyder (1991) notes that elites have a monopoly over two types of information. First, information concerning foreign affairs is often confidential and known only to a few officials. Thus, some elites are the only ones to know the true extent of external threat a nation faces. Normal citizens are not able to count the number of tanks on their borders or receive information about the capabilities of a potential adversary. Second, elites have a monopoly over "expert" opinion, whereby information is interpreted and generally accepted by the populace or even other elites (see Gibbs 1995; Page and Shapiro 1992).

Information centralization mechanisms, by supplying these monopolies, create a foreign-policy facts deficit that allows elites to inflate an external threat. If people are aware of some past hostile actions by another state, and are told about an impending attack, they do not always have the information necessary to refute these elite assertions. Even if the people were unsure about the veracity of elite claims, it seems logical that they would err on the side of caution and support military preparations. Of course, it is difficult for elites to construct international threats out of thin air. For instance, it is unlikely elites could manage a successful campaign to inflate the Canadian threat in the United States, or the Malawi threat in Germany, if there was no international provocation. But where citizens know of past hostility and have prior negative attitudes toward a potential adversary, the opportunity to exaggerate international threats instrumentally is present. For example, German fears of French territorial gains, as well as increasing Russian strength, had historical precedent in past wars and territorial disputes before World War II (Albrecht-Carri 1958). The obverse incentive toward insincere threat deflation is unlikely in any institutional context; any leader has much to lose from being conquered or taken advantage of internationally.

The interaction between public suspicions and information asymmetries is graphically represented in figure 3. If the public is not suspicious of an adversary and does not expect an attack, it is less likely, given moderate information asymmetries, that the external threat can be seriously inflated, as compared to a relevant public that is highly distrustful of a rival. Yet the gap narrows when information asymmetries are very high because leaders will have a relatively free hand in sculpting information and images to fit their conception of international threats (Snyder 1991). Thus, the previous use of information asymmetries to create enemy images makes threat inflation more successful in the future. Elites can attempt to jump from the trusting to the suspicious curve. Likewise, greater external threats and bellicose tactics from a rival can increase suspicions under low asymmetries and make future threat inflation possible.

Information asymmetries are not uniformly distributed around the world but vary with the information level of the populace and the press freedoms in a state. Information asymmetries are defined by what an elite knows that the populace does not. A free press can diminish information

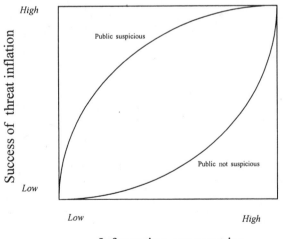

Information asymmetries

Figure 3. The relationship between threat inflation, information asymmetries, and public suspicions.

asymmetries by providing the populace with alternative points of view and independently verified information. The greater the number of outlets for information, the harder it is for leaders to control public attitudes and use propaganda to support their own policies. For example, Gladstone and Disraeli spent almost a decade debating British intervention in Turkey to turn back Russian advances. The debate was published in the press and information was presented from both sides directly to the literate public and indirectly through word-of-mouth. Through the mechanism of open, though admittedly limited, debate, the public was able to form a complex view of the situation, rather than demonizing the Russian threat and over-reacting. Although initial Russian gains in Turkey in 1877 swelled support for Disraeli's tough international policies, by 1880 Gladstone had argued against intervention and returned the Liberals to power. Through relatively open and sophisticated debate, where multiple viewpoints were presented, Gladstone was able to fight off threat inflation and interventionist policies (Swartz 1985).

Conversely, when information-centralized mechanisms are unchecked, elites have the ability to widen information asymmetries to promote an external threat. In 1853, before the Second Reform Bill was passed in Britain, the press and other elites did not have information on foreign threats. This information deficit allowed Palmerston to use Russophobic speeches and articles to inflate the Russian threat to Turkey and to avoid his opponents' government reform measures (Snyder 1991, 199–200). In more extreme examples, Hitler's and Kim Il Sung's control of information in Germany and North Korea facilitated threat inflation and the maintenance of rivalry (Bergmeier and Lotz 1997; Cummings 1997). Further, the presence of legalized opposition party voices decreases the propaganda tools at the regime's control. An informed populace is more likely to hold a complex view of a rival because they will be able to draw on information from multiple sources, as opposed to holding simple enemy images (Gross-Stein 1998; Ottosen 1995; Hermann and Fischerkeller 1995).

It is important to note that private information does still exist, even in democracies with a free press and an informed populace. As Gibbs (1995) notes, covert operations and confidential information are only known, by definition, to a small number of people. Frequently, the populace will be interested in these key pieces of information. Thus, even in the most democratic states, some information centralization mechanisms and informa-tion asymmetries exist. Page and Shapiro (1992) find that public opinion on foreign policy in the United States is prone to elite manipulation when compared to domestic issues. The populace is relatively ignorant of inter-national policy and has little day-to-day experience with foreign affairs. Thus, even when a free press, decentralized information, and opposition voices are present, some manipulation is possible, especially in the face of a credible external threat (McGinnis and Williams 2001).

It is also possible that continued rivalry brings specific benefits to an interest group that is important to the leadership. Lebow (1981) and Sny-der (1991) suggest that oftentimes arms buildups are supported domesti-cally by private corporations that benefit from military expenditures. The corporate opposition to the START treaties in the United States is an exam-ple of this dynamic, whereby rivalries fueled growth for a few companies that had a strong influence on the leadership (Lebow 1981).

Rivalry Outbidding and De-escalation

Information centralization and asymmetries directly affect the attractive-ness of de-escalation. As noted in the previous section, elites may have an incentive to inflate external threats for their own purposes, a process I call rivalry outbidding. In this process, the public can become very distrustful of an adversary as elites use propaganda to justify tough foreign policy moves. The more successful this process, based on the information asym-metries discussed above, the harder it is for a leader to de-escalate a rivalry.

Through outbidding, leaders can be caught in their own rivalry traps. By using threats to centralize power, they are unable to de-escalate a rivalry because of public pressure, even when cooperation might make objective sense. For example, in India, Nehru provoked negative public opinion to-ward Beijing through the control of information. His rhetoric was calcu-lated to quell dissent and credibly threaten China during their border crisis in 1962. Yet when China did not back down, Nehru favored de-escalation because of the much stronger military position of the Chinese. Unfortu-nately for Nehru, his propaganda campaigns were successful and domestic political opinion was highly bellicose. Any conciliatory gestures were deemed treason by Congress and by newspaper editorials (Maxwell 1972, 185–218). A similar situation constrained the junta in Argentina during the Falklands Island dispute, after Britain had responded to the initial threat.

If a leader will likely be deposed or replaced when de-escalation is attempted, it is a less-attractive option, all else being equal. On the other hand, if a leader has nothing to fear or the public is ambivalent concerning the policy toward a rival, de-escalation is more likely. This process is similar to what McGinnis and Williams describe as a "rivalry as prison" effect (2001, 28). They note that if a significant proportion of the politically relevant public perceives the rival as a severe threat to national security, international policy that leaves the state vulnerable will be resisted (see also Nincic 1989).[5]

Rivals play an important role in either further exacerbating rivalry outbidding or propping up the arguments of relative doves. If the other rival acts in a way that is consistent with the prognostications of hard-liners, peace initiatives will be stillborn. A leader may choose not to make peaceful overtures to a bellicose rival, even when they would be in the country's best interests.

A failed peace overture increases the susceptibility of a leader to criticism of being too weak or impractical. In Israel, Barak's peace overtures toward Palestinian chairman Yasser Arafat were only partially met, with devastating electoral consequences. The al-Aksa intifada significantly eroded the Israeli public's support for cooperation with Palestine (Yaar and Hermann 2000). Further, Chamberlain's appeasement of Hitler only came under public and elite vilification after it became clear that Hitler was not reciprocating (Albrecht-Carrié 1958). In an extreme case, de-escalation is highly unlikely if there is the perception within the leadership that a show

---

5. McGinnis and Williams (2001) also suggest that policies that "seem dangerously bellicose" will be resisted by the public. As the emphasis on information asymmetries in the previous section suggests, it is easier to sell bellicosity than peace, given information asymmetries and the security dilemma that unilateral de-escalation engenders. Further, as explained below, if the relevant public is distrustful of a rival, there is an incentive for elites to produce more bellicose policy to compete with other elites that may take a hard line against a rival. Of course, if the public is generally supportive of, or ambivalent about, a putative rival, elites can be constrained from bellicose action. For example, Nixon had to compete with Robert Kennedy, George McGovern, and then various Democrats in Congress to be seen as the leader who de-escalated the U.S. rivalry with China (see Tyler 2000).

of "weakness" will lead to a surprise attack by the rival. Lebow (1981) notes that many putative opportunities for de-escalation were ignored because of these fears, particularly in the Middle East since 1948 and in Europe leading up to World War I.

Even if an adversary offers concessions, the other party does not know whether the rival will keep its promise, inducing a credible commitment problem (Lake and Powell 1999; Lake and Rothchild 1998). When political opponents can use negative public opinion to depose the peace-making elite, even offers of peace are unlikely to be kept. For example, Campbell (1980) notes that a major force facilitating the de-escalation of the rivalry between the United States and Great Britain was the decrease in negative public perceptions of the British in the United States. As Britain became more democratic and years passed without new international confrontations, American elites could no longer count on public support for anti-British policies. Thus, peace overtures after the Venezuelan border crisis were more credible than previous de-escalatory attempts.

A great deal of coordination is needed between two states to orchestrate a bilateral de-escalation and illustrate credible restraint. This coordination is made easier if the costs of future rivalry are high to both adversaries, and these costs are mutually recognized. For instance, a mu-

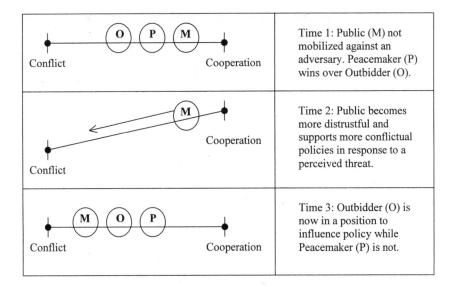

Figure 4. Description of rivalry outbidding in response to international threat.

tual threat can make continued competition more expensive by drawing resources away from a conflict with the third party. A shared external threat also makes overt conflict and war between the two rivals more costly because it would weaken both rivals to the benefit of the third competitor. In these cases, the specific benefits of de-escalation for each rival are less opaque to the other. The greater the shared threat and the salience of that shared threat, the more probable is de-escalation.

Rivalry Outbidding and Escalation

The decision to use propaganda to inflate threats not only makes de-escalation unattractive but simultaneously makes escalation more likely. Other elites can challenge inaction in the face of international provocation. If a leader or political opponent uses propaganda to create negative stereotypes of an international rival, future international policy decisions will be constrained by that decision. For example, if a president creates a condition of extreme popular hatred for an international adversary by using information centralization mechanisms to widen information asymmetries, the popular international distrust could reward elites promising escalatory tactics.

As the rally-'round-the-flag literature predicts, international conflict may breed greater internal support for the current regime. This is especially likely when the international target is unpopular domestically, and the leader's policy attempts to outdo the rival in some way. Focusing on rivalry outbidding suggests that other political challengers, not just a leader, may benefit from a rally (Vasquez 1993; Snyder 1991; Colaresi 2004). If a leader does not wave the banner, another elite has the ability to play the role of national protector.

Dynamic two-level pressures suggest that the rally-'round-the-flag effect depends on what other flag is being challenged. If the other country is perceived as an external threat, it will propel mobilization. A confrontational policy by Britain toward France is less likely to mobilize public support for the leadership today than it would have two centuries ago when the two states were locked in a heated rivalry (Albrecht-Carrié 1958). Dramatically, the United States public greatly increased its support for bellicose policies around the world after September 11, 2001.[6] The Qaeda threat led directly to support for military action in Afghanistan against the organization perceived as responsible for the September 11th attacks. However, increased threat perceptions and support for hawkish policies echoed in the U.S. decision to launch Operation Iraqi Freedom. Political elites suggested that Iraq was part of the war on terror, and that a Qaeda-Iraq alliance had been formed. Those citizens who saw a link between al-Qaeda and Iraq were more likely to support the war in Iraq (Kaufman 2004).

Figure 4 graphically illustrates this process more generally. If we consider a unidimensional policy space that ranges from support for conflict to support for cooperation with a rival, we can denote the median public preference as M. For simplicity we can imagine that leaders are chosen relative to their proximity to M. If public opinion supports cooperation, a peacemaker (P) has a better chance of gaining support. Yet if the median public preference shifts toward more conflict as a result of external threat or elite manipulation of information, an outbidder (O) can win more support than the peacemaker. In fact, there is an incentive for peacemakers to become outbidders under circumstances of public suspicion. Therefore, one can think of external threat and threat inflation as "tipping" the conflict-cooperation continuum and drawing the public into supporting more bellicose policies.

In the India-China border dispute, Nehru was eventually forced to react to other elites' calls for action. Members of Lok Sabha denounced the road that China had built through the Aksai-Chin region and called Nehru's previous pro-China stance, "weak and appeasing leadership" (Maxwell 1972, 131). Further, Lebow reports that the Jana Sangh party passed a resolution that called for immediate military action (1981, 188). It seems highly likely that any U.S. president who did not act militarily in Afghanistan would have come under extreme criticism. For example, Democratic presidential candidate John Kerry attacked George W. Bush's Afghanistan policy not as excessively hawkish but as being too weak and failing to utilize sufficient force to capture al-Qaeda leader Osama Bin-Laden.[7]

---

6. See Colaresi (2005) for a discussion of this opinion dynamic in historical perspective. Davis and Silver (2004) find that September 11th not only increased public support for war but also decreased public support for institutional protections of civil liberties.

7. For example, see John Kerry's speech at Temple University, September 24, 2004.

In a competitive regime where elites are vying for power and where a rival is threatening, someone is going to use the rally effect, especially if the leader leaves this opportunity open to others. In 2004, Israeli Prime Minister Ariel Sharon seemed caught in a similar self-constructed dilemma with respect to Palestine. After years of warning of the Palestinian threat and justifying military action in the West Bank (Shlaim 2001), Sharon faced extreme pressure within his own party to continue hardline policies (Yaar and Hermann 2004). In sum, negative public perceptions of the rival and high political salience can make escalation more likely.

Military Opportunities to Change the Status Quo

When we are discussing escalation, the military means to change the status quo must be present. Therefore, another factor that increases the probability of escalation is the appearance of a relatively low-cost opportunity to change the status quo. When a state's current policy trajectory leads to expectations of high costs in the future, one way leaders can lower the costs is by changing the status quo. This process follows the logic of preemptive wars. If one state will be at greater risk in the future, when an adversary has had a chance to use its industrial capacity for military production, a preemptive strike and escalation may cancel or postpone the dim view of the future.

As the states approach capability parity, the benefits of preemption decrease, owing to the decrease in the probability of winning a confrontation. Thus, the greater the likelihood of a state being able to alter the status quo, the more likely is escalation, when all else is equal. For example, Japan attempted to alter its increasingly costly situation before World War II by escalating its rivalry with the United States and other Asian countries (see discussion later in this chapter). With few raw materials and severe economic problems, Japan encroached upon a weak China and Chinese-controlled Manchuria. Had international opposition been stronger, the decision to escalate might not have been so attractive. Conversely, Pakistan has been seeking a way to change the status quo with India in Kashmir, but its militarily weak position has rarely lent itself to a low-cost escalation opportunity.[8] In the Pakistani case, there is little chance that escalation will change the status quo (Thorton 1999).[9]

However, what constitutes an opportunity for escalation will depend not just on the overall military balance between states, but also on potential locality-specific opportunities. As the September 11th attacks in the United States demonstrated dramatically, even a weak group can injure a superpower, given the right circumstances. In previous decades, both cold war superpowers encountered local conditions that leveled the battlefield, for example, in Vietnam and Afghanistan.

Dynamic-Two Level Pressures and Pearl Harbor

The well-documented case of Japan's decision to attack Pearl Harbor exemplifies the process by which expectations of future costs mixed with a mobilized and under-informed populace to increase the risk of rivalry escalation. In the 1930s, Japan was facing severe constraints on raw material imports as a result of world economic depression (Ike 1967). In search of self-sufficiency and greater control over Asia, the Japanese leadership began forcibly forming a Greater East Asian Co-prosperity Sphere. As Japan conquered Manchuria and the major Chinese cities, the United States placed increasingly strict economic sanctions on Japan. This act led first to an embargo on fuel and scrap iron, and then to the freezing of all Japanese assets in the United States in July 1941. The United States continued to insist that only when Japan withdrew its forces from China and refrained from further aggressive international action would the embargo be lifted. No compromise solution short of retreat was proposed (Feis 1950; Levi and Whyte 1997).

The embargo led to dire predictions about Japan's future ability to compete with the United States. Butow quotes the Japanese chief of military affairs section of the War Ministry as comparing Japan to a fish in a pond from which the water was gradually being drained (1961, 245). Thus,

8. One exception to this was the Rann of Kutch crisis, where the ambiguity of the border and the lack of Indian supply lines provided a localized opportunity for conflict.

9. Note that a change in the military balance, or an advance in nuclear weapons delivery systems, could alter this diagnosis.

while the situation was not yet desperate, in the near future it would be. The inability of the Japanese to secure the rural regions of China, and the United States' obdurate control over the Philippines, meant that a substitute for previously available materials would be hard to find. The Japanese leadership believed that "maintaining the status quo would permit the embargo to progressively reduce Japan's strength, leading eventually to [an] intolerable outcome" (Levi and Whyte 1997, 8).

Thus the costs of continuing the status quo were quite high for Japan. If the Co-prosperity Sphere trajectory continued, more resources would be needed to overcome stiffening resistance just as those necessary inputs were drying up. In reaction to these projections, the Japanese weighed two options against continuing the status quo: (1) de-escalate and make concessions to the United States or (2) escalate and attempt to alter the status quo by challenging the United States militarily (Russett 1967).

De-escalation was not an attractive choice because of the demands of the United States and the domestic situation within Japan. While Public Minister Konoye Fumimaro, Minister of Home Affairs Hiranuma Kiicharo, and Foreign Minister Hideki Tojo, among a few others, were initially supportive of negotiating with the United States to end the embargo, the failure of preliminary talks led even moderates to downplay the expected success of de-escalation (Ike 1967). Giving up Manchurian and Chinese raw materials in exchange for the renewal of American import shipments may have allowed Japan to recover from depression, but would also have the almost certain effect of reducing Japan to a third-rate power (Russett 1967).

Domestically, the previous use of information centralization mechanisms to inflate the need for expansion, and the hostility of the United States, decreased the likelihood of de-escalation further. Snyder notes that throughout the 1930s the Japanese public was "fed a diet of slanted interpretations" that led to a general impression that threats facing Japan were much graver than the elites themselves believed (1991, 141). Although the United States posed an impressive military obstacle, the Japanese leadership under Tojo could not embrace de-escalation because it "would surely have discredited the military leadership that had trumpeted a policy of war and expansion" (149).

Moreover, historical examples had shown that Japanese politics did not favor moderation in international affairs (Levi and Whyte 1997). For example, in 1930, even before the military propaganda machine was in full swing, the reform-minded prime minister Osachi Hamaguchi, who attempted to cut military expenditures and limit Japanese naval power, was assassinated. His assailant, a member of the Aikokusha, or Patriotic Association, was subsequently pardoned and remained politically active even after World War II. The reasons for both the assassination of the prime minister and the commuted sentence was the weak and "treasonous" foreign policy pursued by Hamaguchi. Increasingly wide-ranging right-wing assassinations were carried out again in 1932, 1936, and 1941 (Deac 1996, 21–23). Under these circumstances the dovish Sato Naotake was replaced by the comparatively bellicose Konoye Fumimaro, and then Konoye replaced with the hard-line Tojo (Conroy and Wray 1990). It was believed that the growing internal discontent in the country could only be quelled by international conquest and increasing access to raw materials (Conroy 1955).

Escalation was also risky. How would the Japanese intimidate the United States into backing down? What opportunities were present? While an internal report in Japan quantified the Japanese war-making capacity at only 10 percent of that of the United States (Miwa 1975, 126–27),[10] Pearl Harbor was chosen as the point of attack "to maximize Japan's chances of success" (Levi and Whyte 1997, 13). The strategic decision was based on the element of surprise and the hope that the United States would not be willing to fight a protracted war after initial Japanese gains (Ike 1967). However, there were few delusions about the probability of success. Levi and Whyte (1997) suggest that even hard-liners Nagano and Sugiyama downplayed the likelihood of victory. Instead, they argued that there was a chance, however small, that the future could be made brighter by striking first.

This admittedly risky escalation was a response to certain losses by the elite if the status quo was maintained or if retreat was ordered. Continuation of the status quo would lead to a probable fight with the United States when Japan was even weaker than it already had been, or to complete retreat. De-escalation would likely result in a change in leadership. There

---

10. General Hajime Sugiyama ordered the report destroyed immediately upon hearing its conclusions, another example of information asymmetries resulting from foreign policy information centralization institutions.

were a number of competitors waiting to take control of the government if Tojo and his leadership attempted to appease the United States and reverse course (Ogata 1964, 48). In the years leading up to Pearl Harbor, even non-military elites were successfully staking out hard-line international policies to mobilize domestic support for private power ambitions. Therefore, the choice was between an almost certain loss for the decision makers if they de-escalated or did nothing and an unlikely but possible gain in the event of escalation.

In the Pearl Harbor case, as the dynamic two-level pressure theory predicts, the expectation about the future costs of rivalry led to a change in rivalry behavior, while domestic incentives for escalation influenced the direction of the change. Economic embargoes and a tough stance by the United States made future victory unlikely if the status quo was allowed to continue. At the same time, domestic public opinion previously mobilized against conciliatory gestures reduced the incentives for Tojo and other elites to appease the United States. Therefore, escalation was preferred to de-escalation. The Pearl Harbor example could be placed in the top left-hand box of figure 2. Outbidding pressure and pessimistic future expectations increased the probability of war and escalation.

Conclusion

This chapter presented the dynamic two-level pressure theory of rivalry escalation and de-escalation. Both domestic and international politics influence the probability of observing cooperation or conflict within a rivalry. These multilevel forces can be distilled into three key concepts. First, future expectations concerning a state's threat level influence immediate decisions. For example, if a state's power relative to a rival is decreasing and the future threat horizon looks bleak, continuing the status quo will be unattractive. Second, the presence of foreign policy information asymmetries and a public distrustful of a rival creates conditions that are ripe for rivalry outbidding. Elites may compete with each other to show that they are the toughest and strongest on defense matters vis-à-vis the rival. During this process, the public may become even more extreme in their distrust of the rival. Rival bellicosity, in the form of threats or military actions, can accelerate the fear-mongering process. Outbidding results in pressure to avoid cooperation with a rival and momentum toward promoting continued competition and even escalation. Finally, whether or not domestic and international pressures manifest themselves in outright military escalation depends on the presence of an opportunity to change the status quo. In the following chapters, I test whether the theory predicts the turning points in three rivalries (Somalia-Ethiopia, Egypt-Israel, and United States–China), and then in a larger-scale statistical examination.

3 Zooming In

Introduction to the Case Studies

I USE A DUAL quantitative-qualitative approach to probe the explanatory power of dynamic two-level pressures. By analyzing the historical record of specific pairs of states, I can track distinct policies, events, and motivations. Complementarily, I also create approximate measures (see chapter 8) of dynamic two-level pressures in a much wider array of cases to cross-validate whether the case study findings are peculiar to just a few rivalries. Therefore, the following case studies and statistical analysis serve to reinforce each other. The case studies of Somali-Ethiopian, Egyptian-Israeli, and Sino-American rivalry each allow the reader to directly compare the dynamic two-level pressure prognostications with historical events.

There are, of course, several disadvantages to the use of case studies. Primarily, for the present analysis, information on perceptions and intentions is not always available. Even when information on domestic and international events is recorded, their interpretation is open to debate. However, the contextual information present in diplomatic and personal histories comes closer to approximating the inner workings of rivalry decision making, although imperfectly, than a large-n statistical data analysis alone.

Case Selection

I selected three cases for in-depth historical examination: the Somali-Ethiopian, Egyptian-Israeli, and Sino-American rivalries. Following King, Keohane, and Verba (1994), I chose cases that include significant variation on the independent (or causal) variables of interest. In the context of testing the dynamic two-level pressure theory, this method suggests finding cases with differing expectations of future costs and with distinct domestic outbidding environments. The Somali-Ethiopian, Egyptian-Israeli, and Sino-American cases include both longitudinal and cross-sectional variance on these key concepts. For example, the leadership in Somalia was quite optimistic that their goals could be achieved without major escalation when the rivalry began, but this perception slowly changed, and, by 1976, projections were quite pessimistic. On the other hand, Egyptian and Israeli expectations changed from war-ready to peace-seeking between 1948 and approximately 1975.

In addition, the ability of some states to use propaganda to inflate external threat fluctuates within the sample. In the highly centralized systems of Somalia (after the Barre coup), Egypt, and China, leaders had a relatively free hand in caricaturing their enemies, while the free press in democratic Somalia (pre-1969), the United States, and Israel constrained attempts to inflate threats. Similarly, the level of outbidding and its success oscillated over time within each rivalry. The theory predicts that external stimuli such as more bellicose tactics from an adversary can increase the success of rivalry outbidders. Therefore, we should also be able to map the success of outbidders within the cases over time. Each case includes a cast of players vying for the role of outbidder, including Barre, Farouk, Dayan, Nixon, Begin, and Lin Biao.

Similarly, there is considerable variation in how these rivalries interacted with each other. At least one state within each of the three rivalries attempted to either escalate or de-escalate tensions at different points in time. For example, Somalia moved to appease Ethiopia early in the rivalry, but then reversed course in the early to mid-1970s. Likewise, Egypt and Israel went from fighting three wars from 1948 until 1973 to serious negotiations in 1974. The Sino-U.S. relationship was transformed from war in Korea in 1950 to détente in the early 1970s to the possibility of renewed conflict in the post–cold war world. Therefore, there are actually more than three cases under examination, as periods of escalation, maintenance, and de-escalation are available for analysis in each study. In each rivalry phase I present graphs of the ebb and flow of competition using the Conflict and Peace Databank (COPDAB) (Azar 1993) and World Event Interaction Survey (WEIS) (McClelland 1999; Tomlinson 1993), respectively. These conflict scales are based on news reports and represent intense conflict as low numbers and cooperation as high numbers (Azar and Sloan 1975; Goldstein 1992).

Questions

Several questions guide the case study analyses of rivalry behavior that follow. I use the following questions to focus the comparisons both across and within cases (George 1979):

1. What were the issues under contention, and how important were they to each party? This question specifies the benefits of continued conflict, which must be contrasted with the costs. The more important the issue, the less likely is de-escalation. Stakes involving the survival of the state are assumed to be the most pressing following Brecher and Wilkenfeld (1997).

2. What were the leadership's expectations about the future costs of conflict? This question deals with the costs of likely rivalry trajectories. If the foreign policy leaders were optimistic about attaining its goals by following its current policy trajectory, we would not expect any change in behavior, ceteris paribus. Yet if the costs of future contention are perceived to be high because of mounting economic costs, a new rising threat, or the perception that a war is inevitable, a change in rivalry behavior is likely. Leaders are defined in this study as the elites who have substantial foreign policy decision-making power within the government apparatus and include presidents, prime ministers, foreign ministers, defense ministers, and influential cabinet or opposition ministers.

3. Do elites have information centralization mechanisms they can exploit? If yes, did they use them? The resulting information asymmetries give elites the opportunity to inflate external threats and build domestic enemy images of their international adversaries. If the public is highly mobilized against the adversary, de-escalation is less likely because the leaders will look weak by making concessions. Conversely, escalation is more likely because other elites can saber-rattle and pull support away from more pacific leaders.

4. Was there an opportunity to escalate the dispute? If a state perceives high expected future costs and can not de-escalate the competition because of domestic pressure, leaders may seek an opportunity to escalate.

Whether this opportunity is present depends on the capability balance of the states and the perceived benefits of moving first.

The answers to these four questions serve to produce predictions about each case over the course of the rivalry. I will present and analyze these questions in each phase of the rivalry, during periods of maintenance, escalation, and de-escalation. If the expected future costs of conflict are high compared to the benefits, if the domestic political situation is mobilized against a rival, and if the adversary is unlikely to reciprocate cooperation, de-escalation is unlikely and escalation comparably more probable. Alternatively, if the expected costs of future conflict are high, but domestic public opinion is not mobilized against an adversary and there is a high probability of reciprocation, de-escalation is likely. Finally, if the benefits of maintaining the rivalry in the future outweigh the expected benefits of escalation or de-escalation, no change in rivalry behavior is expected.

Sources

The case studies rely on information from diplomatic and personal histories, as well as original government documents where available. In all cases, there are abundant primary and secondary sources to reconstruct the cases. As Lustick (1996) notes, many times historians themselves disagree over the interpretation of past events and the interpretation of choice may be incorrect. For example, Shlaim (2001) describes a number of disagreements concerning Israeli history, including the heroics of the 1948 war and the leadership characteristics of Prime Minister Eshkol. Also, Tyler (2000) dissects opposing opinions of U.S. policy toward China. In each case study, the contradictions in historical interpretation are explained in relation to their bearing on the argument, where applicable.

Alternative Explanations

It is important that the explanatory powers of other theories are also weighed against the available evidence. For example, a more parsimonious theory such as reciprocity may better explain rivalry behavior in certain instances. Some may argue that the two-level frame of this analysis, using both domestic and international variables, is unnecessary and unduly complicated. Therefore, I compare the predictions of the dynamic two-level pressure theory with Snyder's domestic-centric theory of over-expansion and escalation. As noted previously, Snyder suggests that elites use information asymmetries to inflate threats and receive specific benefits from escalation. If the international level is unnecessary, Snyder's theory is a more parsimonious alternative to the dynamic two-level pressure model. Moreover, Snyder's expectations dovetail with a monadic understanding of the democratic peace, whereby greater levels of democracy and transparency lead to less conflict (Russett 1993).

I also analyze the possibility that domestic politics did not play a role in the escalation or de-escalation of international rivalries. Instead, states may only be reacting to their adversary's previous actions. Some research suggests that reciprocity is a norm in the international system (Goldstein 1992). If rivals only react to the behavior they perceive from an enemy, a multilevel model would be of little added value. Yet it is likely that states deviate from pure reciprocity, by both overreacting and underreacting in certain situations. Therefore, does the dynamic two-level model outperform an international reciprocity explanation, explaining initial choices as well as the residual variance? The answer is particularly important because the deviations from previous rivalry behavior, escalation or de-escalation, remain largely underscrutinized in rivalry research.

4 Ruin Before Reconciliation
The Somali-Ethiopian Rivalry

THE STRATEGIC RIVALRY between Somalia and Ethiopia followed a winding and complicated course from 1960 to 1988. After Somali independence in 1960, incidents of low-level conflict between the Mogadishu and Addis Ababa governments were followed by limited détente in 1967. The uneventful late 1960s and early 1970s could be considered the quiet before the storm. Somalia invaded the Ethiopian-controlled Ogaden in 1977, attempting to take over the disputed territory by force. After Ethiopia defeated Somalia with Soviet help, both states continued to threaten the other until a peace treaty was signed in 1988.

The purpose of this chapter is to test what effect dynamic two-level pressures had on these changes in Ethiopian-Somali interactions. As expressed above, this perspective suggests that escalation in rivalry behavior will be associated with pessimistic future expectations, a mobilized domestic outbidding environment, and a military opportunity. Similarly, de-escalation is expected to spring from high expected future costs of rivalry and a demobilized outbidding environment. In the course of the analysis, the dynamic two-level-pressure explanation will be contrasted with other conventional one-level theories, such as those based on reciprocity and democratic institutions.

Background

The late-twentieth-century conflict between Ethiopians and Somalis can be traced to the fourteenth century, when Abyssinian leaders, in order to gain access to the sea and to proselytize Muslims, entered what is today northern Somalia. Abyssinia was a center of Christianity in Africa, and the

45

push toward the sea was cast as a type of crusade. These raids continued into the sixteenth century, as the Abyssinians met stiff resistance from the native Somalis. The Somalis united behind Ahmed Gurey, and the fighting and animosity continued through Portuguese and Ottoman invasions. However, the dynamics changed considerably when the European great powers arrived in the area.

The nineteenth-century European colonial rush in the Horn of Africa was to leave three long-standing legacies for Somali-Ethiopian rivalry: (1) groups of Somalis were ruled by separate governments; (2) the territorial boundaries between the colonial entities were unsettled; and (3) external repression incubated Somali nationalism (Greenfield 1994, 104). Companies and representatives from Italy, Britain, France, and Russia arrived in the nineteenth century to secure treaties and agreements with Somali chieftains and dignitaries on the coast. In what would become an important geopolitical maneuver, chieftains in the north and east of Somalia signed agreements with Italy, Britain, and France. This move left the central Ogaden region contiguous to Ethiopia on one side and distinct decentralized protectorates on the other. The imposition of state boundaries on Somali territory was considered particularly onerous because the Ogaden played a central role in the transhumance economy. Nomads and pastoralists relied on herds of cattle and camels for subsistence. The maintenance of the herds depended upon unimpeded movement to fertile grounds each season. The Ogaden was a hub for this seasonal rotation. In the colonial search to secure territory, not only were impediments to pastoralism erected, but the Ogaden was also cut off from the other Somali protectorates (Greenfield 1994, 105).

During this time, Ethiopia was able to remain uncolonized, and eventually to extend its own territorial domain. The Ethiopian emperor Menelik II led an internal arms build-up culminating in the subjugation of the Oromo and Somali people living at the eastern outskirts of the empire. Menelik conquered the city of Harer in the Ogaden in 1887 and shortly thereafter was able to control parts of the Ogaden where Somali residents had signed colonial protectorate agreements (Holcomb and Ibssa 1990, 88; Greenfield 1994, 105). Although the Somalis in the Ogaden were briefly united with Italian Somaliland in 1935–40, the British had promised the exiled Ethiopian leader Haile Selassie broad sovereignty when World War II concluded. In 1954, Ethiopia again took control of the Ogaden. By this time, many Somalis were living in French Somaliland (later Djibouti) and the Northern Frontier District (NFD), which eventually became part of Kenya. Thus, one major colonial legacy in the Horn of Africa was the cordoning off of Somalis from each other. In 1960, when Somalia declared independence, over 250,000 Somalis were living outside its borders, almost 10 percent of the total population of Somalia (Laitan and Samatar 1987).

Another colonial development that echoed in future Somali-Ethiopian relations was the inchoate territorial boundaries between Somalia and Ethiopia. While Ethiopia claimed control of the Ogaden, their only major presence was in the cities of Harer and Jijiga. The "provisional administrative line," between Ethiopia and what would become Italian Somaliland was hand-drawn by Menelik on a map that was either lost or discarded before 1908, when the boundaries were to be formally defined. Maybe the clearest example of the confusing boundaries was that in 1934 an Italian garrison was found well inside Ethiopian territory, claiming to have been based there for many years, to the ignorance of Ethiopian authorities. Between 1935 to 1948, dominion over the Ogaden went from Ethiopian to Italian control and then back to Ethiopian jurisdiction. By 1955, Ethiopia was pushing the British out of the Haud and other areas with military force, further muddying the territorial boundary. Upon independence, Somali government officials challenged their borders with Ethiopia, French Somaliland, and, starting in 1964, Kenya.

Throughout the colonial period, the perceived slights to Somali freedoms and recognition ignited and fanned the flame of Somali nationalism. Just as Somali people rallied around Ahmed Gurey during the early Ethiopian raids, Sayyid 'Abdille Hassan mobilized the forces of Pan-Somalism during the colonial period. Derisively called the "Mad Mullah" by the British, Sayyid organized men in the British protectorate into a six-thousand-man fighting force, and in 1900 recovered looted stock from an Ethiopian garrison in Jijiga (Laitan and Samatar 1987, 57). Through word of mouth, Sayyid was able to recruit help from most of the major Somali clan families, including his own Dulbahante clan, but also the Majeerteen, Isaaq, and Hawiye (Laitan and Samatar 1987, 57–58). Active resistance continued until Sayyid's death in 1920. Even as Britain and Italy attempted to transition out of colonialism, the Somali Youth League (SYL) was beginning to recruit paramilitary forces and to protest any move toward Ethiopian control over Somali-claimed territory. The SYL led serious protests and revolts throughout the 1940s and 1950s, the most serious in Harer. As an officer of the British War office stated, "the one thing that the Somali people will not tolerate at any price is that the Ogaden should revert to Ethiopia" (Greenfield 1994, 106–7). Ethiopian attacks in the Ogaden region only further incited Somali nationalism and reduced clan differences (Greenfield 1994, 106–8). In Ethiopia, the ruling elite considered the Ogaden as one piece of their multiethnic state (Ofcansky 1993b).

Upon Somali independence on July 1, 1960, many Somalis were residing in Ethiopia, territorial boundaries between Somalia and Ethiopia were disputed, and Somali popular opinion supported the Pan-Somali movement. Each of these facts made for an unstable international situation that would frame future Somali-Ethiopian relations. The Somali constitution explicitly questioned the border with Ethiopia and French Somaliland. The Somali flag includes a five-pointed star. Two of the points make reference to British and Italian Somaliland, united in 1960. The other three represent the Somalis living abroad (in Ethiopia, French Somaliland/Djibouti, and Kenya/Northern Frontier District). Woodward (1996, 125) notes that the Somali saw conflict with Ethiopia and its other neighbors "less as 'foreign' policy, than the policy of completing the independence of Greater Somalia." Across the Ogaden border, the fact that Ethiopia had military preponderance as well as internationally recognized control of the disputed territory did not predispose Addis Ababa to appease Somali opinion (Lefebvre 1991; Tiruneh 1993).

Issues under Contention

The main issue under contention in the rivalry was the Ogaden territory. Its importance was based on Mogadishu's perception that the Ogaden was integral to Somalia's pastoral economy. Equally powerful was the Somali belief that the Ogaden represented a symbol both of the Pan-Somali movement and of past liberation struggles against Ethiopia. For Ethiopia, the Ogaden represented its own multinational character and integrity. Addis Ababa controlled a number of distinct regions, including Eritrea, Tigray, and the Ogaden. Giving the Ogaden the freedom to choose between Somalia and Ethiopia was perceived as tantamount to unraveling Ethiopia itself (Woodward 1996, 125–27; Greenfield 1994, 105–7; Laitan and Samatar 1987, 134–35).

1960–1964

Rivalry History

Early conflict in the Ogaden took the form of Somali support for the Western Somali Liberation Front (WSLF) and Ethiopian repression and policing of the Pan-Somali movement. The Mogadishu government organized and armed the WSLF force and deployed it in the Ogaden in 1961. The objective of the WSLF was to agitate for the unification of the Ogaden under Mogadishu's rule (Woodward 1996, 125). Ethiopia countered the WSLF with a crackdown on tax evasion and increased livestock confiscation in the Ogaden. However, confrontations in the contested region remained largely nonmilitary at this stage (Samatar 1993, 29). Before 1964, violent military clashes between Somali and Ethiopian forces were rare, although Ethiopia continued to consolidate its control over the region (Laitin and Samatar 1987, 136.)

By June 1963, Ethiopian emperor Haile Selassie had publicly rejected the Ogaden claim for self-government, triggering riots and protests in Hodayo, in Eastern Ethiopia. The Western Somali Liberation Front, fueled by this potential insurgency, reached a mass of three thousand men. As the guerrillas continued to agitate against Addis Ababa's authority, Ethiopia sent reinforcements into the Ogaden to gain control of the situation. This action spurred Somali military intervention in January 1964. At that time, the Somali National Army (SNA) launched ground and air attacks within Ethiopia while stepping up assistance to the guerrillas (Ofcansky 1993b, 196–202). The Ethiopian air force retaliated with strikes against Feerfeer, Beledweyne, and Galcaio in Somalia. The fighting ended in March 1964, when Somalia and Ethiopia signed a cease-fire. Later, an accord in Khartoum was agreed upon, organizing the withdrawal of troops from the border. As a result of the 1964 fighting, Ethiopia demonstrated its military superiority and stepped up its suppression of the WSLF. Ethiopia also proved that it could launch successful strikes within Somalia proper.

In the early 1960s, there were several notable diplomatic victories for Ethiopia and defeats for Somalia on the Horn. When Kenya became independent in 1964, the Somalis living in the Northern Frontier District were within Kenyan territory, despite arguments from Mogadishu concerning Somali unity. As a result, Somalia broke off diplomatic relations with

Britain, which was responsible for orchestrating the Kenyan boundaries. Somalia then began arming insurgents in the NFD. The Kenyan government quickly put down the revolts and signed a mutual defense pact with Ethiopia. Laitan and Samatar (1987, 134–35) argue that perceptions of Somali aggression in both capitals spurred the alliance, pushing Kenya into the Ethiopian diplomatic corner.

Ethiopian-Somali conflict intersected more directly in French Somaliland/Djibouti during this time. Ethiopia had recently constructed a railroad link to Djibouti. If Somalia was able to gain jurisdiction over the French-controlled territory, this important Ethiopian trade artery was likely to be cut off. The French colonial authority, to avoid a conflict with Ethiopia, refused to unite French Somaliland/Djibouti with Greater Somalia. Although Somalia attempted to incite protests and riots in Djibouti through propaganda, no progress could be claimed by Mogadishu (Greenfield 1994, 107; Keller 1993, 97–103). Somalia ruled out military action in Djibouti because fighting a war against European powers and Ethiopia was deemed unattractive. Therefore, in 1964, the Ogaden, NFD, and Djibouti points of the Somali star remained outside of Mogadishu's orbit. Figure 5 illustrates the quarterly highs, lows, and means for rivalry using event data. During these years there was relatively low-level conflict and volatility, as compared to other periods. This fits the narrative descriptions of rivalry maintenance, as both states avoided large-scale wars and broad compromises.

Conventional Explanations

An analysis based on international actions and reactions fails to explain the major driving force of rivalry maintenance between Ethiopia and Somalia during this period. While Somali funding to the WSLF was matched by Ethiopian police actions, and Somali army movements eventually spawned an Ethiopian air attack on Somali territory, the action-reaction sequence was asymmetrical. Ethiopian air assaults were much more bellicose and devastating than Somali incursions into the Ogaden. What a reciprocity perspective ignores altogether is Mogadishu's motivation to continue pushing its claims in the Ogaden, despite facing a much stronger rival. Here, domestic political pressure was key, as Pan-Somalism was domestically popular.

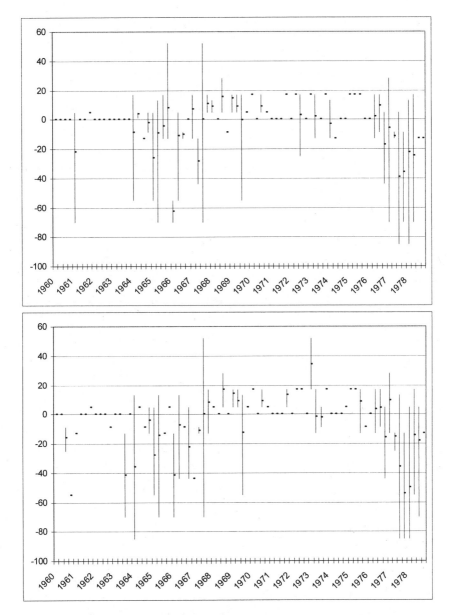

Figure 5. Somali-Ethiopian conflict and cooperation, 1960–1964. *Top:* Somali-to-Ethiopian events; *bottom:* Ethiopian-to-Somali events. COPDAB scale -100 to 60. Smaller numbers represent more conflict, 1960–1964 in frame.

However, common domestic explanations of international conflict also misdiagnose the causes of conflict and limits on cooperation in Somalia and Ethiopia. Coalition building and democratic peace theories suggest that the more democratic and free state will be less bellicose. This prediction is not borne out during this period. It was the more democratic Somalia that initiated and funded the WSLF operations in the Ogaden, and it was Somalia that continued to press its territorial claims in the NFD and French Somaliland. One could argue that the democratic institutions in Somalia capped escalation and military conflict short of war, yet other variables are needed to explain why Mogadishu continued to maintain its rivalry with Ethiopia.

Dynamic Two-Level Pressures

Dynamic two-level pressures more thoroughly explain the major patterns of the 1960 to 1964 period. The consistent strategy for Somalia during this period was the construction and maintenance of the WSLF and the building of a national army, while Ethiopia stalled, counterpunched, and remained militarily superior. Although tensions were high and shots were fired across the border, war was avoided and disputes limited in scope and duration. The absence of high expected future costs, and the presence of domestic pressure to continue the rivalry, made extreme policy choices unattractive. While Ethiopia did have a military option, other factors mitigated the incentive to escalate. Therefore, rivalry maintenance was the most likely course because the leadership in both states expected to win/keep the Ogaden by following their current policy trajectories.

Future Expectations

From 1960 until 1964, both Somalia and Ethiopia expected the costs of rivalry to be moderate to low. The Somalis were optimistic that eventually Pan-Somalism would triumph, and the Ethiopian leadership believed that its military superiority would deflect any calls for concessions in the Ogaden. This dual optimism can be seen in both the domestic costs of rivalry and the external pressure other rivalries exerted on Somalia and Ethiopia.

From the beginning of Somali independence in 1960, Pan-Somalism was the lodestone of foreign policy. Yet this policy had to be interwoven with domestic development. At that time, 65 percent of the population relied on pastoral or semipastoral tasks for subsistence (Laitan and Samatar 1987, 107). This dependence left little opportunity for export earnings and a commercial class, leaving the prospects for economic growth looking dim.

Yet there were several reasons for optimism on the Somali side. First, Somalia was able to receive an unprecedented amount of foreign aid. Mogadishu collected over $200 million in foreign economic assistance through the early 1960s, doubling the sub-Saharan average. This cash influx led to the construction of new government buildings and eventually to a quintupling of the military (Laitan and Samatar 1987, 107–8). Another reason for hope was the Somali expectation that it could achieve a "Greater Somalia" rather cheaply. On all fronts, and especially in the Ogaden, the Somali government believed that multinational states could not survive in an era of nationalism (Laitan and Samatar 1987, 136). Thus, the Somalis in Ethiopia, Kenya, and French Somaliland would be directed back to Somali sovereignty either through international negotiations, plebiscites, or internal rebellions within the bordering multinational states.

As for the Ogaden specifically, Somalis believed that Ethiopia would fragment when Haile Selassie died or was deposed. This expectation came from past experience; Ethiopia had not had a smooth dynastic transition for the last two hundred years. Almost thirty years of disarray separated the reigns of Menelik and Haile Selassie, and therefore the Somali leadership believed that all they had to do was put the country in a position to mobilize Somali and Oromo sentiments in the Ogaden and wait. To this end, the Somali government organized and funded the WSLF, which was to become Mogadishu's tool for prying the Ogaden away from Ethiopia. The WSLF remained separate from the SNA, serving the dual purpose of cheaply infiltrating the Ogaden and not arousing a general escalation to war (Laitan and Samatar 1987, 129–34).

Ethiopian calculations were much simpler. With a military six times greater than the Somali equivalent, and an economy that, while not prosperous, was steady, there was little reason to compromise with Pan-Somali sentiments. Competing with the Somalis did not draw significant resources away from the economy because Ethiopia already had ample hardware and manpower, funded by the United States with promises of more (Ofcansky 1993a, 291). In contrast to Somali preoccupations with Ethiopia, Addis Ababa focused its attention on securing trade routes and diplomatic initiatives around the region and globe. Ethiopia was particularly successful at securing beneficial agreements with France regarding Djibouti and the new rail link, and with the new Kenyan government in signing the mutual defense agreement (Lefebvre 1991; Marcus 1995).

Domestic Rivalry Outbidding Environment

In Somalia, the early years of independence saw a moderate level of threat inflation from elites. As noted, the popularity of the Pan-Somali movement made any gesture renouncing Somali claims on the Ogaden highly unlikely. The first administration, led by President Aidan Abdullah Osman and Prime Minister Abdirashiid Ali Shermarke, had unanimous support from all parties in the national assembly in "all matters affecting unification" (Latian and Samatar 1987, 73). Although Pan-Somali aims were popular, the Ogaden was not the only point of discussion. President Osman was from the Hawiye clan, which has few links to the Ogaden region. He and Prime Minister Shermarke suggested a vote on independence in French Somaliland (which Somalia later lost in 1967) and negotiated with Kenya concerning the NFD. In 1962, Kenyan nationalist Jomo Kenyatta and opposition leader Ronald Ngola were invited to Mogadishu for friendly talks concerning the state of the NFD. When these talks failed, Somalis began supplying the resistance fighters in the NFD but refused to send troops. Therefore, contention in the Ogaden shared the stage with negotiations and conflict elsewhere.

The pressure to escalate tensions was mitigated by Somali institutional incentives and low information asymmetries. First, the Somali press was not only free from most forms of government control and censorship, but was thriving. After camels, a radio was touted as the most prized Somali possession (Laitan and Samatar 1987). Threat inflation was unlikely to be successful, because no one group controlled the tools of propaganda. Radio broadcasts kept the masses informed of the treatment of Somalis abroad, but also of the need to integrate the North and South, increase literacy, and spur industrialization (Hooglund 1993, 170–72). Further, the constitution gave parties the freedom to organize and publicly run for government offices. This freedom supplied an incentive to many opposition forces to voice criticisms of government policy in public (Laitan and Samatar 1987, 69). Limited information centralization mechanisms, owing to the free press and legally protected opposition, led to smaller information asymmetries that could be used by a leader or challenger to mobilize mass opinion behind an invasion of the Ogaden.

The Ogaden question was not as important or salient in Addis Ababa as it was in Mogadishu. There was not general antipathy toward Somalis in Somalia from the Ethiopian people, and Ethiopians did not feel threatened by Somali forces. Although some opposition groups were present in the universities, they protested for more domestic development rather than for a tougher foreign policy. The government did have control over the tools of propaganda, including radio and print publications, but elites, including Haile Selassie, were unlikely to consolidate power by steeling the country against a Somali menace. The public was not suspicious of Somalis, and the information centralization mechanisms that did exist were not being used to inflate the Somali external threats (Ofcansky 1993a, 291–93).

Opportunity for Escalation

It is clear that Somalia's chances to take the Ogaden from Ethiopia by force were slight. Ethiopia had six times the quantitative military capability, according leading indicators (Singer 1987). There were also important qualitative advantages enjoyed by the Ethiopians. The Ethiopian air force included a squadron of F-86 jet fighters that could penetrate Somali air space without opposition. Also, the United States was sending personnel to train the Ethiopian army, and some four thousand Ethiopians received training in the United States. Interestingly, this group included future leader Mengistu Haile Mariam, who attended classes at the University of Maryland. Somali training lagged behind until well after the 1962 grant from the Soviet Union (Ofcansky 1993b, 182–83). The Somali strategy illustrated their position of weakness. While slowly expanding the military in relative terms, the funds to the unconventional WSLF guerrilla force were viewed as the best hope for successfully bringing Somali control to the Ogaden (Woodward 1996, 125–26).

Conversely, one could argue that Ethiopia did have an opportunity to escalate the dispute. It could launch strikes on Somali cities quite close to Mogadishu. In fact, as discussed above, attacks of this type occurred in 1964, and they illustrated Somali weakness, particularly to air strikes. Nevertheless, Ethiopian incentives for escalation, apart from opportunity, were lacking. They controlled the Ogaden and did not claim any additional territory in Somalia.

Summary and Analysis

During the early period of Somali-Ethiopian interstate rivalry, dynamic two-level pressures were pushing both countries toward maintaining, but not significantly escalating or de-escalating, the dispute. The expected benefit of continued rivalry and conflict far outweighed the prospective costs for Somalia and Ethiopia. In Somalia, domestic pressure to build a Greater Somalia, and elite perceptions that this could be accomplished at low cost, made de-escalation unpopular and politically dangerous. In comparison, immediate escalation was unnecessarily costly and risky. For Ethiopia, the costs of holding off Somali claims were quite minimal, given the qualitative and quantitative military advantage Addis Ababa enjoyed. Also, the benefits of holding the Ogaden were viewed as integral to suppressing and deterring other internal nationalist movements.

The incentives for elites to inflate international threats and outbid other political opponents were largely absent. Somalia nationalism suffused the Pan-Somali movement but concentrated not only on the Ogaden, but also on the NFD and Djibouti. Therefore, an escalation in the Ogaden would not create a Greater Somalia by itself. Further, the democratic structure of the Somali government, press freedoms, and decentralization of government information did not allow any one group to control propaganda and mobilize the masses for their own interests. No single group of elites controlled the radio stations, policy debates, or other levers of information. Pan-Somalism was popular, but it shared the public policy stage with issues relating to domestic development. In Ethiopia, the Ogaden was not a salient issue that could be used to mobilize the masses or gain public office. Although Haile Selassie did control the means of propaganda, these tools were used to spur opinion against Eritrea and other internal enemies.

Taken together with the lack of opportunities for escalation and de-escalation, the dynamic two-level logic presented earlier suggests that both sides would continue to maintain their rivalry, without significant escalation or de-escalation. If military conflict was to break out, as in 1964, both states had an incentive to keep the conflagration from reaching all-out war. Somalia perceived that its chances to unify the Ogaden would be better in the future, and Ethiopian defense of the status quo would limit escalation and de-escalation.

1965–1969

Rivalry History

The attacks in 1964 and failure to create a united Somalia led to a robust policy debate in Mogadishu. These deliberations saw their clearest articulation in the 1967 campaign between former president Osman and former prime minister and current president Shermarke. Osman had supported a greater Somalia and had run the country with Shermarke during the conflicts in 1961 and 1964. His previous defeat was directly related to the military and diplomatic failures during that period. Shermarke was perceived as the strongest supporter of expansion and Pan-Somalism at "all costs" (Laitan and Samatar 1987, 74). Mahammad Igaal, Shermarke's choice for prime minister, favored a more nuanced approach, in which Somalia would ally with the United States and tacitly renounce its territorial goals. In return, Igaal proposed that Somalia would gain economic aid and be rewarded with admission into the East African Community.

From 1967 until the 1969 coup, Somali policy attempted to de-escalate tensions with Ethiopia, in order to cajole aid from the United States and join the East African Community, while at the same time continuing to build up its own military. Igaal stopped supplying the WSLF in Ethiopia and other groups in Kenya, and in a joint communiqué, Igaal and Haile Selassie agreed to a cooperative military commission to monitor the Ogaden border. The two states also agreed to set up direct commercial and telecommunication links and terminated the state of emergency in the Ogaden.

Despite limited cooperation, Somalia continued to spend 40 percent, or $58 million, more of its GNP on military projects than the African average. Igaal was also careful to ensure that Somalia would not renounce its rights to protect the Ogaden residents (Laitan and Samatar 1987, 138–39). To illustrate Somalia's continued interest in the Ogaden, Igaal issued a formal protest and a threat to end détente when Ethiopia enforced a tax on Ogaden livestock. Not surprisingly, these contradictory policies produced little movement on either front. No progress was made on the Somali application to the East African Community, and Ethiopia continued to enjoy military superiority (Keller 1993, 99–103). Selassie was careful during this period to avoid both military and diplomatic entanglements relating to the Ogaden, while he focused on increased student demonstrations and other liberation movements.

The events data in figure 6 again show a pattern of rivalry maintenance with a few notable exceptions. Somalia's mean cooperation scores were generally higher than those from Ethiopia, mirroring Igaal's policy of limited détente. In addition, the continued balancing of cooperation with continued threats is reflected in the increased variance in rivalry interactions during this period.

Conventional Explanations

Igaal's limited peace initiative in 1966 is not adequately explained by either domestic variables or reciprocity, although domestic explanations do play an important role in the slight change in Somali policy trajectory. During this time, Ethiopia did little to reciprocate Somali compromises, and in fact undercut Igaal's support by failing to back Mogadishu's bid for East African Community membership. Conversely, the democratic institutions of the Somali state helped Igaal present his message of domestic development to the people and rally support for peace. The political triumph of peace over bellicosity may have been unlikely in a nondemocratic context. Two important questions that are not explained by either conventional argument are: (1) Why was the Somali peace initiative so limited, as Igaal refused to give up Mogadishu's claims on the Ogaden? and (2) What correlates with the timing of the policy change, since the democratic institutions were present previously and changed little during this period? A constant is little help in explaining the variance in rivalry interactions.

Dynamic Two-Level Pressures

From a dynamic two-level-pressure perspective, Ethiopian-Somali conflict was altered by the rising Somali costs of competition and the mounting

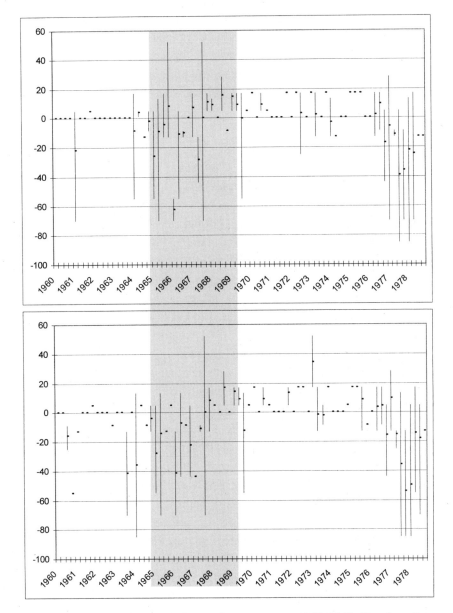

Figure 6. Somali-Ethiopian conflict and cooperation, 1965–1969. *Top:* Somali-to-Ethiopian events; *bottom:* Ethiopian-to-Somali events. COPDAB scale -100 to 60. Smaller numbers represent more conflict, 1965–1969 in frame.

salience of French Somaliland in the eyes of Somalis in the mid-1960s. While Ethiopia's position remained firm, Somalia was forced to reanalyze its Ogaden policy as a result of domestic doubts and military defeats. These changes led to a general pessimism about Pan-Somali aims and led the rivalry toward temporary and limited détente.

Future Expectations

Laitan and Samatar note that after 1964, Somalia began to feel the rising costs of pursuing Pan-Somali principles (1987, 178). In response to the repeated failure of negotiations with Britain over the NFD, Somalia broke off diplomatic relations with London. Although this break was a clear signal of discontent, it cost Somalia approximately $1.3 billion in promised international aid. Similarly, the high spending on defense had curbed domestic development, and the Somali economy remained largely agrarian.

There were some notable economic successes. Somalia was not dependent on a foreign source for sugar, and livestock exports continued to grow. Also, the irrigation and road infrastructure continued to improve throughout Somalia. However, the country could not overcome its dependence on foreign assistance. A United Nations Food and Agriculture Organization (FAO) report in 1967 highlighted the severe deterioration of grazing land in northern Somalia, which in turn reduced arable land and increased Somali dependence on foreign grain (Laitan 1993, 125–26).

Somalia's failures in domestic development were exacerbated by its lack of success internationally, as the three errant points of the Somali flag seemed to have drifted farther away. The NFD became part of Kenya, as irredentist revolts there were successfully repressed. French Somaliland remained separate, and the Ogaden was still controlled by Ethiopia. In fact, the Somali claims in the Ogaden were more tenuous in 1965 than in 1960. The military defeats in 1964 had illustrated Ethiopia's broad military superiority, and the unconventional guerrilla tactics of the WSLF had led to strikes on Somali territory. Most distressing was the fact that with each military battle, more Ethiopian troops poured into the Ogaden. The administration of Harer and Jijiga became more centralized and Ethiopian rule and tax collection became more prominent (Woodward 1996, 125–26). The costs of continuing to battle Ethiopia intermittently would only worsen the problems with the domestic economy, while also scaring off needed foreign aid.

International support was also lacking for the Somali cause. Mogadishu made numerous attempts to have the Ogaden problem adjudicated by the Organization of African Unity (OAU) and the former colonial powers. However, because of Ethiopia's clout, and the multinational character of many other African states and great powers, few allies could be found for the Greater Somalia cause. For example, the Soviet Union refused to acknowledge Somali claims in the Ogaden because they were afraid it would set an irredentist precedent for their own multinational empire (Woodward 1996, 125–26). Likewise, the United States supported Ethiopian sovereignty, both because it did not want to extend a rationale for civil wars and irredentist claims elsewhere in Africa and because Washington maintained a base in Ethiopia. The United States did agree to provide assistance for a minimal five-thousand-troop Somali army, an insufficient force for anything but defense (Ofcansky 1993a, 208–14). Little to no international pressure was brought to bear on Ethiopia to compromise.

In Ethiopia, the situation remained relatively stable. Although Ethiopian GDP remained stagnant, Addis Ababa had proved capable of holding off Somali claims and dealing with the WSLF in the Ogaden. Support from the United States continued and even increased throughout the 1960s (Ofcansky 1993a, 291). Despite this support, there were two events that hinted at future problems. First, student demonstrations for land reform and an end to corruption increased in frequency and intensity. Second, the Eritrean Liberation Front (ELF) had transformed itself from a primarily Muslim movement exiled in Cairo to a nationalist organization (supported by Syria and Iraq) that included urban Christians. These insurgencies did not yet amount to a challenge to the regime or Ethiopian control of Eritrea and did not worry Selassie (Schwab 1985, 103–4).

Domestic Rivalry Outbidding Environment

Developments in French Somaliland temporarily shifted Somali attention from the Ogaden region. In 1966, French president Charles de Gaulle made a state visit to Djibouti, stirring numerous protests by Somalis seeking independence. The French responded with armed repression and forced deportation. Because Somalia was unwilling to take the refugees, a camp was set up near the port of Djibouti. Mogadishu responded with verbal warnings and a campaign to raise public awareness of these injustices (Gorman 1991, 37–38).

With Somali public attention split between the Ogaden and Djibouti, escalation in the Ogaden was temporarily less salient. In the 1967 presidential election, former prime minister Shermarke ran against the incumbent Osman. The central difference between the two candidates was that Osman favored internal economic development while Shermarke prioritized pressing Pan-Somali claims. Rallying around the mistreatment of the Somalis in Djibouti, Shermarke and Pan-Somalism again proved popular, following the SYL model. Even though Shermarke promoted Igaal, a moderate, to prime minister, the leader of the executive branch made it clear that Somalia would not give up its claim on the Ogaden. As long as Igaal walked the thin line between reducing the threat from Ethiopia and not offering any tangible concessions in the Ogaden, he could hold the government together. Yet this policy also depended on cooperation from Ethiopia. If Addis Ababa looked like it was taking advantage of Somali weakness, détente was not likely to last (Samatar 1993, 33–36).

The Ethiopian situation remained similar to the early 1960s period. Selassie remained in control and Somali-Ethiopian conflict was not highly salient domestically, as protests and public attention centered on government corruption and increased development. Selassie's power was not conditional on Somali-Ethiopian conflict. Instead Addis Ababa continued to portray itself as the embodiment of independent Africa (Woodward 1996, 32).

Opportunity for Escalation

The Somali opportunities for escalation remained virtually unchanged during this period. Although Soviet support began to reinforce Somali power, even the target 14,000-man army was not a threat to Ethiopian sovereignty in the Ogaden. Similarly, the WSLF continued to operate in the Ogaden but had little hope of starting an irredentist revolution. With both conventional and unconventional forces unlikely to liberate the Ogaden successfully or to impart significant costs on Ethiopia, escalation remained an unattractive option.

For Ethiopia, punitive or preventative military action against Somalia became more costly after 1966 because of the rising Eritrean nationalist movement. By 1966, The ELF was emerging as a viable threat to Ethiopian forces. The insurrection was far from succeeding in its goals, but it continued to tie down considerable numbers of Ethiopian troops and armor. Although Ethiopia had the manpower to fight in Eritrea and the Ogaden simultaneously, this outcome was not desirable (Schwab 1985, 103–4).

Summary and Analysis

The configuration of prospective costs, domestic outbidding, and opportunities explains the changes and continuities in Somali-Ethiopian relations from 1965 to 1969. The combination of rising prospective rivalry costs in the form of economic development problems, a moderate domestic outbidding environment, and a pessimistic military outlook made Somali de-escalation likely. These factors also explain the low intensity of Igaal's détente initiative. Igaal could not remain in control if Somali claims to the Ogaden were abandoned. The Ethiopian constellation of costs and low outbidding suggests that they would maintain control over the Ogaden and continue to collect taxes and consolidate their rule. On the other hand, remaining open to limited de-escalation and freeing up resources to fight in Eritrea was a relatively cheap strategy. Ethiopia did not offer a federalized structure or a major compromise but would accept any de-escalation in Somali threat and would permit some pastoral activities. The crackdown on the Ogaden livestock tax is one example of the continued Ethiopian consolidation of the region in the face of limited Somali de-escalation. The major concession made by Addis Ababa, giving pastoralists the right to graze in the Ogaden lands, could easily be taken away at any time and did not threaten their centralization plans.

1969–1974

Rivalry History

The Shermarke-Igaal stalemate was shattered by a coup d'etat in 1969 that left Muhammad Siad Barre in charge of the government. From 1969 to 1974, Barre moved to construct regional alliances in the Organization of

African Unity. This effort resulted in a joint Somali-Ethiopian plan to develop the Ogaden. By 1974, Barre had signed a Treaty of Friendship and
Cooperation with the Soviet Union and had begun significantly upgrading
Somali military potential, narrowing the military gap with Ethiopia. The
influx of 150 T-35s, 100 T-54 tanks, and 50 MiG fighters, as well as
bombers, ground-to-air missiles, and Soviet advisors, led Somali planners
to think that the failures of 1964 would not be repeated. Not including foreign aid, Somali military spending more than doubled from 1967 to 1974
(Brzoska and Pearson 1994, 180–88).

While Somalia was growing stronger through external aid, internal divisions weakened Addis Ababa. Ethiopia undertook military action in
Gojam to collect agricultural taxes in the late 1960s, but the army was
forced to retreat in 1969. More fundamentally, separatist movements in
Eritrea severely weakened Haile Selassie's external projection capabilities.
The ELF and the Eritrean People's Liberation Front (EPLF) continued to
mobilize supporters to the cause of Eritrean independence. By 1973, the
rebel organizations had become a serious internal threat to the Ethiopian
regime, and in early 1974, the EPLF won an important battle at Asmara
(Turner 1993, 46–48).

Internal dissent mixed with famine to produce an Ethiopian revolution in 1974. Growing from a provisional army revolt over food and water
in Welo and Tigray to a mass protest, the new ruling Derg deposed and imprisoned Haile Selassie on September 12. The Derg was composed of low-
ranking military officers, and it elected Major Mengistu Haile Mariam as
chairman. The ensuing power struggle between Mengistu and various
leaders left Ethiopian leadership unclear, although Mengistu was eventually victorious (Tiruneh 1993, 60–70).

Despite this volatility, no major war or compromise was initiated by either party. In 1973, when a U.S. drilling company discovered the prospect
of natural gas in the Ogaden, both countries mobilized their forces to
claim any possible profit, but no war or battle ensued. Conversely, in negotiations in December 1973, both countries were unwilling to compromise and tensions increased. As Gorman notes, "neither party was willing
to press the issue," and either escalate to war or compromise (1991, 40). Although Barre was willing to de-escalate in Kenya and Djibouti, this option
was not persuasive in the Ogaden. For Ethiopia, even the Asmara dispute

did not shake the Ethiopian belief that it needed to hold the Ogaden to protect its territorial and multinational integrity (Keller 1993, 103). Again, when we turn to a quantitative representation of these rivalry interactions in figure 7, a rather stable pattern of limited conflict emerges. Neither state pushed the envelope toward escalation, despite a few threats at the beginning of Barre's tenure.

Conventional Explanations

On the surface, reciprocity would seem to be a likely explanation for the rivalry interactions during this period. Both states matched mobilizations in 1973 but avoided war. Similarly, neither state was willing to cooperate in the ensuing negotiations. But reciprocity does not explain why Barre began his arms buildup at the same time that Ethiopia was suffering a growing famine. More important, the domestic incentives for continuing the rivalry in both capitals are not considered by such an analysis. A focus on coalition building and domestic politics might anticipate more Somali bellicosity under Barre, as the government became much less democratic. However, this increase in autocracy and cartelization did not correlate with conflict, as Barre restrained from launching an invasion of the Ogaden in 1974.

Dynamic Two-Level Pressures

Instead of ignoring the interaction between the domestic and international levels of analysis during this time, a focus on expectations about the future, domestic outbidding environments, and opportunities for escalation fills the holes left by the more conventional explanations. Barre maintained the rivalry, through increased arms buildups and the avoidance of compromise, because he expected Somalia to be in a stronger position later. In addition, the domestic coalition supporting his rule strongly favored continuing the Somali claims on the Ogaden. In Addis Ababa, although famine and revolution had raised the expected future costs of rivalry for the Ogaden, there was no domestic pressure to change strategies, and no international opportunity to change the status quo by force.

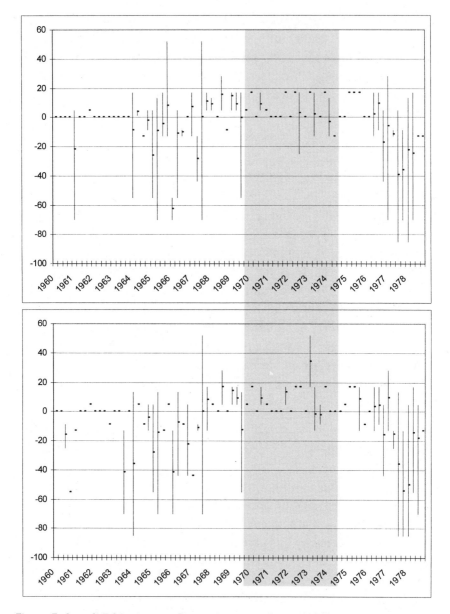

Figure 7. Somali-Ethiopian conflict and cooperation, 1970–1974. *Top:* Somali-to-Ethiopian events; *bottom:* Ethiopian-to-Somali events. COPDAB scale -100 to 60. Smaller numbers represent more conflict, 1970–1974 in frame.

Future Expectations

In 1969, the landscape of Somali-Ethiopian relations began to change. On October 20, Siad Barre took control of the government after a coup d'etat. As clear head of the ruling Supreme Revolutionary Council (SRC), Barre began to improve the Somali economic and military outlook. Barre was able to get considerable aid from the European Community's Development Fund, the World Bank, and the Soviet Union. Although aid had been flowing into Somalia since independence, the Barre regime ended much of the corruption that siphoned off public money for private gain. Poverty and illiteracy decreased, agriculture was diversified, and general health improved owing to a vigorous immunization program. Most important, the famine that was to spread through Ethiopia was averted in Somalia with external help (Gorman 1991, 40–41).

Even more dramatic than the domestic development was the military buildup Barre was able to facilitate. In 1969, Somalia had a 10,000-man army and a small air force. But through the early 1970s, the Somali military more than doubled in size and effectiveness. The 1972 visit of Soviet foreign minister Andrei Grechko to Somalia marked the acceleration of arms transfers from the Soviet bloc to Mogadishu. Somalia had received $32 million in support from the Soviet Union in earlier years, but this figure increased markedly after 1969, when the Soviet Union became Somalia's major arms supplier. With the promise of more economic and military aid in the future, Barre was quite optimistic that Somalia would be in a strong position to bargain for the Ogaden in the near future (Gorman 1991, 40–42; Ofcansky 1993b, 208–10). Thus, the expected future costs of rivalry were decreasing for Somalia because of the military and economic improvements.

The situation was reversed in Ethiopia. The drought in the Tigray and Wallo provinces spurred the most dramatic change in Ethiopian expectations. By 1972, with the rains still stalled, people began leaving the countryside. In 1974, estimates of the dead reached 100,000 (Farer 1976, 12; Gorman 1991, 41). Famine alone was enough to induce pessimism in Ethiopian projections about the future, but the perceived inaction of the government also increased domestic discontent. The drought began in two provinces that had already been home to demonstrations against the government in the 1960s (Woodward 1996, 32). Scarcity fueled the flames of rebellion further. The biggest catalyst for the coming revolution was the popular perception that the government was acting to cover up the famine rather than dealing with the problems (Gorman 1991, 41).

Dissent was greatest in the military and universities. By February 1974, violence erupted in Asmara, when officers and enlisted men in the army's Second Division mutinied. Rebellion spread to Harer and Addis Ababa, with Selassie reorganizing his cabinet and replacing the prime minister to help quell the protests. With the revolution continuing, members of the armed forces began organizing the Armed Force Coordinating Committee (AFCC), later known as the Derg. (Gorman 1991, 41–42).

In this context, a triangular conflict in Eritrea erupted anew. The ELF and EPLF fought against each other, and each fought against the Ethiopian army. Casualties were estimated at over 1,200 and reflected the ferocity of the conflict (Turner 1993, 46–47). Violence also flared in Begendor and Gojjam (Gorman 1991, 43). This internal fighting sapped the military and economic edge Ethiopia held over Somalia. As Gorman (1991, 43), notes, the disparity between an ascending Somalia and a descending Ethiopia "bade poorly for the future of Ethiopian-Somali relations." For the time, Ethiopia remained strong enough to fight off a Somali attack, with continued American assistance. There was also hope that the Derg would restabilize the country, but this hope was much more fragile in 1974 than it had been ten years earlier.

Domestic Rivalry Outbidding Environment

The institutional changes in Somalia, precipitated by Barre's coup, placed the tools of propaganda in the government's hands and increased the information asymmetries between the leadership and the populace. The democratic government was disbanded and replaced by the SRC, the new un-elected ruling body. While the twenty-five-man SRC did rule by majority vote, debates were rarely published or made public, and public input was seldom sought. More fundamental, the SRC killed and jailed civilian officials who were not susceptible to "re-education" (Samatar 1993, 37–43). The tendency of Barre and the SRC to centralize power in their own hands found its culmination in Law Number 1, which gave the SRC the power of the president, the national assembly, the council of ministers, and most of the powers the courts previously held. This concentration of power reached its peak with Barre, who was head of state, president of the SRC, and commander-in-chief of the armed forces. Barre also had the power to control the press from Mogadishu. All radio broadcasts were censored by the SRC in order to carry out a propaganda campaign aimed at increasing support for Pan-Somali goals. This government also oversaw the publication of all newspapers and magazines that circulated in the country (Hooglund 1993, 170–72).

The Ogaden issue took on special importance given the motives of the coup and the coalition supporting Barre. In 1969, the coup had been popular because of both the domestic promise to end corruption and the international focus on Pan-Somalism. The SRC announced that "existing treaties were to be honored, but national liberation movements and Somali unification were to be supported" (Samatar 1993, 36–37). However, the irredentist Somali claimants were treated unevenly. Barre eventually ceded the NFD to Kenya in a number of speeches and public gestures, and French Somaliland/Djibouti had become less important since the vote against independence in 1967. Conversely, Barre's personal rule relied upon a tripod of clan allegiances, commonly referred to as the MOD. This grouping represented Barre's own Mareehaan clan, Barre's mother's Ogaden clan, and Barre's son-in-law's clan, the Dulbahante. At times, fully half of the SRC consisted of members of these three clans. As is obvious, the Ogaden clan had a special interest in compounding Somali military power and confronting Ethiopia on the Ogaden claims. To keep the coalition together, Barre had to be tough and uncompromising to the Ethiopians. While détente was possible with Kenya and Djibouti, de-escalation with Ethiopia, without some gains in the Ogaden, was likely to topple Barre's government (Samatar 1993, 40–43; Laitan and Samatar 1987, 140).

The dual forces of government centralization and a coalition mobilized against an external enemy locked Barre into a policy of confrontation with Ethiopia. Barre now had the tools to mobilize public opinion, as well as the institutional motivation to confront Ethiopia. As the country continued to amass arms through its relationship with the Soviet Union, domestic pressure to escalate mounted. When Selassie fell in 1974, Barre was pressed by his MOD coalition into forming a military plan to take the Ogaden. Although he held out against escalating at that time, outbidding pressures were building. Both the Ogadeni and Dulbahante leadership made it clear that Barre's position depended on the success and maintenance of the Ogaden claim (Lewis 1991, 90–91; Samatar 1993, 40–43). In Ethiopia, the Ogaden issue remained of low salience, as both the drought and Eritrean insurrection were perceived as higher priorities.

Opportunity for Escalation

The postcoup years saw Somalia gaining military strength quite rapidly. While this improvement increased the optimism about the future because more arms were expected, it also opened up an opportunity in the present to escalate the conflict. The capability ratio between Ethiopia and Somalia remained two to one. But with dissent in Eritrea and the dissolution of the Selassie regime, Somalia would be able to commit all of its forces to an Ogaden conflict, while most experts estimated that Ethiopia could only commit half of its troops to an Ogaden operation (Gorman 1991, 67). Similarly, the qualitative increase in Somali arms, in the form of T-34 tanks and MiG-15 and MiG-17 aircraft, plugged some of the deep holes in Somali defense that had become evident in 1964. A reinvigorated and Soviet-trained air force would not leave border cities as vulnerable to punitive Ethiopian strikes. Also, the tank and armored personnel carrier reinforcements would allow for a rapid deployment of a large number of troops. Maybe for the first time, Somali capabilities were in striking distance of Ethiopian control of the Ogaden (Brzoska and Pearson 1994, 180–90).

In Ethiopia, conversely, the ability to initiate and win a military engagement with Somalia was dwindling. With more troops committed to Eritrea, and morale running very low because of the perception of government inaction during the famine, Ethiopia's quantitative advantage was not matched with qualitative force. The situation was not yet dire. Even after the Derg deposed Selassie, U.S. arms continued to flow into the country. While the United States was postponing a general aid agreement to Ethiopia, it increased the dollar sum of arms shipments, which included aircraft and tanks, to Addis Ababa. The United States also attempted to counter Soviet support in Somalia by providing Ethiopia with F-5 fighters from Iran, and $200 million worth of surplus arms directed from Vietnam (Ofcansky 1993a, 291–94).

Summary and Analysis

Between 1969 and 1974, Barre's fits and starts toward escalation correlate with the shifts in dynamic two-level pressures. First, the inflow of arms from the Soviet Union, coupled with Ethiopian internal dissent, meant that an opportunity for escalation was present. Second, Barre's centralization of power under the SRC and his domestic coalition (MOD) made contesting the Ogaden an attractive political decision. The tools of the state could be used to mobilize citizens against Ethiopia and in support of escalation. Yet the Somalis were still one step away from the edge of escalation. Barre was able to hold off escalation in 1974 because it looked like any battle would be easier to fight later rather than sooner. As Somalia gained strength, and Ethiopia became weaker, the costs Somalia expected to pay in acquiring the Ogaden decreased (Gorman 1991, 41). Barre believed that by holding course and maintaining Somali momentum, he could be the liberator of the Ogaden. Thus, the final piece of the escalation puzzle, high expected future costs of maintenance, was still missing. Ethiopia, with its combination of moderate expected costs and low outbidding, also had an interest in maintaining the rivalry status quo. They were not in a position to escalate, but also believed de-escalation would prove too costly for the Eritrean battle.

1975–1978

Rivalry History

The Ethiopian-American alliance began to split in the mid-1970s over the new Derg government. In 1975 the United States postponed an economic aid package to Ethiopia. Although the United States did not believe that the new Ethiopian government was "intrinsically anti-U.S.," the administration doubted the new regime's dedication to its alliance with Washington. Even before the break with Washington had become public, the Derg sent a delegation to Moscow to negotiate an arms deal in December 1976. That same month, the United States announced its intention to close the Kagnew air force base and reduce the number of U.S. personnel in Ethiopia by September 1977. In response, Ethiopia evicted American military personnel and terminated the lease on the Kagnew station (Ofcansky 1993a, 291–94). In February 1977, U.S. secretary of state Cyrus Vance suggested that all grant military assistance to Ethiopia be terminated because of growing human rights violations. Therefore, just as Somalia was peaking in military power, Ethiopia was losing its main benefactor and had yet to receive aid from the Soviet Union, currently Somalia's principal ally.

After the Ethiopian revolution, Barre was under pressure to plan for the liberation of the Ogaden. The Somali leader's first step was to "lighten his load of enemies" (Laitan and Samatar 1987, 140). Through statements and meetings, Barre assured the Kenyans that Somalia had ceased support for dissidents in the NFD. Likewise, in 1975, when the French promised equal treatment for the Somalis in Djibouti, Mogadishu agreed not to interfere in decolonization. Having freed his hands to the north and south, Barre reorganized the WSLF in order to coordinate operations within the SNA for a potential Ogaden operation (Laitan and Samatar 1987, 141).

Despite these preparations, there were several reasons Barre himself was not enthusiastic about declaring war in 1975. First, Barre was going to be head of the OAU, and war in the Ogaden would make hosting diplomatic meetings awkward. Second, he believed that there was still a chance that Somalia could gain more through peaceful negotiations. Finally, the Soviet Union had told Barre that military aid would cease if Somalia attacked the Ogaden.

Eventually, Barre allowed regular army personnel to join in battle with the WSLF in early 1977. By July, 35,000 regular and 15,000 guerrilla troops had attacked the Ogaden region. Somali forces were successful in the first wave of attacks. After two months of fighting, Somalia controlled 90 percent of the disputed region and the city of Jijiga (Ofcansky 1993b, 184–85).

The tide turned definitively when the Soviet Union switched sides. The alliance about-face was caused by both ideological and geopolitical factors. When forced to choose, Moscow viewed Ethiopia as the more important and influential state. In addition, the rift between Ethiopia and the United States offered a window of opportunity to usurp American power on the Horn. In August 1977, all Soviet aid to Somalia ended, and Soviet military advisors left Somalia directly for Addis Ababa, taking most of Somalia's military maps of the region with them. The Soviets then supplied Ethiopia with $1.5 billion in military equipment, over seven times the aid Somalia had received in the previous three years. A Soviet-Cuban-

Ethiopian force swept back through the Ogaden, encircling Jijiga and forcing a Somali retreat.

The graphs in figure 8 dramatically show the increase in conflict and volatility during this period. What is of particular interest is the timing of the trend toward conflict. The 1974 Ethiopian revolution did not spur an immediate escalation from Barre. Instead, Somali bellicosity, and with it Ethiopian conflict, increased in late 1976. By 1977 the Ogaden war was in full swing for both parties, accounting for the high mean conflict levels and low cooperation scores in that year and 1978.

Conventional Expectations

Reciprocity, by definition, cannot explain Barre's decision to invade the Ogaden. Ethiopia did little to ignite the offensive. After seventeen years of intermittent threats and counterthreats, Barre sent 40,000 troops into the disputed territory, unprovoked militarily. Similarly, a purely domestic theory does little to explain the escalation because the changes in Somali institutions had long since occurred. Barre's increased centralization may have increased the probability of escalation, but some other dynamic must explain the timing. Why did Barre refrain from escalation in 1974, only to invade the Ogaden in 1977?

Dynamic Two-Level Pressures

As noted in the previous section, Somalia already possessed a mobilized outbidding arena and an opportunity for escalation in 1974. By 1977, extremely high expected future costs were added to the equation, as Moscow moved close to Addis Ababa. This configuration of a pessimistic future outlook, previous threat inflation, and a newly modernized army increased the probability of Somali escalation.

Future Expectations

The greatest shock to expectations about the future in the region occurred with the rumbling of realignment by the superpowers. The Derg propaganda became increasingly socialist, and Addis Ababa began making overtures to the Soviets. In 1976, an Ethiopian representative met with Soviet

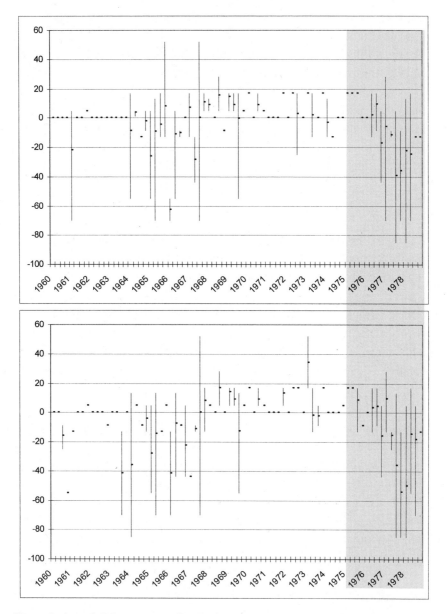

Figure 8. Somali-Ethiopian conflict and cooperation, 1974–1978. *Top:* Somali-to-Ethiopian events; *bottom:* Ethiopian-to-Somali events. COPDAB scale -100 to 60. Smaller numbers represent more conflict, 1974–1978 in frame.

officials to discuss the possibility of an alliance (Africa Research Bulletin 1977, 43–61), and by December of that year, the Soviet Union had pledged $100 million in arms to Ethiopia. Simultaneously, the United States and Ethiopian began to shy away from each other (see Gorman 1991, 52).

The cutting of Ethiopia's most important alliance tie, coupled with a growing Moscow–Addis Ababa relationship, left Somalia in a peculiar position. Barre had been quite successful in using the Soviet Treaty of Friendship and Cooperation to strengthen the Somali military. As noted above, Somalia had gone a long way toward creating an opportunity for escalation. In addition,

> Ethiopia's shift towards the Soviet Union also created some temporary problems for its [Ethiopia's] armed forces, most of which were trained only in the U.S. on American, not Soviet [style] weapons. Somalia, on the other hand, had only Soviet weaponry. While the transition to Soviet aid put Ethiopia at a temporary disadvantage, there were clearly implications in the trend of the balance of forces that bade ill for Somalia. (Gorman 1991, 68)

Ethiopia would soon begin to integrate the Soviet and American weapons, and the Soviet Union was moving further away from Somalia. Although alliance ties were not formally broken between the Soviet Union and Somalia until November 1977, Barre was making overtures to the United States through Saudi Arabia and to North Yemen much earlier. By July 1977, the Soviet Union had ceased shipments of arms to Somalia and continued to accelerate its support of Ethiopia (Ofcansky 1993b, 294–96). Therefore, "Somali leaders may have believed that future opportunities to recover the Ogaden would be limited in view of the trends in international support on the Horn" (Gorman 1991, 68).

There was some hope for Somalia in overtures from the United States. In June 1977, President Carter sent Dr. Kevin Cahill, a friend and physician, to Barre, to negotiate U.S. aid, but the official message from Washington said only that the United States would "consider sympathetically" Somalia's defensive needs. There is some debate about whether the message insinuated that the United States would ignore any escalation in the Ogaden. No amount of financial or military aid was promised. Although Saudi Arabia did pledge military aid, it could not counterbalance the arms

Ethiopia was projected to receive from the Soviets (Greenfield 1994; Gorman 1991, 61–68).

Ethiopia had $100 million worth of arms landing on the ground from the Soviet Union, while Somalia had some ambiguous nonbinding discussions with the United States. The longer Barre waited, the stronger Ethiopia would become. Thus, Barre faced a closing window of opportunity to take the Ogaden. Ethiopia was transitioning to the Soviet alliance and arms, and Somalia had no formal alliance with the United States to match. Somalia's projected future costs of rivalry were extremely high.

Domestic Rivalry Outbidding Environment

The question still remains, even if Barre thought the future was looking bleak, why not de-escalate in the Ogaden? De-escalation had been Barre's policy in the NFD and Djibouti in the early 1970s. In these cases, Barre made public statements relinquishing Somali claims on foreign territory and the Somali people that inhabited them. This same policy prescription was highly unlikely in the Ogaden because of the domestic outbidding arena that Barre had helped to create. During the previous five years, Barre had centralized power and rearranged the country's military structure. These changes benefited the members of his MOD coalition, but special treatment was given to the Ogadeni. Most of the officers in the SNA were from the Ogaden clan, and their support of Barre was conditional on his plans to take the Ogaden. The Ogaden clan was also central in linking together the Mareehaan, who were not generally well respected in the country, and the Dulbahante against a countercoalition of powerful clans. The Majeerteen, Hawiye, and Isaaq clans had been the power brokers during civilian rule from 1960 to 1969, and every president or prime minister during that time was from one of these three clans.

This countercoalition stepped up its criticism of Barre in 1974 (Laitan and Samatar 1987, 91–92). To protect himself, Barre took a hard line on the Ogaden. He integrated the WSLF into the SNA in 1974, and also stepped up funding to the guerrilla group (Gorman 1991, 78). While Pan-Somalism remained very popular, the clans residing in Djibouti and the NFD were not pillars of Barre's rule.

De-escalation was possible in Kenya and Djibouti because there was little incentive for the opposition to outbid Barre and call for attacks on the region. For example, the Harti clan segments in the NFD were not central to government power, and therefore a call for the liberation of the NFD would not mobilize the population relevant to leadership selection (Lewis 1991, 90–91). On the other hand, in the Ogaden, liberation was wildly popular among the central clan in the government coalition.

Hostile Ethiopian actions also accelerated both public and elite support for a militant hard line on the Ogaden. Laitan and Samatar noted, "most Somalis feel that under Ethiopian suzerainty Somalis get little but retribution" (1987, 136). The main Ethiopian government presence in the Ogaden was tax collection, and there were no state-sponsored schools in the Ogaden for the first decade of Ethiopian control. The jailing and harsh treatment of dissidents also elicited Somali sympathies. Most important, the stories of Ethiopian army members stealing camels and cattle from Somali nomads, and the 1964 air strikes within Somalia, fueled the enmity toward Addis Ababa. In comparison, the Kenyan government had not tipped the scales against itself in the same way. Somalis in Kenya could become full citizens and were not repressed in the same manner. Also, Kenya had never attacked Somali territory. Therefore, in the NFD, there was less for Somalis to mobilize against.

In Ethiopia, the incentives to mobilize support against Somalia remained as they were in the previous years. The Derg government continued to deal with insurrection in Eritrea and Tigray, and while the WSLF stepped up its activities in the Ogaden, the other rebellions were more salient and threatening (Turner 1993, 48–49). Therefore, there was little domestic elite pressure during this period to attack Somalia. Mengistu continued to hold the Ogaden, and the status quo was acceptable.

A power struggle in the Derg also broke out during that time. On November 23, 1974, fifty-nine political prisoners were executed, including General Amay, who had been the head of state. Following this "bloody Sunday," Tafari Benti became head of state, yet by 1976, a triangular power struggle involving Mengistu, Tafari, and Major Atnafu was underway. Internal hostility came to a head in February 1977, when a shootout erupted at the Grand Palace in Addis Ababa. Tafari and most of his supporters were killed. By November, Atnafu had been killed also. During this internal power struggle, Mengistu was unlikely to relinquish control over the

Ogaden to Somalia, possibly encouraging further resistance. Mengistu had taken swift steps to mobilize the army in reaction to Eritrean independence and would not do anything to jeopardize the territorial integrity of Ethiopia (Turner 1993, 54–56).

Opportunity for Escalation

As noted, Somalia had opportunities to escalate at any time from 1974 to 1977. Although Somalia was at an eight-to-one population disadvantage and a two-to-one military personnel disadvantage, these figures did not represent the true balance of forces. Resistance movements in Eritrea, Tigray, as well as Wallo and Arussi, meant that the population the Derg government could call on for service was less then twenty-eight million. Further, given internal dissent, Ethiopia's full force could not be mobilized in the Ogaden. U.S. State Department Intelligence estimated that only one-half of the Ethiopian force could be safely deployed to the Ogaden as after the uprisings in 1974 (Gorman 1981, 67, 67n. 59). This still left Ethiopia with a nominal personnel advantage, but that neglects the lack of training in the Ethiopian military. Gorman (1991, 67) suggests that only one-third of the Ethiopian military was ever ready for battle. When you add the overall advantage of the Somali tanks, armored personnel carriers, and training, "the balance of forces in July was apparently in Somalia's temporary favor" (Gorman 1991, 68).

Summary and Analysis

Not only the timing but also the direction of Somalia's change in rivalry policy is consistent with dominant dynamic two-level pressures during this period. None of the other Somali-claimed territories carried the same domestic salience as the Ogaden, especially to the MOD coalition. By at least early 1977, with the flip-flop of Soviet allegiance on the Horn, Somali policies reflected a pessimistic future outlook, a mobilized public, and an opportunity for escalation. As predicted by the dynamic two-level theory, this interaction of international expectations and domestic mobilization led to a general escalation by the strengthened Somali forces.

1978–1983

Rivalry History

The resounding defeat in the Ogaden left Somalia in a fragile position. With 8,000 troops killed, a decimated air force, and a lost alliance, the prospects for the Greater Somalia project looked dim. Barre attempted to ally with the United States, offering the use of the Berbera base built by the Soviets. But as technological changes made a communications station in East Africa less important to Washington, the forthcoming aid never reached earlier levels. Also, in the aftermath of the war, possibly as many as two million refugees entered Somalia, straining the already weak economy. An attempted coup in 1978 by a group of Majeerteen army officers illustrated the growing domestic discontent.

The Ethiopian victory led to the further consolidation of the Ogaden region and allowed Mengistu to begin supporting dissident groups representing the Isaaq, Majeerteen, and Hawiye clans that opposed Barre's rule. Ethiopia's military superiority also accelerated after the war. From 1979 to 1989, the Ethiopian army grew by over 400 percent to about 350,000 soldiers, while during the same period the Somali army grew by less than 50 percent to 54,000 (Keller 1993, 104).

Mengistu supported the raids in January 1982 by the Somali National Movement (SNM) and used Somali Salvation Democratic Front (SSDF) units to punish WSLF guerrillas and a small SNA force that had infiltrated the Ogaden. On June 30, 1982, approximately 8,000 Ethiopian troops and Somali dissidents attacked the border towns of Ferfer, Balambale, Galcaio, and Guldogob. Although repulsed in Galcaio and Ferfer, the Ethiopian-led force took control of Balambale and Guldogob. The combined guerrilla-army force represented less than a tenth of Ethiopian manpower and underscored the weakness of the Somali forces. However, Mengistu did not press his advantage, and he even withdrew fresh reinforcements that had arrived from Warder (Greenfield 1994, 112–13n. 14). This was a limited punitive strike in response to Barre's continued maintenance of Somali claims. Despite success on two fronts, Mengistu held back further escalation, choosing instead to maintain the rivalry.

Figure 9 presents the WEIS scores of conflict (lower scores) and cooperation (higher scores) for the post-1979 period. It can be seen that there are few cooperative interactions in the years after the Ogaden. Also, there is only intermittent conflict registered, especially on the Somali side.

Conventional Explanations

There is little doubt that Barre continued to maintain Somali claims on the Ogaden for domestic reasons. As noted, his rule, to a large extent, relied upon support for the Ogaden cause. Had Somalia been more democratic, it is possible to argue that de-escalation would have been preferred in Somalia, given the growing poverty and civil strife. A broad-based government may not have needed to heed the electoral clout of the Ogadeni clan, as did Barre. Domestic politics did not serve as the sole motivation for Ethiopian actions. Mengistu was an autocratic ruler at the time and indeed did launch an attack in 1982. Nonetheless, that attack did not involve the bulk of Ethiopian forces and was limited in nature from the outset (Greenfield 1994). If there were any changes in the rivals' domestic institutions, Barre's rule became more cartelized and totalitarian as he crushed his opposition. The reasons that Barre moved from escalation in 1977 to maintenance in 1979 involve more than purely domestic logic.

It is also apparent that reciprocity and the international action-reaction sequence in the rivalry were not symmetrical during this time. Although in some ways Ethiopian support for the SNM mirrored Somali backing of the WSLF, Ethiopian conflict was much harsher than Somali actions, as the 1982 raid illustrates. Why neither state seriously offered to de-escalate the rivalry during this period, especially Barre, remains to be explained despite reciprocity.

Dynamic Two-Level Pressures

Dynamic two-level pressures changed in two ways after the war. Somalia squandered its opportunity to escalate, not only losing Soviet support, but then having Moscow's might arrayed against it. Barre had little hope of changing the status quo militarily. As domestic outbidding remained salient in Mogadishu, and the MOD clan still supported Barre's rule, de-escalation with Ethiopia was also unattractive. Another change was that Mengistu's security increased after the war, and he was able to turn his at-

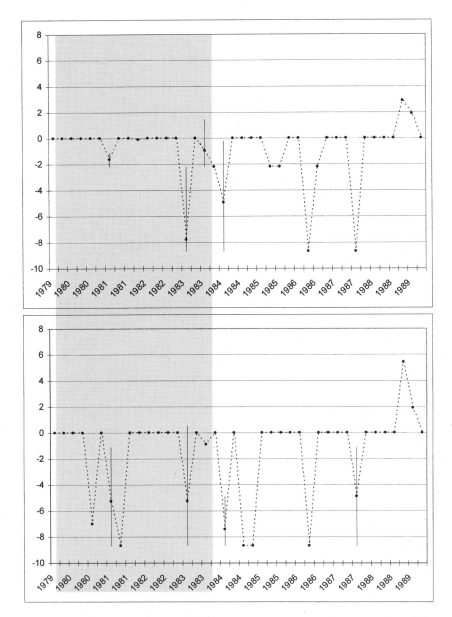

Figure 9. Somali-Ethiopian conflict and cooperation, 1978–1983. *Top:* Somali-to-Ethiopian events; *bottom:* Ethiopian-to-Somali events. WEIS scale -10 to 8. Smaller numbers represent more conflict, 1979–1983 in frame. Dotted lines connect the means.

tention to other domestic threats. Therefore, the future looked bright in Addis Ababa, but bleak in Mogadishu. In short, the rivalry was maintained because Barre had no opportunity, and Mengistu had little reason, to change the status quo during this time.

Future Expectations

The Ogaden war only accelerated the decline of Somalia and the ascent of Ethiopia, which had been expected in 1977. Internal divisions in Somalia began to trouble Barre's regime almost immediately after the war. In 1978, Majeerteen officers attempted to overthrow Barre. Although they failed in deposing the leader, the group was able to set up the SSDF in Ethiopia, with funds from Addis Ababa. The avowed goal of the organization was to replace Barre. In the north, Issaq dissent supported the formation of the SNM, created in London in 1981 but operating from bases in Ethiopia and supported by South Yemen. The SNM was able to launch an attack on Barre's troops in January 1982, and the SSDF, backed by substantial Ethiopian military personnel, attacked Somali territory in August 1982. Somali domestic instability was exacerbated by between 650,000 and 2 million refugees who had fled Ethiopia during the war and by a rising debt crisis (Laitan and Samatar 1987, 146–51). Also, domestic production of exports such as canned meats and bananas had fallen as much as 85 percent since 1975 (Laitan and Samatar 1987, 117).

The military situation looked equally dire for Somalia. In the Ogaden war, Somalia had lost fully half of its air force, three-fourths of its tanks, and its social cohesion. The inconsistent alliance with the United States never matched the scale or intensity of previous Soviet arms deliveries. The United States pledged only "defensive" military assistance in return for the use of the Berbera, Mogadishu, and Chisamayu airfields. In 1979, Barre asked for $2 billion and received only $40 million worth of military aid. While China sent American F-6 fighter bombers to Somalia in 1981, this supply could not close the growing air power gap with Ethiopia (Ofcansky 1993b, 208–13). For the near future, Somalia was forced to fight growing domestic discontent while dependent on the IMF for debt relief, and on the United States for defensive military needs.

Expectations about the future were much brighter in Ethiopia. Although the Tigray People's Liberation Front was able to hold its ground against the government in several instances, prospects for a government victory in Eritrea looked promising. The ELF and EPLF had begun fighting each other, with a significant escalation in internecine conflict in 1980. Meanwhile, Addis Ababa was able to commit more troops to Eritrea while Cuban reinforcements secured the Ogaden. The alliance with the Soviet Union remained strong, with Moscow promising $2 billion worth of weapons to support "Red Star," a program intended to roll back the Eritrean revolution (Woodward 1996, 95–97).

Domestic Rivalry Outbidding Environment

In response to domestic insurrection, Barre stepped up his repression of the opposition clans. In 1979, Barre sent his Red Berets to cut the water supply to a Majeerteen subclan that was related to the founder of the SSDF. In the following months, two thousand subclan members died of thirst. The Victory Pioneers, an urban militia group that supported Barre, stole livestock and harassed and assaulted members of the dissident Majeerteen clan. With the SSDF and SNM emerging as major threats to Barre's leadership tenure, the government did not move to mobilize support against Ethiopia. Instead, internal threats and repression took on paramount salience.

Barre still felt domestic pressure to maintain Somali claims in the Ogaden despite the high costs. The dissent from other clans only reinforced Barre's reliance on the MOD coalition. Moreover, he continued to support the WSLF intermittently, after a short hiatus because of U.S. pressure. U.S. Department of State analysts argued that Somalia remained committed to another attempt in the Ogaden (Hooglund 1993, 176). Mengistu continued to be highly unpopular in Somalia, and both the SNM and SSDF were generally considered treasonous organizations for even associating with Ethiopia (Laitan and Samatar 1987, 93). In addition, various cosmetic institutional changes, implemented in a new constitution in 1979, did little to alter Barre's power or coalition. By 1980, power resided unequivocally in the hands of Barre, the SRC, and the MOD coalition (Laitan and Samatar 1987, 92–94).

In contrast to Barre's reliance on the Ogadeni clan to hold his ruling coalition together, Mengistu's sovereignty depended on the Amaharas, who had little interest in the Ogaden or Somalia, apart from supporting

territorial integrity. Although Barre's attack on the Ogaden increased enmity towards Mogadishu, and domestic opinion supported destabilizing
Barre, Mengistu had relative autonomy in deciding the means to deal with
Barre. The immense institutional powers under Mengistu's control allowed
little room for Somali irredentism. Even the SNM and SSDF, while being
supported by Ethiopia, did not ask for the Ogaden to be returned to Somalia in a putative post-Barre world. Therefore, little domestic outbidding
pressure was brought to bear on Mengistu (Greenfield 1994, 107–8).

Opportunity for Escalation

As described earlier, Ethiopia continued to enjoy a military advantage over
Somalia in the post-Ogaden Horn. Addis Ababa had significantly more
mechanized armor and, high-tech aircraft, and more troops at its disposal.
The secure relationship with the Soviet Union gave Ethiopia access to new
arms shipments, as well as spare parts. Likewise, the use of Cuban troops to
guard the Ogaden lessened the multifront burden on the Ethiopian army.
The lack of matching U.S. support further eroded Somali chances to take
back the Ogaden successfully. In addition, the newfound SNM and SSDF
anti-Barre allies could be used in conjunction with conventional forces to
destabilize Somalia (Ofcansky 1993a, 1993b).

Summary and Analysis

One major question concerning this period of rivalry is, why did Barre not
attempt to negotiate a settlement? Obviously, if one just focuses on the
costs of rivalry, the situation in 1980 looked similar to that of 1964. Somalia had been as soundly defeated in 1961 and 1964, in admittedly limited
interactions, as they had been in the 1977 war. There was little hope of an
external savior. Yet in 1964 Somalia attempted a subtle shift in policy
under Igaal, where tensions were conditionally and temporarily reduced.
In 1980, Barre did not attempt to de-escalate the rivalry.

One reason suggested by dynamic two-level pressures is that the outbidding environment had changed from 1964 to 1980, although the costs
were similar. In 1964, Somalia was a newly formed democracy with a free
press, a broad franchise, and limited information asymmetries between
elites and the public. Under this institutional structure, Igaal was able to

stay in power by selling peace and domestic development to the relevant electorate. Although there was pressure to continue Pan-Somalism, hardliners like Shermarke could not significantly inflate the Ethiopian threat. By 1980, the information centralization mechanisms at Barre's disposal were significant. There was no free press and no legal opposition. More important, Barre's rule depended not on a broad franchise of voters who would benefit from domestic development plans, but on the relatively rich MOD coalition, centered around Pan-Somali claims in the Ogaden. Barre was unlikely to de-escalate despite the high costs because his coalition depended on continued maintenance of the Ogaden claims. The threat from the SNM and the SSDF did not yet threaten Barre's position in power; the 1978 coup was put down, and the Red Berets remained capable of crushing dissent. Short of backing down, Barre oversaw and planned the reinfiltration of the WSLF and the SNA into the Ogaden.

In Ethiopia, the victory in Eritrea and continued Soviet support left Addis Ababa in its strongest position in two decades vis-à-vis Somalia. The only question was how best to use its growing advantage. If we trichotomize Mengistu's decision into de-escalation, escalation, and maintenance, the extreme choices seemed to make little objective sense. There were few reasons for Mengistu to compromise on the Ogaden when Ethiopia remained, and expected to remain, in a position of strength. Likewise, a major escalation or an attempt to attack the Somali government directly seemed unnecessarily costly. Mengistu could hope to achieve security and stability in the Ogaden by continuing to pressure Barre with the SNM and SSDF, while consolidating the Ogaden and the border with Somalia. Thus, Mengistu's strategy appeared similar to Barre's choice to support the WSLF in the early 1970s, while building an arsenal of Soviet arms. Tactical raids were supported, but general war was avoided.

1983–1991

Rivalry History

By the early 1980s, the refugee problem as well as the strains of conflict with Ethiopia had begun to erode Somali state power. Attacks by dissident groups in 1983 exacerbated the already squalid refugee conditions. To deal with the refugee problem, large amounts of foreign aid were received throughout the 1980s, averaging about $70 million per year. However, much of this aid never reached the refugee camps and was diverted by Barre to the army for use in domestic repression. Also, Barre and his supporters attempted to recruit army members from the refugees to use against other clans, such as the Isaaq in the north. Woodward (1996, 183) reports that Barre even raided the houses and stores of indigenous Somalis looking to supply troops from his own clan. The internal situation in Somalia had degenerated to such an extent that over one in every four people in the country was in danger of starvation at the end of the 1980s (Woodward 1996, 183).

Ethiopia also had its own growing domestic problems in the middle to late 1980s. The Eritrean People's Liberation Front, taking advantage of the Ethiopian preoccupation with the Ogaden, captured most of the small towns and regions in Eritrea (Woodward 1996, 95). While the Ethiopian government was able to push the Eritrean Liberation Front (ELF) and EPLF into a general retreat with Cuban help immediately after the Ogaden war, the EPLF broke out of its trenches in 1984. As civil war again raged in Eritrea, the Tigray Peoples Liberation Front (TPLF) was able to attack government positions in the heart of Ethiopia. In 1988, the EPLF scored an important victory by overrunning an Ethiopian base at Afabet. The following year, the TPLF created the Ethiopian People's Revolutionary Democratic Front (EPRDF), which unified many other different dissident groups, including the Oromo Liberation Front (OLF). The combined forces in the EPRDF swept through the countryside with over half of the Ethiopian forces stationed in Eritrea (Woodward 1996, 95–99).

Barre and Mengistu moved toward compromise in 1986–88. In 1988, both governments agreed to end assistance to dissident groups, to exchange prisoners from the Ogaden war, and to facilitate the repatriation of refugees (Woodward 1996, 127–28; Lewis 1991, 92–93). The disappointing reaction to this peace accord in Somalia came in the form of a major assault by the SNM and a general feeling that Barre had sold out national pride. The opposition in Somalia compared the 1988 peace accord to the Hitler-Stalin pact of 1940 (Woodward 1996, 70). The reaction in Ethiopia was more muted, but the agreement did not save the Mengistu regime. As revolution spread in both countries Barre was forced to flee by tank from Mogadishu in 1991, and Mengistu left Addis Ababa four months later. With Somalia descending into a chaotic civil war, and with no central government in Mogadishu to continue to contend with the rivalry, external conflict became less salient for both parties.

The graphical analysis of the events data in figure 10 also represents the presence and timing of de-escalation in the rivalry. It is of note that the variance in interactions between the rivalries is very low during this time. The downward spikes in conflict prior to the third quarter in 1987 were threats and small skirmishes along the Ogaden, mostly between Ethiopian-backed Somali opposition forces and Barre's troops. The mutual peace agreement in 1988 is the highest recorded level of cooperation in the rivalry since the Igaal years.

Conventional Explanations

The action-reaction sequence of reciprocity aids but does not explain the move toward de-escalation in the mid-1980s. The promises and mutual easing of tension in 1986 culminated in the 1988 agreements. It is doubtful that Barre would have compromised on the Ogaden without a reciprocal promise from Mengistu. But this supposition does not clarify why Barre decided on de-escalation in the first place, or why Mengistu was only interested in compromise after the battle at Afabet.

The 1988 peace accords between Somalia and Ethiopia would also not be predicted by the coalition-building theory. Mengistu had solidified control of the Ogaden in 1978 and pushed further into Somalia in 1982. Ethiopian support for the SNM also expanded Mengistu's reach in the Horn. Why then, with no change in institutional structure, did peace prevail (at least temporarily) in 1988? Likewise, Barre had stepped up support for the WSLF in the early 1980s. Yet leading up to 1988, the cartelization of politics only increased, with narrowing clan favoritism and repression (Laitan and Samatar 1987, 93–94). Why did Barre sell out the interests of his supporting coalition in 1988 by renouncing the WSLF? Again, something else, more than reciprocity and coalition building, is needed to explain this diversity of interaction.

Dynamic Two-Level Pressures

The interaction between domestic and international forces supplies a more thorough explanation for the movement toward and timing of de-escala-

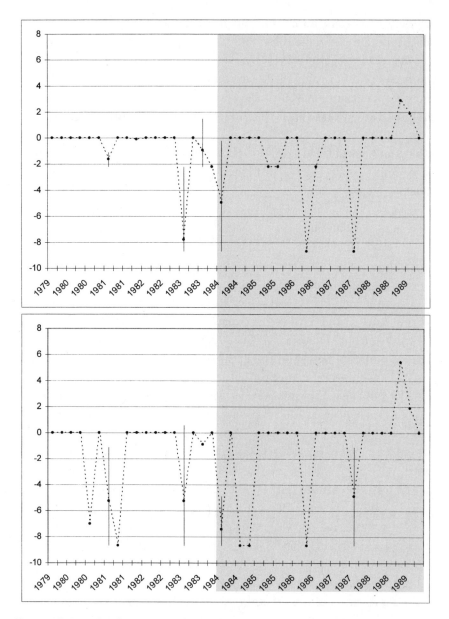

Figure 10. Somali-Ethiopian conflict and cooperation, 1984–1989. *Top:* Somali-to-Ethiopian events; *bottom:* Ethiopian-to-Somali events. WEIS scale -10 to 8. Smaller numbers represent more conflict, 1984–1989 in frame.

tion in the Somali-Ethiopian rivalry. Starting in 1982, Barre's restructuring of the military and high-level government offices decreased internal pressure to take back the Ogaden. Members of the Ogaden clan were replaced with Barre's own Mareehan clansmen. This domestic restructuring, coupled with the high prospective costs of maintaining the rivalry, given economic and refugee problems, and military defeats, made de-escalation likely.

Ethiopia also was suffering from domestic turmoil, decreasing the already low salience of the Ogaden issue in Addis Ababa. This unrest led to a generally pessimistic outlook. Therefore, by 1988, a reading of the dynamic two-level pressures suggests that both countries would seek to de-escalate their rivalry.

Future Expectations

After 1983, the internal turmoil in both Somalia and Ethiopia expanded. The first major Somali dissident group, the SSDF, continued to wage guerrilla war on government positions, and although it met with little success, the SSDF redirected valuable and scarce Somali resources. The SNM proved to be more effective. The mainly Isaaq dissidents were able to ally themselves with smaller clans in northern Somalia, formerly British Somaliland. These alliance ties, in conjunction with Ethiopian and South Yemeni aid, allowed the SNM to broaden its fight in the north. The Hawiye clans, occupying the central Abgaal region, where Mogadishu is located, remained loyal to Barre for the first part of the 1980s. These clans held important military and bureaucratic positions, and had fewer grievances than the Isaaq or Majeerteen. Barre had to use all of the state resources to suppress the SSDF and SNM. The $80 million in additional military aid from Washington, given in response to Ethiopian support to the SNM in 1982, was used to repress the Isaaq and Majeerteen rebellion, rather than to arm against Ethiopia. By 1987, even the WSLF was halting military operations in the Ogaden (Woodward 1996, 68–70).

The Somali economy was also deteriorating. In 1983, Saudi Arabia terminated the import of Somali cattle, sheep, and goats because of suspected disease in some livestock. Some believe that the import ban was related to heavy investing in Australian cattle by many Saudi businessmen (Laitan 1993, 132–36). This change created a large budget deficit, worsening the debt crisis and an already bad economic forecast for Somalia. Manufacturing fell from 1980 to 1987, and the World Bank projected that Somali GDP per capita had declined 1.7 percent from 1980 to 1989. The bleak outlook remained despite help from the IMF and the restructuring of Somali debt payments by the Paris Club. The escalation of interclan warfare during this period only exacerbated the dreary economic outlook.

In Ethiopia, domestic unrest was also heating up. From 1978 until 1983, Ethiopian forces, backed by Cuban troops and Soviet aid, had reduced the ELF to a small-scale operation and forced the EPLF into general retreat. Yet after the rout, the EPLF remained entrenched in Nacfa, and army discipline remained strong. In 1984, the EPLF launched a major offensive against Ethiopian positions. Although war would continue for more than seven years, the 1984 operation proved to be the beginning of the end of Ethiopian control over Eritrea. Additionally, the 13,000 regular Cuban soldiers had left Ethiopia earlier that year, increasing the defense burden on the Ethiopian army (Woodward 1996, 96–97). Even more troubling were the Soviet signals in 1987 and 1988 that they were reducing aid to Ethiopia and disengaging from the Horn.

The disengagement of communist support and the success of the EPLF spurred on other dissident movements in Ethiopia. The TPLF was able to mobilize peasant dissatisfaction within central Ethiopia to challenge Mengistu's rule. In the course of the Afabet capture, the EPLF killed or imprisoned 18,000 Ethiopian troops and took control of Ethiopian military equipment. Subsequently, the TPLF was able to destroy four Ethiopian army divisions and by April had captured Adirgat in northern Tigray and cut the main road from Addis Ababa to Eritrea.

The Ethiopian economic horizon also looked barren. In 1984, a new drought had begun in large swaths of Ethiopia, including Eritrea, Tigray, and Welo. In the north, there was almost total crop failure. Relief was hampered by the civil war, which siphoned off aid and cut off transportation routes. Famine continued in 1985 and spread further in 1986 to the south. In all, 3.8 million people were dependent on external food aid, with few prospects for renewed domestic production. Locust and grasshopper plagues in 1986 only continued the string of Ethiopian economic troubles. Thus, the prospective costs of external rivalry were extremely high to both Ethiopia and Somalia as a result of internal dissent and economic problems.

Domestic Rivalry Outbidding Environment

As may be expected under these dire economic circumstances and social conditions, both Somalia and Ethiopia, but particularly Somalia, spent less energy mobilizing the populace against each other. Radio propaganda in Mogadishu was turned against the Isaaq SNM and other dissident groups. While Ethiopia was implicated by its support of the SNM, Barre's tactics were aimed at stemming the growing tide of rebellion against his own regime. Barre also began to give preferential treatment to his own Maree-han clan over the other MOD coalition members (the Ogaden and Dulba-hante), who were viewed as less trustworthy. This favoritism eroded much of Barre's domestic power base, but particularly the anti-Ethiopian elements. The salient threat was domestic in focus (Woodward 1996, 68–70). Ethiopia remained unpopular within Somalia, but this enmity was not mobilized by the man who held the power of propaganda, at least in the middle to late 1980s. Even the SNM and SSDF had given up hope for Somali claims on the Ogaden. The situation worsened when Barre was involved in a near-fatal car crash in 1986, spurring a power struggle on the chance that Barre would not survive. In response, power was further consolidated in the hands of the Mareehan clan. Barre's ruling coalition was no longer contingent on Ogadeni claims, as the MOD alliance crumbled (Lewis 1991, 93).

In Ethiopia, a similar situation was unfolding. Mengistu remained firmly in control of the Derg and the Communist party apparatus, even after the ersatz institutional changes in 1987. Information was still controlled by the central government, and the Derg leadership. Domestic opposition around Addis Ababa, famine, and military defeats at the hands of the EPLF and TPLF left Mengistu attempting to rally the population against internal, not external, threats. Keeping the Ogaden remained important, but in 1987, the new constitution gave the territory limited autonomy, with little backlash at Mengistu. Keeping a tight grip on the Ogaden was

not as important when other provinces were already in open revolt and Somalia was in such a weakened position. Mengistu did not have to worry
about being outbid on hostility toward Somalia, only toward domestic dissident groups.

Opportunity for Escalation

After 1983, neither country was in a position to escalate the Ogaden conflict. Barre needed to use the military to quell domestic discontent. By that
time, the Isaaq, Majeerteen, and Hawiye clans were in open revolt. During
the mid- to late 1980s, human rights groups began reporting that the military was being used against SNM and the SSDP, as well as the newly formed
United Somali Congress (consisting of Hawiye clan members) in the heart
of Somalia. The highly trained Red Beret units were continually used
against these groups, and army officers were purged because of a lack of
"presidential loyalty" (Samatar 1993).

Although Ethiopian forces remained superior, escalating internal violence reduced their external fighting potential. The military had suffered
losses to the EPLF and the TPLF. In 1986, a group of Ethiopian army officers
mutinied in Eritrea. By February 1988, elements of the Second Revolutionary army were in revolt against Mengistu. Further, in early 1989, a coup
was launched against Mengistu, during his visit to East Germany. The coup
did not succeed, but the subsequent purges of military personnel again de-
teriorated Ethiopian military effectiveness.

Summary and Analysis

Dynamic two-level pressures explain why Barre was the first to seek de-escalation and to follow more closely the precepts of the peace treaty. As
noted, Barre changed the domestic outbidding environment he was operating in, by dismantling the MOD coalition. With the constantly high future costs of rivalry, the domestic changes correlate with the first peace
overtures Barre made through Kenya and Djibouti to Mengistu. At the
time, Mengistu was not ready to reciprocate cooperation. It would not be

until 1986 that Barre and Mengistu met face-to-face in Djibouti and not until 1988 was a peace agreement signed.

Ethiopian reticence between 1982 and 1988 can be explained by the changes in prospective rivalry costs over that period. Until 1982, the Red Star campaign had kept the Eritrean revolution contained, but drought in the mid-1980s, Soviet disengagement in the late 1980s, and finally the major military defeat at Afabet in March 1988 eroded Mengistu's optimism. Therefore, the need to lower external costs by de-escalating their rivalry with Somalia was not necessary until 1986, or at the latest March 1988. The terms of the peace treaty were identical to prior agreements that both states had previously rejected (Ofcansky 1993b).

Although Barre and others have suggested that Mengistu was not faithful to the peace treaty and continued to support Somali dissident groups, tensions between the two countries declined considerable from 1988 to 1991. Internal unrest and the growing probability of a leadership change in both countries proved a more salient threat than the military force of the other.

Conclusion

The dynamic two-level model of rivalry interaction explains more of the ups and downs of Somali-Ethiopian rivalry than either reciprocity or coalition building. The theory predicts that changes in rivalry behavior will be related to the prospective costs of future rivalry, the domestic outbidding environment, and the opportunities for escalation. High future costs mixed with a public mobilized against an enemy are more likely to lead to escalation. Alternatively, high future costs in the face of an ambivalent public are more likely to lead to de-escalation, as the leadership attempts to shift resources from the rivalry toward domestic development or other threats that may be more salient. The probable success of escalation in the form of an equal or positive capabilities balance also increases the chances of escalation.

Table 1 suggests the explanatory power of dynamic two-level pressures in the Somalia-Ethiopia context. The only combination of factors that led to war was high costs, high rivalry outbidding, and the presence of an op-

Table 1

Somali and Ethiopian dynamic two-level pressures

Years	Costs	Outbidding	Opportunity	Prediction	Observed
Somalia					
1960–64	Medium	Medium	Low	Maintain	LC
1966–69	High	Medium	Low	Maintain	LC
1970–74	Low	High	High	Maintain	LC
1975–77	High	High	High	Escalate	War
1978–82	High	High	Low	Maintain	LC
1983–91	High	Low	Low	De-escalate	CO
Ethiopia					
1960–64	Low	Low	High	Maintain	LC
1966–69	Low	Low	High	Maintain	LC
1970–74	Medium	Low	Medium	Maintain	LC
1975–77	Medium	Low	Medium	Maintain	LC/War
1978–82	Low	Low	High	Maintain	LC
1983–91	High	Low	Low	De-escalate	CO

LC: Limited conflict/limited cooperation
CO: Cooperation

portunity for escalation. Together these forces increased the probability that Somalia would initiate war in 1977. The configuration of high costs and low rivalry outbidding, with no opportunity to escalate, led to de-escalation in 1988. When these facilitative factors are not present, in each case, Somalia and Ethiopia chose to maintain their rivalry, rather than upset the status quo.

5 Peace (Not) Now
The Israeli-Egyptian Rivalry

THIS CHAPTER INVESTIGATES the period of Egyptian-Israeli rivalry between 1948 and 1979. Not only did the two states fight three wars during that time, but they also significantly de-escalated tensions after 1974. What explains this variation in rivalry interaction? Why did war in 1948, 1956, and 1967 serve to perpetuate conflict, but the 1973 war serve as a catalyst for cooperation?

Background

The rivalry between Israel and Egypt is rooted in the events leading up to Israeli statehood. Beginning in the late nineteenth and early twentieth centuries, both Egyptian and Jewish groups sought their own states. At the time, British colonial territory was the target of the two nascent movements' ambitions, as London controlled Egypt and Palestine. Egyptian nationalism was institutionalized in the Wafd party, which was run by Sa'ad Zaghlul. In 1924, Egyptian King Fuad authorized elections, with the Wafd winning a landslide victory. Jewish hopes for statehood were pursued by Zionist organizations led by Theodor Herzl, Chaim Weizmann, and David Ben-Gurion. The Zionists hoped to create a Jewish-controlled territory in Palestine. To this end, the group worked to increase the Jewish population there from 20,000 (3 percent of the population) in 1880 to 85,000 (14 percent) in 1914 (Sachar 1981, 22). In addition, the Zionists lobbied British prime minister Lloyd George for support. After the fact, Israeli politicians have pointed to the Balfour Declaration, signed in 1917, as a pronouncement of British backing for a "Jewish National Homeland" in Palestine. However, the document was vague both in its wording, including some

95

promises to the indigenous population, and in its mandate, excluding any details about governance powers and timing.

Through the 1930s, both the Egyptian nationalists and Zionists continued to press for statehood. In Egypt, the lack of colonial autonomy helped to fuel the rise of militant right-wing groups such as Ikhwan (the Muslim Brotherhood) and Misr al-Fatat (Young Egypt). Terrorism increased in Egypt, mostly against the colonial authorities. Zionists continued to facilitate Jewish migration to Palestine, and the Jewish population reached 500,000 (41 percent) in 1939. This immigration occurred despite increases in anti-Jewish protests by Arabs in Palestine (Hourani 1991, 333–53).

Until the 1930s, Egyptians had largely ignored the growing Jewish immigration into the Levant. However, there was an increasing movement toward "Pan-Arabism," led by figures such as Haj Amin, the Mufti of Jerusalem, that transcended purely national issues. Zaghlul had stated that "our problem is an Egyptian problem, not an Arab problem" (Sachar 1981, 31). But in 1929 and 1931, anti-Jewish riots in Palestine attracted considerable attention in Egypt. Ikhwan and Misr al-Fatat seized on the issue to destroy Jewish property in Egypt. King Farouk, after taking the throne from Fuad, used Pan-Arabism and the Arab "plight" in Palestine to divert attention from continued British occupation and a stagnant economy. Farouk organized the Conference on the Defense of Palestine in June 1938 and sent a delegation to demand an Arab Palestinian state from London (Hourani 1991, 353–55, Gershoni 1981, 35–44).

With the rise and conquests of Hitler's Nazi Germany, anti-Semitism became more popular in Egypt and in the Middle East in general. Both the Wafd party and the palace saw German victory as a path toward an independent Egypt. General Aziz Ali al-Misr, of the Egyptian army, was discovered to have spied on British troop movements for the Italians and attempted to fly to Vichy-Lebanon with a number of sensitive documents to escape. Also, King Farouk wrote a series of letters to Hitler hoping for an Axis victory. In return, Hitler promised Egyptian independence after the war. Another Axis supporter in the Middle East was the Mufti of Jerusalem, who visited Mussolini and Hitler and was promised an Arab Palestinian state in return (Sachar 1981, 38–39).

The Zionists found themselves in an uneasy alliance with the British. In 1939, British prime minister Neville Chamberlain had signed a White Paper severely limiting Jewish immigration to Palestine and giving the

Arab population a veto of any future immigration changes. This had the practical implication of undoing even the limited and vague language of the Balfour Declaration. Throughout the war, Jewish immigration numbers were reduced. To stop illegal immigration, the British blockaded the coasts of Palestine.

The White Paper induced a split in Zionist policy toward Britain. Some extremist groups such as Etzel and Lech'i began assassination campaigns against British commissioners. But most Zionists supported the British cause against the Nazis. Jews in Palestine produced weapons for the British to use, and 136,000 men and women enrolled in the national service volunteer corp. By 1942, Palestinian Jews made up 25 percent of the British front line in the Middle East. In 1944, a "Jewish Brigade" was formed and fought on the Italian front. Also, the Haganah, a Jewish militia, gathered intelligence in Vichy Syria (Sachar 1981, 38–40). The Zionist policy toward Britain during the war was articulated by Ben-Gurion: "we will fight with the British against Hitler as if there were no white paper; we will fight the white paper as if there were no war" (quoted in Shlaim 2001, 23). Therefore, World War II served to ally Arab nationalism with the Axis powers against the British and mainstream Zionists.

After the war, the British began to accelerate their plans to disengage from Egypt. In October 1946, London set September 1, 1949, as the date for the full evacuation of Egypt. However, the question of who would control the Sudan border and the canal, both important issues for Britain, remained unanswered. Because extremist Egyptian national groups such as Ikhwan and Misr al-Fatat had killed one prime minister and threatened to do the same to any other politician who negotiated with the British, the new premier, Mahmud Fahmi al-Nuqrashi, killed a compromise agreement that would have called for phased withdrawal. Nuqrashi wanted the British out of Egypt with no equivocation (Hourani 1991, 348–49; Gershoni 1981, 78).

At the same time, a growing proportion of the Jewish population in Europe wanted to immigrate to Palestine, but the new British Labor government continued its ban on immigration to the colony. British intransigence led the Zionist leadership to reject the notion of a "Jewish National Homeland" with limited autonomy in favor of a Jewish national state with full sovereignty (Sachar 1981, 42–43; Shlaim 2001, 20–25). Although Zionists had been almost evenly split in 1937 on whether to partition Palestine into separate Jewish and Palestinian states, by 1942 partition was generally accepted. The scope of Jewish hopes for sovereignty continued to grow. At a meeting in the New York Biltmore Hotel in May 1942, the participants, who included Weizmann and Ben-Gurion, agreed to pursue a Jewish state that encompassed the whole of Palestine, rather than just the small territory that Jews currently inhabited (Shlaim 2001, 23). By 1945, members of Etzel and Lech'i stepped up demonstrations and protests and even bombed the British Intelligence headquarters in Jerusalem's King David Hotel in July 1946. To help fulfill the Biltmore program, the Haganah began illegally transporting Jews into Palestine.

With the blockade on Jewish immigrants becoming increasingly costly, the British called for American aid. But conversely, President Truman campaigned for the immediate admission of 100,000 Jews into Palestine. A joint British-American commission created the "Grady-Morrison Report" in 1946, which called for two separate provinces (one Jewish, one Arab) under British control. Yet because it also included strict immigration controls, the Zionists and Truman both rejected the report. Adding to London's Palestinian dilemma was the tide of world opinion, which was sympathetic to the plight of the Jews after the Holocaust (Sachar 1981, 44–45).

The British announced in February 1947 that they were turning Palestine over to the United Nations because of the rising costs of keeping the territory. By August, the UN General Assembly voted for the termination of the British mandate, for the partition of Palestine into separate sovereign states, and for Jerusalem to remain under UN trusteeship. This plan was accepted by Ben-Gurion, the Zionist leadership, and the United States, as well as the Soviets, but was rejected by the Arabs. Despite Arab protests, on November 29, 1947, the UN General Assembly voted to accept the transition plan that would lead to two separate states on October 1, 1948. After the British announced that they were pulling out in May, Ben-Gurion proclaimed the Republic of Israel.

Issues under Contention

The issues under contention in the Israeli-Egyptian rivalry changed over time, moving from a question of rights and reparations to a territorial dispute. Throughout the period from 1948 to 1979, the issue of the rights of the Palestinians was questioned. Israel's policy toward both non-Jewish in-habitants and refugees who fled to the surrounding Arab countries was harshly criticized. These people constituted a majority of the population before independence, and they posed a demographic problem for Israel. Egypt, in no small measure to boost its Pan-Arab prestige, continued to support the rights of the Palestinians to return home and argued for Israeli reparations.

However, after 1956, and especially after 1967, Egyptian-Israeli con-flict included disagreements about territorial boundaries. The territory under dispute included the Gaza Strip, the whole of the Sinai, and particu-larly Sharm al-Sheikh. Although Israel did not have a historical claim to the Sinai, it wanted to create a security buffer zone there to stop the infil-tration of Egyptian-supported guerrilla groups (Shlaim 2001, 161). By 1967, Israel had captured the Sinai and kept the territory because of con-tinued security concerns (Quandt 1993, 57–58). On the other side, Egypt had a historical precedent for holding the Sinai, including the Gaza Strip and Sharm al-Sheikh (Sachar 1981).

1946–1948

Rivalry History

As Ben-Gurion prepared to create Israel, the British attempted to work be-hind the scenes to undermine the transition. London suggested that King Abdullah of Transjordan, a British ally, occupy the Arab portion of Pales-tine quickly, therefore continuing British influence in the region. Also, the British gave no help to the nascent Jewish government apparatus. As Arab guerrillas from Iraq and Syria increased their attacks on Jewish farms in 1947, the British disarmed the Jews as reprisals were planned. Finally, the British announced that they were pulling out on May 15 rather than in Oc-tober, catching the unprepared Zionist leadership by surprise.

Ben-Gurion and the Jewish regime began to speed up the collection of money, equipment, and resources to combat an increasingly desperate sit-uation. Groups of Arab irregular forces were already attacking Jewish farms and convoys and had seized the strategic highlands. The Zionists' war matériel included only a few thousand rifles and several hundred mortars and guns. However, in April and May, the Haganah was able to recapture the strategic heights that protected the coastal highways and eastern Galilee. Training regiments were stepped up as the Haganah, soon to be the Israeli Defense Force, prepared itself for war.

As expected, when Ben-Gurion proclaimed the Republic of Israel on May 15, 1948, Syria, Transjordan, Egypt, and Iraq attacked, and the War of Independence began. Egypt's participation was spearheaded by King Farouk, who used the Palestinian issue to place Egypt (and himself) at the forefront of the Arab world. Farouk's main challenger was King Abdullah of Transjordan. Armed intervention in Palestine by the Arab powers had been discussed as early as June 1946 and was supported by Abdullah, Salih Jabr of Iraq, and Haj Amin. Egypt, Lebanon, and Saudi Arabia each urged caution. Egypt's reasons for avoiding conflict were that it had no territory to gain, unlike Jordan, in an ensuing fight, and that it did not claim sovereignty over the disputed territory. Yet what Farouk made clear was that if Abdullah went to war, he would have to march also. Farouk would not allow Transjordan to dominate the Arab world and the newly formed (1945) Arab League (Sachar 1981, 49; Gershoni 1981). When Abdullah sent his Arab Legion into the West Bank in April, Farouk countered. By late April, Egypt had drawn up plans for a loosely coordinated Arab attack when the British mandate ended.

Although the young Israeli republic was overmatched from a population standpoint, the Arab armies found themselves at several strategic disadvantages. The Haganah was able to field 30,000 men and women on May 15, 1948, while initially the Arab states only mustered 25,000. Similarly, by December the Haganah/IDF had almost double the Arab states' strength (Shlaim 2001, 35). Although, the Haganah/IDF's weapons were inferior, troops coming from Baghdad had to travel 700 miles to fight at Haifa, and the Egyptian communication lines had to stretch 250 miles. Most important, the Arab countries never fully coordinated their attacks. Despite these disadvantages, General Naguib was able to lead his 10,000 Egyptian troops to within 16 miles of Tel Aviv and control the Negev roads. Moreover, the Arab Legion conquered the Jewish old city quarter of Jerusalem.

The tide of the battle turned with the June 11 UN cease-fire. During that time Israel was able to collect more weapons and artillery, especially from Czechoslovakia. While the Arab armies were able to increase their forces to 45,000, Israel fielded at least 60,000 troops as fighting resumed in

June. Moreover, infighting between Egypt and Jordan interfered with coordination. For example, Abdullah vetoed the appointment of an Egyptian commander-in-chief for the total invading force. When the battle resumed, Israel was able to launch an offensive to retake and expand its territory. By December, Israeli forces were attacking Egyptian territory in the Sinai.

Figure 11 illustrates the quarterly international interactions between Israel and Egypt during their rivalry. This graph plots the high, low, and mean conflict/cooperation scores based on COPDAB. The lower the score, the more bellicose and less cooperative the event. The first few years of Israeli independence illustrate the high level of conflict between the two countries. Although there are a few instances of cooperative actions (those above zero), they are limited. The overwhelming pattern is one of threats and uses of force on both sides, with mean cooperation scores among the lowest in the whole rivalry.

Conventional Explanations

A focus on international actions and reactions explains elements of the 1948 war. If we relax the requirement that states must be independent to partake in international interactions, as this period spans the pre-state history of Israel, one could argue that Egypt went to war to counter the Haganah strikes. However, this account is unconvincing upon further investigation. Primarily, Israeli actions were not aimed at Egyptian territory or interests. The UN mandate did not involve any land Cairo claimed. Also, a pure reciprocity explanation ignores the fact that Egypt was a restraining voice in the Arab League debates in 1946. Why would Egypt be against war in 1946, only to speed troops to the front in 1948?

A domestic-centric focus also leaves similar puzzles unsolved. Although Israel was in the process of setting up democratic institutions at independence, Egypt was governed by more autocratic processes. It is consistent with the democratic peace or a coalition-building theory to suggest that the more autocratic and cartelized Egypt would initiate a war. King Farouk could mobilize the masses to march toward war because there were few democratic checks on his power. Of course, this suggestion fails to explain the Haganah offensive, and why Egypt changed its mind about war in 1948.

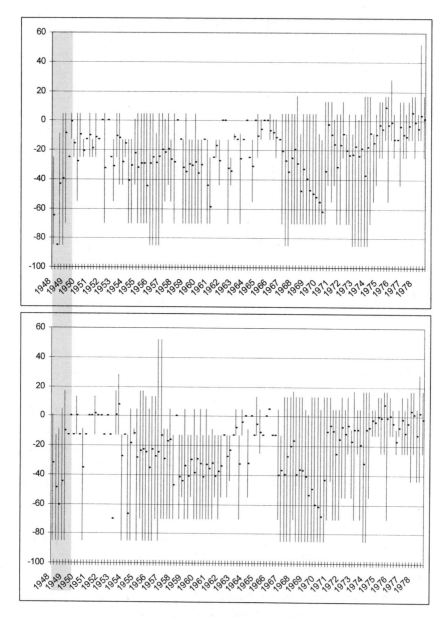

Figure 11. Egyptian-Israeli conflict and cooperation, 1948–1949. *Top:* Egyptian-to-Israeli events; *bottom:* Israeli-to-Egyptian events. COPDAB scale -100 to 60. Smaller numbers represent more conflict, 1948–1949 in frame.

Another conventional explanation for the 1948 war relies on religious and cultural differences between Israelis and Arabs (see Stoessinger 1993). This perspective suggests that war was unavoidable because the two cultural groups harbored historical hatred for each other. Although the general distrust between the two distinct religious groups may have helped to speed mobilization toward war, the historical enmity explanation ignores several important anomalies. First, the nationalist Wafd party had opened friendly negotiations with the Zionist leadership previously, despite these enduring cultural differences. Why would cultural traits lead to conflict in one decade but not another? Second, not all Arab states, notwithstanding their cultural and religious differences with Israel, supported war initially. Jordan and Iraq pushed toward war while Egypt argued against conflict. These rivalry dynamics stretch far beyond simple religious animosity.

Dynamic Two-Level Pressures

Changes in the dynamic two-level pressures operating in the rivalry provide a more convincing explanation of the 1948 war and its timing. Given the configuration of expected future costs, outbidding environments, and opportunities, Egypt would be expected to escalate the dispute after Abdullah moved into the West Bank. If Farouk stayed on the sidelines and did not send troops to invade Israel, Egypt stood to lose prestige in the Arab League (Rabinovich 1991, 16; Heikal 1986, 117). In addition, the highly mobilized outbidding environment in Egypt and throughout the Arab world exacerbated the situation, raising the costs of conciliation with Israel. Finally, a coordinated Arab assault appeared to be an opportunity for escalation. All of these pressures coalesced in 1948, not before, to raise the probability of Egyptian military action.

In Israel, although the future looked costly, the elites did not have an incentive to inflate the Egyptian threat. In fact, threats from Syria and the Palestinian guerrillas were more salient to the Israeli leadership (Shlaim 2001, 24–26). The interaction between domestic and international factors clarifies both who was most likely to escalate (Egypt) and when (after Farouk was sure Abdullah was going to attack).

Future Expectations

After World War II, both Egyptian and Zionist leaderships expected their future relations to be costly. Ben-Gurion was already leading a counteroffensive against guerrilla forces in a quest to protect Jewish settlements. Yet the fledgling governing body had few resources with which to organize and fight. The British remained obstinate in their refusal to help organize the Zionist government, and further, they actively disarmed Jewish farmers who would attempt to defend or punitively attack the raiding fedayeen forces. By 1947, the Palestine guerrilla force, under the leadership of Abdel Qader al-Husseini, had severed the roads between Tel Aviv and Jerusalem. The Jewish offensive military strategy carried out through "Plan D" was successful in decreasing the intensity of Palestinian incursions after 1947. But Ben-Gurion believed that this small-scale battle was only a prologue to a coming conflict with the neighboring Arab states (Shlaim 2001, 30–31; Brecher 1974, 12–20). Moreover, in this next stage of conflict, Israel might be facing the combined forces of Syria, Lebanon, Jordan, Iraq, and Egypt. Although secret talks between Golda Meir and King Abdullah of Jordan showed some promise of mutual understanding (neither wanted a Palestinian state), the Arab states could produce a fighting force approximately ten times greater than the expected Israeli mobilization effort. Also, since Israel was not yet a state, it could not legally procure weapons on the international market.

The rising tide of immigration also posed some problems for the Zionist leadership. While there had been only 56,000 Jews in Palestine in 1918, that number rose to over 600,000 by 1948. Further, the British White Paper limiting Jewish immigration to Israel had artificially raised the demand for Jewish transportation to the Holy Land. When a Jewish state was created, and immigration barriers fell, a flood of Holocaust survivors and other groups were expected to, and eventually did, enter Israel. Specifically, Ben-Gurion expected 2–3 million immigrants after independence (Shlaim 2001, 23). Without substantial help, the new population boom would fall on a weak government and economy. The mail and train services were not operable, and the supply of arable land and housing could not match the expected demand that increased immigration would bring. Therefore, because of the rising military challenge of the Arab states, the lack of an alliance with the British, and rising immigration, the new Israeli state expected the cost of future rivalry to be high.

The expectations in Cairo were also pessimistic, although for different reasons. Since at least 1939, King Farouk had attempted to place Egypt at the head of the Arab world. This policy took the form of organizing a conference in 1938 on the Palestinian issue and competition with the other Arab states to champion Arab independence and imperial withdrawal from the region. As the United Nations began to move toward supporting a Jewish state in 1947, Haj Amin, the Mufti of Jerusalem, began mobilizing support against partition. Abdullah supported a military attack at least in part to ensure that only an Arab Palestine would exist. King Farouk was then faced with the image of a future where Abdullah had de facto control of Palestine, vaulting Jordan, rather than Egypt, toward the leadership position in the Arab world. Furthermore, with the poor economic performance of the Egyptian economy, and its lack of industrialization, prestige was of high value to Farouk (Sachar 1981, 47; Heikal 1986). By April 1948, Abdullah had declared that he would send the Arab Legion into the West Bank upon Israeli independence. Therefore, Farouk expected that inaction was more costly than action.

Domestic Rivalry Outbidding Environment

During this time, Egypt was rife with rivalry outbidding, while the elite bargaining situation was more moderate in Israel. Since 1937, King Farouk had used the Palestinian issue to mobilize support for his regime (Sachar 1981, 34–35). Speeches blaming the Zionists for Egypt's economic and colonial ills found resonance in a society looking for a scapegoat. Around this time, groups such as Ikhwan and Misr al-Fatat began to form and protest against Zionism. Bombings and boycotts of Jewish businesses became routine. As Sachar notes, the king and his advisors "were not laggard in sensing the diversionary usefulness of the Palestine issue and of Pan-Arabism as key weapons in the crown's on-going struggle with the Wafd" (1981, 35). Therefore, to remain in power, Farouk outbid the Wafd on hostility toward the Zionists. This continued through 1948.

While the Wafd leadership had been negotiating with Jewish leaders such as Eliahu Sasson, public opinion was being molded against the Zionists. King Farouk was able to use speeches and his control over information to accuse the Zionists of smuggling gold and weapons out of Egypt, flooding the nation with counterfeit money, and even contaminating the water supply (Sachar 1981, 49). In response to the growing antipathy toward Zionism, the Wafd terminated their high-level meetings with Sasson, and Ikhwan set up recruiting offices to support Palestinian independence. While Prime Minister Nuqrashi remained personally against any military campaign, he also publicly supported intervention in order to keep his job. Therefore, Farouk was able to outbid Nuqrashi and draw the prime minister toward conflict with the Zionists. By 1948, even the faculty at leading universities had joined the leaders of Misr al-Fatat and Ikhwan in calling for military intervention in Palestine.

There was also a second layer of rivalry outbidding pressure on King Farouk. Not only did Egyptian politicians compete with Farouk for prestige, but other Arab politicians such as King Abdullah of Jordan also extended this competition to the regional level. A number of Arab leaders, King Farouk included, were positioning themselves as leaders of the Arab world. In this regional arena, King Farouk faced Arab criticism that he was not doing enough for the Pan-Arab cause and Palestinians. To appear weak in the face of Western and Israeli conflict would have damaged Farouk's standing in the Arab world (Lorenz 1990, 20).[1]

The domestic situation in Israel was equally chaotic, although no group was monolithically mobilizing the populace against Egypt. Although Egypt was viewed as a threat to Israeli sovereignty and existence, more immediate and salient threats came from the indigenous Palestinian uprisings, as well as from Syria and Iraq. There were two factions in the Zionist leadership at the time. Ben-Gurion led the "fighting Zionist" element that rejected an alliance with Britain for a homeland, in favor of a strong independent state. Groups that represented this point of view, such as the Irgun and the Stern gang, attacked Arab civilians, setting off reprisals

---

1. This regional level of outbidding is rather rare. Most leaders seem to weight domestic opinion more heavily than international opinion because of electoral and revolutionary incentives. One reason for this peculiarity may be the traditionally porous borders between the territories and the shared "Arab" history. For more on regional outbidding see Lorenz 1990 and Hasou 1985. I thank William R. Thompson for helping me to see this distinction and to work through its implications.

from the Arab inhabitants (Rabinovich 1991, 76). The "diplomatic Zionism" core was led by Weizmann and supported British help in creating a homeland rather than a state. As the threat to Israel rose and Britain declined to revise its White Paper, Ben-Gurion assumed the leadership position, and support for diplomatic Zionism declined (Moore 1974, 260–62).

A second cleavage in Israeli politics involved Ben-Gurion's faction, which supported accepting a limited Israeli territory as offered by UN resolution 181, and the more militant Lech'i. Led by Menachim Begin, the group wanted all of Palestine, Eretz Israel, to be included under Israeli dominion. Ben-Gurion's faction remained more popular during this period, winning a majority of the seats in pre-independence elections. Therefore, the outbidding environment toward Egypt was moderately mobilized. Although diplomatic Zionism was less attractive under the high threat conditions of the time, people did not swing toward the militant Eretz Israel ideals of Begin (Shlaim 2001, 25). In February 1948, Moshe Sharett stated that "no reduction of Jewish rights either in territory or in sovereignty would be accepted by the Jewish people" (Israeli Department of Information 1960, 35). There was neither a domestic incentive for immediate escalation and territorial expansion nor a large constituency for peace and compromise.

Opportunity for Escalation

The opportunity to escalate tensions resided solely in the hands of Egypt and the Arab states. While still under British dominion, Egypt had a modern army of approximately 300,000 men at its disposal, compared to the Israeli Haganah, comprising 30,000 troops just before Israeli independence. In addition, the quality of the Egyptian arms was far superior to the Israeli weapons. When the added strength of the other invading Arab armies is included in the equation, Israel's position appeared quite weak. What is more dramatic, the joint populations of the invading countries outnumbered the Israeli inhabitants by over 200 to 1. The advantages held by the Haganah were its dedication to the cause, for defeat meant the loss of a Jewish homeland, and its extensive training from fighting both in World War II and against the Palestine irregulars (Sachar 1981, 51; Brecher 1972 58; Peres 1995, 60). Also, as the Arab armies overextended themselves, the Israelis were able to counterpunch successfully from their defensive positions.

Summary and Analysis

In these early years of rivalry, the historical evidence supports the dynamic two-level predictions. Egypt agreed to join the other Arab states in the Israeli invasion only after Abdullah announced his intention to send the Arab Legion into the West Bank. Although this move did not threaten Egypt at the time, Farouk believed that it would decrease Egyptian prestige in the future. Further, Sachar (1981, 49) notes that moderates felt pressure to step up their public attacks on Israel in the face of Ikhwan's assassinations, the king's propaganda, and the mobilized outbidding environment. In Israel, Ben-Gurion did not attack Egypt, but instead ordered the IDF to secure the Golan Heights and other strategic positions on the eastern front. Had Egypt not attacked, it is highly doubtful that Israel would have attacked first (Brecher 1972, 58). Moreover, the lower outbidding pressure in Tel Aviv helps to explain why Israel was open to accepting a two-state solution before the war.

1949–1954

Rivalry History

When the fighting ended on December 29, 1948, the landscape of Palestine had changed remarkably. Even before the war had begun, 175,000 Arabs had fled toward Egypt, Transjordan, and Syria, and by December, 650,000 Arabs, or two-thirds of the total Arab population of Palestine, had retreated. This flight initiated a large-scale refugee crisis for the surrounding Arab countries. As the Rhodes Armistice was being signed on February 25, 1949, Israel controlled eight thousand square miles of Palestine, 21 percent more than they would have claimed under the UN mandate.

Sachar (1981, 62) notes that the Rhodes Armistice was meant to be a temporary fix. While the agreement did end the bellicosity between Israel and all of the Arab states, excepting Iraq, it proposed an untenable status quo. First, the question of what to do with the Palestinian refugees who were now residing in Egyptian, Jordanian, and Syrian territory was left for another day. Also, the Israeli-Jordan line separated many families from their farms, which in turn led to border violence and "incursions." Likewise, the armistice lines left many Jewish farmers on the Syrian side of the border. There was also disagreement concerning the status of Jerusalem, which was split into the Israeli-controlled "new" section and the Jordanian-occupied old city. Finally, the Gaza Strip was carved out of the Israeli Negev territory and given to Egypt. Gaza had become a magnet for refugees fleeing the crisis, and Egypt eventually began recruiting guerrillas from the displaced Palestinians. Egypt also proclaimed the right to blockade the Straits of Tiran, using a loophole in its treaty with Israel (Sachar 1981, 62).

During the next decade, neither country mobilized or attacked the other, even when border clashes between the IDF and Palestinian refugees arose. Similarly, although there were some medium-level negotiations between the rivals in 1953, neither leader felt the need to compromise. Talks in Switzerland collapsed when the participating states could not even agree on the sequence in which issues would be discussed. In communication between Abdel Rahman Sadeq and Shmuel Divon in Paris, the new Egyptian Revolutionary Command Council (RCC) made it known that it could not recognize Israel officially or depart from the Pan-Arab position of intransigence toward Israel. Reciprocally, the Israeli government refused to support Egyptian claims on the Suez as long as the boycott of Israeli shipping continued. There was limited military conflict between the two countries in the early 1950s, as Israel attacked the villages it believed were responsible for harboring refugees who continued to infiltrate Israeli territory. However, none of these incidents escalated to war during this period. In fact, Egypt worked to curb infiltration into Israel, as they kept 250,000 refugees on the Gaza Strip, and they punished and deterred border crossings into Israel until 1954 (Shlaim 2001, 80–84; Heikal 1973, 27; Brecher 1974, 226–54).

The quantitative event data in figure 12 record the drastic shift in conflict patterns after 1949. Not only do the mean cooperation levels increase, but also the variance in conflict decreases substantially. Despite a few border incursions and reactions, this pattern is consistent with rivalry maintenance, where both states were careful to avoid both excessive cooperation and conflict.

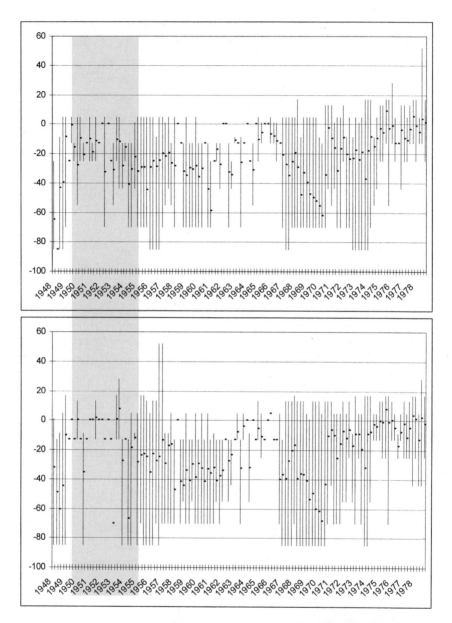

Figure 12. Egyptian-Israeli conflict and cooperation, 1949–1954. *Top:* Egyptian-to-Israeli events; *bottom:* Israeli-to-Egyptian events. COPDAB scale -100 to 60. Smaller numbers represent more conflict, 1949–1954 in frame.

Conventional Explanations

On the surface, the relative quiet of the 1949 to 1954 period suggests the process of reciprocity. Both states matched the limited conflict received from the other and did not deviate from this pattern. Despite this appearance, reciprocity does not explain why Egypt was willing to fight in 1948 but not in 1950, or why Egypt worked to curb infiltration into Israel until 1954, just as Israel was threatening and carrying out raids into the neighboring Arab states. When Israel offered direct negotiations during this time, the idea was rejected by the Egyptians. It follows that Israeli intransigence was more likely because of continued Egyptian hostility, and Egyptian distrust of Israel grew as a result of Israeli border incursions. However, the original source of conflict is ignored. More emphatically, cooperation did not always lead to reciprocated cooperation.

Domestically, as in 1948, Egypt was the more autocratic state, especially after the Free Officers coup in 1952. A focus on institutional constraints and voting suggests that Egypt would be the more bellicose rival, as it was in 1948. However, Egypt did not launch an offensive during this period and even worked actively to avoid conflict with Israel until 1954. Also, Israeli defense spending and military adventures into its neighbors' territory, although limited, does not fit with the presumed pacifying effect of democracy. Despite different domestic institutions, these countries both acted quite similarly, bounding both conflict and cooperation.

Dynamic Two-Level Pressures

During this time, dynamic two-level pressures that might have altered the rivalry status quo in either Israel or Egypt were absent. In Egypt, conflict with Britain remained more politically popular than conflict with Israel. Also, the expectations that the future might be more propitious for any confrontation or reconciliation with Israel delayed any changes in rivalry behavior. Finally, the lack of an easy military option decreased the odds of a substantial change in rivalry behavior.

Likewise in Israel, Ben-Gurion and the majority of the Israeli leadership believed that Israel's position vis-à-vis the Arab world would only grow stronger with time. Thus, in negotiations Ben-Gurion did not feel pressed to compromise, nor in military planning did he feel the need to alter the status quo. The outbidding pressure placed on Ben-Gurion by the hard-line Herut party and the left-wing Mapam party, proved unsuccessful during this period, as voters supported the policy of maintenance as opposed the escalation. The lack of an opportunity for escalation, as in the case of Egypt, made maintenance the likely Israeli policy.

Future Expectations

After the War of Independence, Israel's beliefs about the future were optimistic, especially compared to their expectations in 1948. As Shlaim observes, Israel emerged from the war with "a tremendous sense of achievement, and a confident outlook on the future" (2001, 40). Ben-Gurion himself was steeled by the victory, believing that he could bargain from a position of strength in the future. With this spirit of optimism, Israel began instituting its plan for economic development, and large-scale immigration.

There were still a number of problems for Israel to deal with. First, the Jewish nation had suffered great losses in the conflict, with 1 percent of the total population killed and approximately 10 percent wounded. Second, the loss of the Arab indigenous market, as the Arab Palestinians fled, decreased the potential economic output of the country. Yet even these problems had a silver lining. Immigration was going to replace and then double the Israeli population in the next four years. Also, the evacuation of the Palestinians from Israeli soil solved the great demographic problem that the Zionists had wrestled with for fifty years. In the past, Ben-Gurion worried that a Jewish state would have to rule over a Palestinian majority; now this was no longer the case. Moreover, with increased territory, Israel now had additional room to accommodate the flow of new immigrants. Substantial aid from the United States and West German reparation payments eased the population burden, as well as the nascent Arab boycott of Israeli goods and shipping (Avi-Hai 1974, 176–78).

The security situation in Israel was also improving. The Israeli Defense Force was able to mobilize and arm almost one-sixth of the population in the War of Independence. Arms shipments from Czechoslovakia and other sources on the black market had bolstered Israel's defense potential. Similarly, in 1950, the United States, Great Britain, and France made a firm declaration against any offensive move in the Middle East, promising weapons to those countries in need of self-defense. Therefore, Israel harbored hopes of great power help in any ensuing invasion.

In Egypt, the defeat in the 1948 war sent shock waves of unrest through the country. Many people blamed Britain for the military defeat, and anticolonial and anti-British violence increased. The bombings of Jewish homes and businesses, which had begun during the war, continued throughout the late 1940s. Terrorist groups such as Ikhwan were responsible for killing 250 Jews in 1948, and, shortly thereafter, Prime Minister Nuqrashi was assassinated. With negligible economic growth, the unrest was likely to continue (Sachar 1981, 64–66).

When the Free Officers, led by Gamal Abdel Nasser, successfully gained control of the government in 1952, both economic and social unrest continued (Heikal 1973, 16–18). The 120,000 Palestinian refugees in Egypt continued to drain resources, and the anti-imperialist policies of the new government meant that little to no aid could be expected from Britain or France. In August 1952, a group of textile workers at Kafr el-Dawar near Alexandria commandeered their factory. In the ensuing riot, nine people were killed and twenty-three injured. The trial and death sentences for the leaders threatened more violence and highlighted the possibility of greater unrest in Egypt in the future (Nutting 1972, 43–44).

Despite the riots, Nasser was hopeful that the Free Officers would be able, in the words of Nutting, to "awaken the docile Egyptian masses and liberate them from their age-old servitude" (1972, 38). To some extent, the Free Officers induced some optimism into Egyptian expectations of the future. In 1952, the Revolutionary Command Council abolished the honorary titles of Pasha and Bey that had been the center of corruption and the selling of offices in the palace. The armed forces were reorganized, and senior officers viewed to be "corrupt" or "ineffective" were imprisoned.

Most important, Nasser had hopes that the United States would help Egypt in its bid for independence. Support for this hope came in the form of direct contact with Kermit Roosevelt of the U.S. Central Intelligence Agency. Additionally, commentators such as Walter Lippmann in the U.S. press praised the Egyptian change in regime and the move toward land reform. Ali Sabry, a Free Officer, passed Nasser's messages of friendship to an American contact even before the coup had taken place. Nasser's hopes were buoyed when William Foster, the American assistant secretary for defense, agreed to submit and support Egypt's request for $100 million in military aid (Nutting 1972, 46). Therefore, the Egyptian leadership's ex-pectations of the future costs of rivalry with Israel were moderate. There were many domestic problems to deal with, as well as the restructuring of the land holdings, and the army, but the aspirations for American aid lightened the pessimism.

Domestic Rivalry Outbidding Environment

In Israel, there were three distinct voices in the Knesset. The first and fore-most was that of Ben-Gurion and his Mapai party. Ben-Gurion wanted to continue competing with the Arab countries while creating a democratic Jewish republic. He did not believe the idea that the incorporation of large swaths of Palestinian territory was propitious because it would degrade the democratic base of the republic. Ben-Gurion's position toward Egypt can be summed up in his writing, "Peace is vital—but not at any price" (quoted in Shlaim 2001, 56). The Mapai party won the majority of votes in the 1949 elections and continued to enjoy broad support. The Herut party, led by Begin and consisting of the followers of Ze'ev Jabotinsky and the former Irgun, sought Israeli control of all of Palestine, Eretz Israel. This faction se-verely criticized Ben-Gurion's decision to recognize Jordanian control over Old Jerusalem and the West Bank, despite the Arab Legion's de facto con-trol of those territories. Eventually, this disagreement led Begin to call for a "no confidence" vote against the Ben-Gurion government. A third, smaller coalition, consisting of the left-wing Mapam party and the communists, joined Begin in criticizing the Jordanian agreement. This group also called for a separate Palestinian state in the West Bank that would be friendly to Israel (Brecher 1972, 117–22).

Throughout the period, Ben-Gurion felt only moderate pressure to es-calate tensions toward Egypt. At the time, the Herut party was more inter-ested in contesting Jordanian control over the West Bank and Syrian occupation of the strategic hills north of the Sea of Galilee. More salient still was the UN move to internationalize Jerusalem, leading to the pre-emptive naming of Jerusalem as the capital of Israel. Thus, Begin and Herut were unsuccessful in outbidding Ben-Gurion on conflict with Egypt. While the increased incursions along the Jordanian border induced public opin-ion toward escalation with Jordan and Syria, as Herut and Mapam called for, Egypt's border remained relatively quiet, and thus less contentious politically (Shlaim 2001, 84). When Moshe Sharrett took over as prime minister in 1953, his dovish policies, in comparison to Ben-Gurion's, were not attacked until the status quo on the Egyptian border changed in 1955.

The situation was similar in Egypt. After the war, although elites continued to describe Zionism as a "disease" (Sachar 1981, 64), Britain was viewed as the true villain (Hasou 1985, ii). The RCC's anti-imperialist speeches and dispatches inflamed enmity toward Britain. This situation does not mean that peace with Israel would have been popular in Egypt. Nasser himself noted that any discussions with Israel would have to be secret, for fear of Egyptian and Arab reactions. When Nasser began secret contacts with Israel in 1953, he continually worried that they would be discovered and that his domestic situation would be compromised (Shlaim 2001, 81). This distrust of Israel and Zionism remained latent during the early 1950s because of the salience of the British presence (Sachar 1981, 65–66; Heikal 1973, 26–27).

During this time, Nasser continued Farouk's legacy of promoting Egypt as the leader of the Arab world. Using the Arab League, based in Cairo, and the Voice of the Arabs, a radio station set up in 1953, Nasser transmitted his calls for Arab unity and Egyptian leadership internationally. This regional propaganda campaign increased Nasser's popularity both at home and in the region in general. Nasser's prestige was further boosted by his success in stalling the Baghdad pact and his success at the Bandung conference in 1955 (Hasou 1985, 31–34; Dawisha 1976, 163).

Opportunity for Escalation

Neither the Israelis nor the Egyptians had a clear military advantage during the 1949 to 1955 period. Domestic unrest, military reorganization, and conflict with Britain decreased the mobility and efficacy of the Egyptian military. There seemed little reason to expect a result different from that of the 1948 war, even if some loose Arab coordination could be negotiated. In Israel, the defense force was reorganized and modeled after the Swiss reservist force in 1949, which meant that any mobilization for a large-scale offensive would be very costly. With new immigration necessitating more domestic resources and the United States unwilling to sell offensive weapons to Israel, escalation was an unlikely option. In addition, the probability of conflict with Syria and Jordan meant that any additional troops mobilized against Egypt would weaken the northern and eastern fronts (Brecher 1972, 59–60).

Summary and Analysis

During this period, the logic of dynamic two-level pressures suggests that neither state would significantly escalate or de-escalate its rivalry with the other. The historical record supports this prediction of rivalry maintenance. Israel offered to have direct talks but was unwilling to compromise on statehood or reparations to the refugees. Egypt was even less willing to compromise but continued to avoid provoking a military encounter with Israel. Although high expected future costs, a mobilized outbidding environment, and an opportunity to escalate were present for Egypt in 1948, these conditions were not the case in the following years. Despite different domestic situations, both countries faced similar dynamic two-level pressures, clarifying why the rivals' behaviors were similar. A change in policy trajectory was not needed because both states were confident in gaining stronger leverage in the future, and the mobilized domestic arenas made compromise unlikely.

1955–1956

Rivalry History

In the mid-1950s, Israel's security and economic position was becoming increasingly unstable. Immigration in 1948–53 doubled the Israeli population to 1,200,000, and in 1951 one-tenth of the population was living in tents. In 1953, Ben-Gurion was forced to announce a mandatory 10 percent loan that went to the government from all bank deposits. Internationally, Israel lost all hope of Soviet aid when it supported the United States in the Korean War (Sachar 1981, 78). The Lavon Affair of 1954, where Israeli spies were discovered planning to burn British and American buildings in Egypt, inflated Egyptian enmity toward Israel and undercut diplomatic support for Israel. In addition, with the withdrawal of British troops from Egypt, Nasser found himself in control of ten new airfields, numerous military camps, and a vast network of supply stations. As the boycott on trade, and specifically the naval blockades, continued to erode the Israeli economy, new border incursions from Jordan, Egypt, and Syria decreased Israeli security (Shlaim 2001, 113–17). The final straw for Israel was the proposed delivery of new Russian equipment to Egypt in 1956.

Thus, Israel began mobilizing troops and volunteers and digging trenches in late 1955. With the aid of French arms, especially the Mystere fighter jet, Israel looked to strike Egypt preemptively before the new arms were delivered. An opportunity to escalate the conflict emerged when Israel was approached by Britain and France to cooperate militarily to retake the Suez Canal.

On July 26, 1956, Nasser had nationalized the canal, to great jubilation in Egypt. But this act threatened vital trading lanes for both Britain and France. As part of Operation Musketeer, Israel attacked first, landing paratroopers near Suez, and then a brigade under the command of Ariel Sharon crossed into the Sinai. Next, London and Paris at this point offered a cease-fire that was sure to be rejected by the Egyptians. A day later, British and French forces had entered the battle and began bombing Egyptian air and oil fields. Yet when British forces were only twenty-five miles from their objective, London accepted a cease-fire in reaction to dual U.S.-Soviet pressure to end the fighting. By the termination of the fighting, Israel had broken the blockade of the Straits of Tiran, destroyed most of the Gaza military training camps, and captured the Sinai. Due to U.S. pressure, Israel was forced to withdraw from all of Sharm al-Sheikh, which guarded the Straits of Tiran, and the Gaza Strip, and these territories were eventually put in United Nations trusteeship (Brecher 1972, 198–99; Brecher 1974, 277–82; Bar-Siman-Tov 1987, 81–83).

Figure 13 records the increase in conflict and volatility during this period. The vertical bars representing the range in high to low conflict during each quarter are dramatically longer in this period as compared to the previous five years. Similarly, the mean cooperative levels decrease for both states, marking the period of escalation.

Conventional Explanations

The Israeli decision in 1956 to attack Egypt with the help of the French and British does not conform to an international action-reaction process or to expectations derived from the democratic peace. Likewise, an arms-racing explanation fails to account for the changes over time. It is possible to

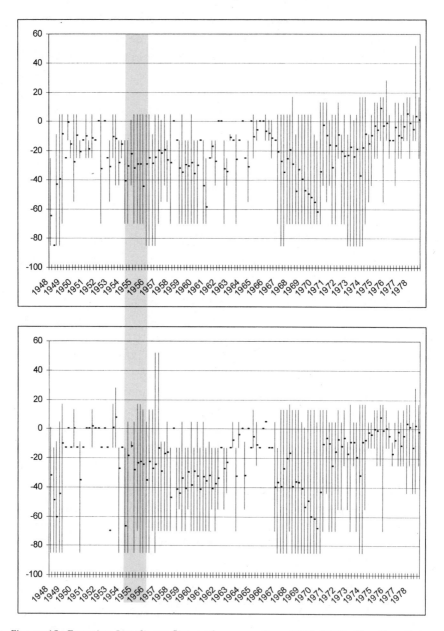

Figure 13. Egyptian-Israeli conflict and cooperation, 1955–1956. *Top:* Egyptian-Israeli events; *bottom:* Israeli-Egyptian events. COPDAB scale -100 to 60. Smaller numbers represent more conflict, 1955–1956 in frame.

argue that the Israeli decision was made in reaction to Egyptian support for terrorist training in Gaza, but this argument fails to explain the intensity of the offensive and what led to Egyptian intransigence in the first place. Put more directly, why would the rivalry follow a pattern of reciprocated but limited conflict in the early 1950s, only to explode into war in 1956? Something in addition to purely international interactions is needed to explain this divergence from past behavior. A similar critique can be levied against an arms-racing explanation of the 1956 war. One could suggest that Nasser's rearming coupled with Israeli bellicosity increased both states' insecurity and pushed both toward war. But this explanation fails to specify a prime mover, begging the question of what caused the arms race. Why race in 1956 but not in 1952?

Similarly, the 1956 war does not fit with an explanation that relies on the pacific nature of democracies. In this case, not one but three democracies took the initiative in attacking an autocracy. Nasser's arms build-up and bellicosity does correlate with increasing autocracy in Egypt after the Free Officers coup, but Cairo did not escalate the conflict. Most emphatically, some process other than a strictly domestic or international one is needed to explain the timing of the escalation.

Dynamic Two-Level Pressures

The configuration of high expected future costs, high domestic outbidding, and an opportunity for escalation created pressure toward Israeli escalation. Economic troubles, mixed with a clouding security situation, served as the motivation for a change in policy toward Egypt. Had Israel merely maintained the rivalry, Egypt could have boasted a much stronger military, as well as more economic power stemming from control over the Suez Canal. And de-escalation with Egypt was domestically impractical. Even Sharrett, a moderate, felt the domestic pressure to escalate the conflict. Finally, Operation Musketeer opened a window of opportunity for escalation with a high probability of success. For Egypt, maintaining the rivalry, rather than altering the status quo, is the predicted policy choice. Escalation made little sense before their new weapons were operational because they would be in a stronger position later. For the same reason, de-escalation was not a priority because the costs of rivalry were manageable.

The mobilized domestic opinion and outbidding environment against Israel also made de-escalation and a breakthrough in negotiations unlikely.

Future Expectations

In Israel, a number of changes took place in 1954–55 that made the status quo look increasingly untenable. First, the Gulf of Aqaba had been closed to Israeli trading in 1954, and in September 1955 Nasser also blockaded the port of Eilat, closing the Red Sea trade routes. The Arab blockade had an accumulating negative impact on the economy, especially when all ships calling on Israel were excluded from Arab trade. Second, increased border violence, as Nasser eased restrictions on, and even supported, fedayeen raids against Israel beginning in 1955, destabilized Israeli settlements in the area. From 1954 to 1956 there were approximately 12,000 incursions of the Israeli borders (Sachar 1981, 90–97).

As the security situation for Israel seemed to be deteriorating, Egyptian expectations were becoming more optimistic. Through contact with Zhou Enlai of China, Nasser was able to negotiate an arms deal with the Soviet Union in August. In the agreement, Czechoslovakia, the major arms supplier to Israel in the 1948 war, contracted to send $320 million worth of arms to Cairo on an interest-free basis in exchange for annual payment in Egyptian cotton. The quality of the war matériel was the highest yet received by Egypt, and included 120 jet fighters, 50 bombers, 200 tanks, 150 artillery pieces, 2 destroyers, and 2 submarines. Syria also received substantial military assistance at the time from the communist bloc. In addition, Soviet and Czech instructors were sent to train the Egyptian force on its new equipment (Sachar 1981, 91; Brecher 1972, 60).

Egypt's regional support also seemed to be increasing, as Nasser signed mutual defense treaties with Syria, Saudi Arabia, and Yemen. And Cairo's strategic position was further strengthened when Britain agreed to end its military occupation of the peninsula on December 6, 1954. Thus, Egypt gained the use of numerous air, naval, and communication stations and the infrastructure for a modern army (Brecher 1974, 254). In the face of this increasing threat, neither the United States nor Britain seemed willing to match the Soviet Union's military commitment to Israel, as both were trying to entice Egypt to join the Baghdad pact (Shlaim 2001, 113). France was the only great power evincing sympathy for Israel, given its own battle with Egyptian-supported Algerian rebels. Therefore, beginning in 1955, Israel's expected costs for the future were high, and Egypt's were moderate to low.

Domestic Rivalry Outbidding Environment

The outbidding environment in Egypt heated up considerably in 1954–55. With the end of British occupation, a bitter enemy had retreated (see Nutting 1972, 71–72). However, Nasser was unable to carry out successful land reform or industrialization. The intelligentsia, including novelists Naguib Mahfouz and Yusuf Idris, began to lead demonstrations protesting the lack of democratization and economic growth in Egypt. Nasser attempted to use Israel as a scapegoat. The Lavon Affair spy scandal, as well as Israel's border policy toward Palestinian refugees, made Israel an ideal diversionary candidate. Anti-Jewish sentiment had been a potent weapon for Farouk against the Wafd after World War II, and Nasser now tried to use the same threat-inflation tactics. First, Nasser announced that only Arabic could be taught in schools and that Jews could not invest in the stock market. By 1955, increased government-sponsored and -supported attacks had begun against the 40,000 Egyptian Jews, and a number of their rights were revoked.

To further his campaign of threat inflation and to silence his critics, Nasser gathered all the tools of state propaganda under his control in 1955. He centralized power by placing Mahfouz under house arrest, shutting down the newspapers, and arresting the leading editors (Meir 1973, 90–93). As Sachar notes, "Israel was singled out as a critical target of Nasser's ambitions" (1981, 92). The Egyptian leader used his public speeches to compare Israel and Zionism to the imperialist powers of the past, specifically Britain. In a newspaper article in 1954, Nasser wrote that Israel was out to "degrade us and to acquire what was in our hands . . . to take our lands . . . deaden our hearts and steal away our minds and this world of ours" (Sachar 1981, 92). Israel was consistently referred to as the "Zionist enemy" (Hasou 1985, 35).

This threat inflation in turn affected Nasser's bargaining position toward Israel. When the United States attempted to induce Nasser to bargain face-to-face with Ben-Gurion, the Egyptian leader answered that he feared assassination and the domestic backlash that would result. Nasser even alluded to the plight of Abdullah after he negotiated with Israel (Heikal 1972, 43–57).

The situation in Israel also became increasingly polarized in late 1954 and 1955. After Ben-Gurion left the government the more dovish Sharrett took power. His prime ministry was plagued by conflict with more hawkish ministers such as Moshe Dayan, the chief of staff, and Pinhas Lavon (Shlaim 2001, 110). As the raids on Israeli territory increased in 1954 and 1955, both Dayan and Lavon pressured Sharrett to respond with military force. After the Anglo-Egyptian agreement, Lavon called for the seizure of Gaza. Dayan wanted a "massive" blow against Egypt and Jordan for not suppressing border incursions, and suggested a raid against Jordan to repatriate 480 sheep that had wandered from the Ein Hashofet kibbutz into Jordan (Burns 1969, 41–44).

At the same time, criticism began to increase in the press, charging that Sharrett was being too weak in response to the border clashes. The attacks increased when a Syrian patrol captured five Israeli soldiers inside Syrian territory, and one of the Israeli officers committed suicide in prison. This event precipitated a verbal harangue by Herut and a call for a no-confidence vote (Shlaim 2001, 115–16). A short time later, Jordanian infiltrators in Ajour killed two Israeli farmers. In a meeting with Golda Meir and Zalman Aran, Sharrett said that retaliation could not be stopped, not because it would help "from the security point of view," but because domestic "anger must be assuaged" (quoted in Shlaim 2001, 116–17). He realized the need to retaliate in order to remain in power. Although direct retaliation was aborted when Jordan captured a number of the infiltrators responsible for the Ajour murder, escalation was only delayed. When negotiations failed with Egypt in 1955, Sharrett's dovish policies were already on the wane. In February, Ben-Gurion took Lavon's post of defense minister, and in November he became prime minister. By June 1956, Lavon resigned his post as foreign minister and resigned from politics. With the increased external pressure on Israel, Ben-Gurion was a wildly popular choice for leader (Shlaim 2001, 123; Brecher 1972, 280–81; Brecher 1974, 261–62). Ben-Gurion's threat inflation took the form of comparing Nasser to Hitler (Avi-Hai 1974, 128).

Opportunity for Escalation

The Israeli general staff believed they had seven months until the Egyptian military "absorbed" its new weapons and posed a major threat to Israeli security. In addition, the IDF estimated that the combined forces of Egypt and Syria would be six times greater than Israeli capabilities after all the Russian military hardware was operational. Therefore, Egypt would have an opportunity for escalation in late 1956, as their new weapons and alliances threatened Israel. But until that time, Egypt would be at a strategic disadvantage (Sachar 1981, 92–97; Nutting 1972, 170).

The Israeli opportunity to escalate appeared via Paris. France viewed Egypt as solely responsible for the uprising in Algeria (Nutting 1972, 124). Thus, as early as 1954, Israel received twelve French Duragen jet fighters. Both Shimon Peres and Ben-Gurion had frequent contacts with Guy Mollet after he was elected the French president in 1956. Mollet sent a shipment of France's latest Mystere jets to Israel early that year. Then, on July 4, 1956, French foreign minister Christian Pineau told the Israeli ambassador that all limitations on arms shipments to Israel were lifted, something neither the United States nor Britain could change (Bar-Siman-Tov 1987, 27–33).

The opening to preemptively strike the rising power in Cairo came when Nasser nationalized the Suez Canal. Both France and Britain were outraged, given the canal's integral importance to international trade. The British were the most severely effected because they owned a controlling share of the Suez Company and one-third of all ships using the canal were British. Further, almost all British oil passed through Suez. The French and British organized Operation Musketeer in response. The British would supply 50,000 troops and one hundred ships, and the French 30,000 troops and thirty ships. Further, Israel would provide a "threat" to the Suez, which would call for military intervention by the French and British forces (Sachar 1981, 100–102; Shlaim 2001, 165–67). Ben-Gurion viewed the French and British forces as essential for success because the new Mystere fighters were not yet operational. But Israeli intelligence did know that only thirty of the hundred new Egyptian MIG fighters, twelve of the forty Illyshin bombers, and fifty of the two hundred new tanks were operational. With the element of surprise and help from two great powers, Ben-

Gurion was confident of success (Sachar 1981, 106; Brecher 1974, 258–59; Avi-Hai 1974, 134; Dayan 1966, 60–61).

Summary and Analysis

As the above evidence suggests, a multilevel explanation of the 1956 war provides a more thorough understanding of the conflict than either a domestic or an international theory could illuminate in isolation. International pressure from Egypt, Syria, and Jordan, amplified by Soviet arms shipments, induced pessimism in Israeli thinking. Simultaneously, these international threats resonated in Israeli domestic politics, pushing Sharrett into a more hawkish position. Finally, only after 1956, when Nasser nationalized the Suez Canal, was a clear-cut opportunity for escalation apparent to Israel. Without the presence of domestic pressure to continue the rivalry, Israel may have been able to reach a compromise with Egypt. And had Israel not felt threatened by increases in Egyptian arms, a risky escalation would not have been as attractive. From Cairo's point of view, the confluence of domestic and international factors created little pressure to change their rivalry trajectory. Continued but limited conflict promised a more propitious bargaining situation in the future. It is the interaction between the domestic and international levels of analysis, rather than the levels themselves, that changed the probability of rivalry escalation in 1956.

1957–1965

Rivalry History

During the decade after the Suez crisis, Israel was reaping the economic benefits of security and thus was unlikely to alter its rivalry with Egypt substantially. In Egypt, Nasser continued his tough rhetoric against Israel, but without the teeth a competitive military would provide. Therefore, both countries maintained the rivalry during this period. Like Goldilocks, the states continued to make sure the rivalry never got too hot or too cold. The Iraqi coup and subsequent upheaval in Lebanon and Jordan in 1958 saw Israel playing only a passive role. Although plans were made to capture the West Bank if Jordan fell under Cairo's sway in a Nasserist coup, this move never was needed, and preemptive action was deemed unnecessary (Shlaim 2001, 200–201). Likewise, in 1960 as Syrian-Israeli tensions mounted, neither country crossed the brink of escalation to armed conflict. Although Nasser transported 50,000 troops into the Sinai, an Israeli countermobilization led to an eventual withdrawal, and the so-called Rotem Crisis passed without war.

As for negotiation, Ben-Gurion began inquiring about a face-to-face meeting with Nasser in the early 1960s. When a London journalist who had interviewed Nasser privately reported to an Israeli contact that Nasser had hinted at a meeting with Ben-Gurion, the Israeli prime minister sent a note in response. However, Nasser turned the idea of a secret meeting down, listing Israeli sins from the previous decade. Even had a meeting taken place, it is unlikely that a serious de-escalation would have resulted. In fact, Ben-Gurion had his own doubts, especially after the tripartite agreement of Egypt, Syria, and Iraq in 1963 (Shlaim 2001, 213). The Israeli leader was unlikely to compromise on the Palestinian issue, and Nasser was unlikely to trade his popularity at home for peace with Israel (Sachar 1981, 125). Again, both states continued their trajectory of nonmilitary conflict and rivalry maintenance. The event data in figure 14 illustrate this pattern. After the threats and recriminations from the 1956 war dampened in the early 1960s, both highly conflictual and cooperative events were rare.

Conventional Explanations

In many ways, the 1957–65 period mirrored Israeli-Egyptian interactions in 1949–55. Both states resisted a final reckoning at the negotiation table and on the battlefield. Just as in the earlier period of rivalry maintenance, reciprocity and domestic political explanations only supply part of the picture. Continued threats from Nasser tended to be answered with Israeli threats, and vice versa, but Ben-Gurion's call for direct negotiations went unanswered. Domestically, both states continued to refrain from escalation, despite different domestic institutions. Likewise, the domestic circumstance changed little in Egypt and Israel, as political leaders continued to feel pressure to avoid compromise. Why would similar domestic circumstances lead to escalation in 1956, but rivalry maintenance in the next decade?

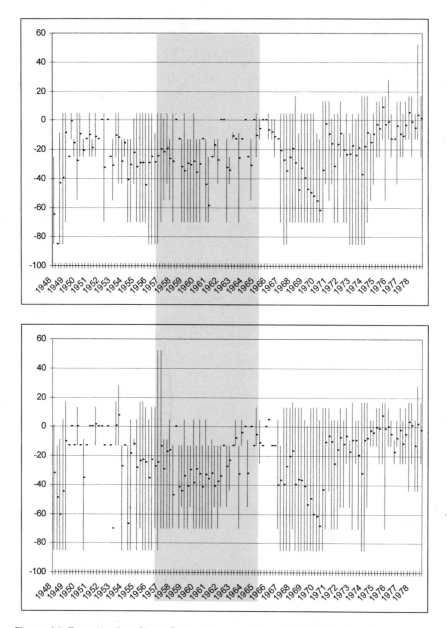

Figure 14. Egyptian-Israeli conflict and cooperation, 1957–1965. *Top:* Egyptian-to-Israeli events; *bottom:* Israeli-to-Egyptian events. COPDAB scale -100 to 60. 1957–1965 in frame.

Dynamic Two-Level Pressures

The pattern of rivalry maintenance during this period is better explained by the lack of pressure in both countries to alter the status quo. Israel was enjoying increased security and economic growth and expected these prospects to continue into the future. Russian financial loans and increased international clout similarly convinced Nasser that continued but limited rivalry would be better than a military or diplomatic showdown during this period. Domestically, the political costs of compromise further added to the continuation of rivalry in Cairo and Jerusalem.

Future Expectations

The end of the Suez crisis marked the beginning of an economic boom for Israel. With the United Nations in control of Sharm al-Sheikh, the Straits of Tiran and, with it, the Gulf of Aqaba were open to trade with Asia. Commerce through the Straits also allowed a network of pipelines to be built, making Israel a major oil transportation center between Iran and Europe. At the center of this economic development was the port of Eilat, where naval traffic doubled between 1957 and 1967 (Sachar 1981, 121; El-Gamasy 1993, 18–19). Expanded security, with the UN buffer zone, made international investment in industrial infrastructure more appealing. In fact, between 1950 and 1969, Israel's industrial output quintupled, and from 1953 to 1965, GNP increased by a factor of 2.5. Another by-product of the increased security was that immigration surged. Between 1956 and 1967 the Israeli population rose from 1,667,000 to 2,384,000. Yet instead of being a burden on the economy, joblessness did not rise, and production increased. This increase was due to a new irrigation system throughout the country that increased the water supply and arable land by 25 percent.

During this time, Israel was able to maintain its military advantage with Egypt, as arms continued to flow to Israel from France and, beginning in 1959, from Germany. The French navy protected Israeli shipping from its bases in Djibouti, and in 1958 conducted joint military maneuvers with the IDF. The Israeli air force received the new Mirage fighters, and the French and Israelis jointly developed the Matra air-to-air missile and the Shavit two-stage rocket. Most important, Paris aided in the construction of a nuclear reactor, which could produce military grade uranium, at Dimona. West Germany sent 50 planes, and in 1964 paid for 2 British submarines and 150 tanks to be delivered to Israel. Finally, the Arab threats were balanced against the newly formed "Alliance of the Periphery" that linked Israel with Iran, Turkey, and Ethiopia (Shlaim 2001, 192; El-Gamasy 1993, 18–19). Therefore, the Israeli expected future costs of rivalry during this period were low.

Although militarily defeated in 1956, Nasser was able to gain significant diplomatic capital from the Suez crisis, as he led his people against the former "imperialists." During this period, Nasser pressed Arab nationalism in Syria, Iraq, and Lebanon and extended his prestige around Africa in Ethiopia, Ghana, and Malawi (Sachar 1981, 132–33). Union with Syria in 1957 was viewed as a mixed but hopeful sign of Arab unity (Nutting 1972, 196). Even when the United Arab Republic was split in 1961 by a Syrian coup, Nasser was hopeful that his influence would spread to Yemen, through a successful civil war there. Further, Nasser was rid of a rival after Qassem fell in Iraq (Heikal 1973, 118–20; Nutting 1972, 268–70).

There was also hope that Egyptian industrial output would increase. In 1957, the Russians promised approximately $75 million in loans at only 2.5 percent interest. Afterwards, the Soviet Union continued to be generous in loaning money to Nasser both for economic development and for military expenditures. For example, the Soviets agreed to help build factories and docks in return for use of the ports at Alexandria in May 1964. To spur a government-led industrial revolution, Nasser created the "Economic Development Organization" and launched a five-year economic plan calling for approximately $300 million in industrial expansion. The jewel of the plan was the building of the Aswan High Dam, which the Soviets supported after the United States reneged on a loan for the project (Nutting 1972, 151). From 1960 to 1965, the Egyptian economy grew by a modest 6 percent.

There were also some dramatic social successes. By 1967, for example, 70 percent of primary school-age children were attending school, and registration at universities had tripled (Sachar 1981, 123). Government sponsored health programs had also improved the medical facilities in the country. Therefore, Soviet aid, Nasser's programs for economic development, and the tangible social programs on education moderated the expectation of future rivalry costs in Cairo.

Domestic Rivalry Outbidding Environment

During this time, Israeli domestic pressure toward escalation subsided. After the Suez war, the intensity of border incursions and fedayeen raids decreased substantially in Israel. Although there were occasional incidents on the Syrian and Jordanian borders, they were neither as frequent nor as violent. In addition, the destruction of the guerrilla bases in Egypt and UN trusteeship in Gaza meant that the Israeli-Egyptian border remained quiet during the vast majority of this period (Mor 1993, 115–19).

Ben-Gurion's popularity peaked after the 1956 victory, and throughout the late 1950s and early 1960s he remained the premier decision maker in international policy (Brecher 1972, 252–53). The only change at home was the strengthening of Mapai's ruling coalition on Ben-Gurion's coattails (Shlaim 2001, 187–89). Therefore, Ben-Gurion and Mapai felt little pressure to inflate the threat from Egypt and escalate tensions until 1963. Even Gahal, the party created when Herut and other right-wing parties merged, became more moderate (Brecher 1972, 174). In the early 1960s, the Mapai party was split internally over disagreements concerning the Lavon Affair. New evidence was announced that some documents were forged in 1954 to blame Lavon solely for the Egyptian operation. In response, Lavon asked Ben-Gurion to absolve him. The resulting schism pitted a group of younger elites, such as Shimon Peres and Giora Yoseftal, against the veteran personalities of Golda Meir, Levi Eshkol, and Isser Harel.

The veteran group seized on the issue of German aid to the Egyptian missile program to outmaneuver their younger counterparts. In July 1962, Egypt tested a surface-to-surface missile that it claimed could target all of Israel. It was further noted that some German scientists had been helping Egypt develop their weapons program. The Herut party joined forces with the veteran Mapai members to mobilize public opinion behind them. This strategy proved successful as Eshkol succeeded Ben-Gurion upon his retirement in 1963. Therefore, promoting conflict with Egypt could still provide domestic benefits, but the current harvest of threat inflation was significantly lower than the pre–Suez crisis atmosphere (Shlaim 2001, 212–16).

Enmity toward Israel and Jews in general continued to be salient in Egypt throughout this period. After the Suez crisis, Nasser took his frustrations out on the remaining Jews in Egypt. Of the 28,000 Jews still in Egypt at the time, 3,000 were imprisoned without charges, 8,000 were ordered to leave the country on four days' notice, and another 14,000 were "encouraged to leave" (Sachar 1981, 121–22). By 1961, only approximately 3,000 Jews remained in Egypt.

Nasser also nationalized the press and industry, continuing to centralize information and power in his own hands. Even before taking over the press, Nasser was issuing anti-Israeli propaganda. In a Radio Cairo broadcast in 1963, Nasser argued that "Israel is the cancer, the malignant wound in the body of Arabism, for which there is no cure but eradication" (quoted in Sachar 1981, 126). He frequently called for the destruction of Israel and blamed the Jerusalem government for subverting Egyptian growth and prosperity. Thus, Nasser continued to mobilize the public against Israel, a task made easier by the residual bitterness left from the two earlier military defeats. The rivalry outbidding environment in Egypt was tilted against compromise with Israel. There were few voices calling for peace, and they were drowned out by the calls to maintain the rivalry and "liquidate" Israel (Sachar 1981, 121–26; Nutting 1972, 271, 296–98; Meital 1997, 5–7). Nasser remained wildly popular throughout the period (Hasou 1985, 37).

Opportunity for Escalation

Despite Nasser's rhetoric, Egypt had little opportunity to escalate its conflict with Israel. Even if the capabilities of Egypt and Syria were added together after the 1957 union with Syria, the military balance was not in their favor (Shlaim 2001, 192). Increased immigration, industrialization, and military aid from France and Germany ensured that Israel remained secure. Nasser himself noted that Israel was too strong to confront in the early 1960s (Leng 2000, 145). This reality was reinforced when, after the Suez crisis, the Russians stated they would not support escalation against Israel. In 1960, when Syrian leaders proposed war with Israel, Nasser is said to have fetched a letter sent previously from Khrushchev stating the Russian position (Nutting 1972, 170).

Summary and Analysis

It is only when the international and domestic levels are integrated that a coherent explanation of the events, and lack thereof, during this period is found. Even though domestic pressure was lighter in Israel in 1963, as compared to 1956, there was little movement towards de-escalation. Because expectations for the future were optimistic in Israel, no change or compromise was needed. Similarly, in Egypt the lack of an international opportunity to change the status quo, the domestic pressure to avoid recognizing Israel, as well as the expectation that the future would bring a stronger bargaining position, made rivalry maintenance more likely.

1966–1970

Rivalry History

By 1967, Nasser was facing increased domestic and regional criticism. His constituency was the target of propaganda from Iraq and Syria accusing him of allowing Zionist aggression in the north. Simultaneously, Israel was losing support from the west as al-Fatah began stepping up its attacks from Jordan and Syria. Also, Syrian and Israeli tensions were rising, over both the border incursions and the diversion of the Jordan River. Damascus wanted Egyptian guarantees of support in any conflict. In response to the perceived Arab threats, the right-wing Israeli parties pressured Eshkol into forming a unity government. The outcome was the formation of a national government of unity that included the right-wing Herut party and foreign policy hawk Begin, for the first time.

The events of late spring 1967 began with Nasser forcing the United Nation to withdraw from Gaza and Sharm al-Sheikh, while also announcing the closure of the Straits of Tiran. This move was an escalation in tensions with Israel that stopped just short of war. Nasser gained previously lost territory, without a shot being fired, because U Thant, the UN secretary general, ordered the international peacekeeping force to retreat (El-Gamasy 1987, 24–26).

Israeli decision makers were outraged at Nasser's retaking of Sharm al-Sheikh and the closing of the straits. In June, Israel launched a coordinated aerial bombardment and land assault to break the blockade. After a mere six days of fighting, Israel had secured the whole of the Sinai and the Gaza Strip from Egypt. Their conquest included Sharm al-Sheikh, as well as the Golan Heights from Syria and the West Bank and old Jerusalem from Jordan. The Arab armies and air forces were eviscerated because of impressive Israeli intelligence. In the campaign, Egypt alone lost approximately three hundred planes, six hundred tanks, and 20,000 troops, while Israel lost fifty planes, eighty tanks, and 800 troops (Sachar 1981, 159).

The fighting stopped only long enough for Egypt and Syria to rearm with Soviet weapons. At the Khartoum Conference in the summer of 1967, the Arab states issued the "three no's": no peace with Israel, no recognition of Israel, no negotiation with Israel concerning any Palestinian territory. More dramatically, from February 1969 to August 1970, Nasser mounted his "War of Attrition," against Israel. As Lewis (1990, 26) states, "given the wide disparity in the populations of Israel and Egypt, Israel could not long tolerate trading casualties with the Egyptians." In retaliation, Israel launched a series of air raids on Cairo and on important oil facilities deep in Egypt. The fighting only stopped when Israel feared direct Soviet intervention in response to the shooting down of four Soviet-piloted planes in July 1970. With American prodding, Israel accepted a cease-fire and UN resolution 242 setting out a vague program for peace in 1970.

Figure 15 illustrates this escalation, as the relative quiet of the early to mid-1960s was shattered by highly volatile conflict and descending mean cooperation scores. In fact, the event data record the most bellicosity for both states in 1967 since the last period of escalation one decade earlier.

Conventional Explanations

There is little doubt that the spiral of Egyptian and Israeli threats helped to precipitate the Six Days War. The international actions and reactions led from threats of war to massive Israeli strikes in response to Nasser's mobilization. However, the timing of each threat and the continued momentum toward greater escalation did not follow a symmetrical path. Threats were not answered in kind but were amplified by each party. Nasser's threat to the United Nations was met by Israeli calls for escalation. Israeli threats were parried by Nasser's mobilization, which in turn was countered by an overwhelming Israeli preventative strike. Why would Egyptian mobilization during the Rotem crisis only lead to a temporary escalation in tensions, while Nasser's mobilization in 1967 spurred massive Israeli strikes?

Moreover, domestic political changes and democracy levels do not explain this threat amplification and escalation. Although Nasser may have

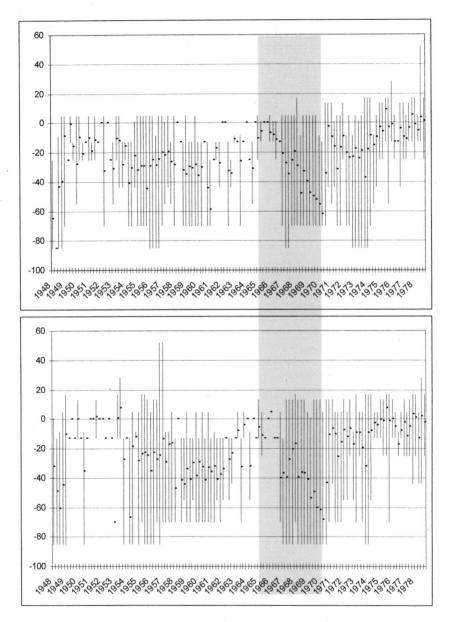

Figure 15. Egyptian-Israeli conflict and cooperation, 1966–1970. *Top:* Egyptian-to-Israeli events; *bottom:* Israeli-to-Egyptian events. COPDAB scale -100 to 60. Smaller numbers represent more conflict, 1966–1970 in frame.

initiated the crisis by ordering the UN out of the Sinai, Israel eventually met threats with overwhelming force. Thus, it was the more democratic state that escalated the crisis to war, or at the very least continued the escalatory spiral toward war.

Dynamic Two-Level Pressures

Dynamic two-level pressures identify strong currents toward escalation in both states by 1967, although at different intervals. Egyptian expected future costs rose first, coalescing with a mobilized domestic outbidding environment to make the current rivalry trajectory unattractive. Nasser moved to assuage this pressure by retaking the Sinai and by ejecting the United Nations. In Israel, it is only after the retaking of Sharm al-Sheikh by Egypt that some change in behavior was needed. Since compromise was unpopular in both states, the only room for movement in the rivalry was upward, toward confrontation.

Future Expectations

The domestic situation began to change in late 1965 and early 1966 for both countries. During that time, Nasser's continued borrowing from other countries caused a balance-of-payments deficit of $200 million. Over the past decade and a half, Egypt had borrowed $1 billion from the Soviet bloc, accounting for 14 percent of Soviet support to the third world. More disconcerting was the fact that this aid did not bring modernization and efficiency. The Egyptian economy remained largely agricultural, and what industrial goods were produced continued to be of poor quality and reputation. In 1966 and 1967 growth slowed considerably, and in those years there were food shortages and growing unemployment. In response, protests became frequent in Cairo.

The Yemeni conflict also consumed Egyptian money and arms. Sachar describes the Yemeni civil war as a "meat grinder of Egyptian resources" (1981, 125). From 1962 through 1965, the number of Egyptian troops in Yemen increased from 20,000 to approximately 60,000. This conflict consumed nearly the entire energy of the Egyptian army (El-Gamasy 1993, 17–18) and further undercut economic growth.

To pay the mounting bills of war and failed development, Nasser drew

closer to the Soviet Union. In 1966, the USSR and Egypt signed an agreement exchanging the Soviet use of four Egyptian ports and three airports
for increased military equipment. Despite this deal, economic growth continued to be slow, and the tide of the Yemeni civil war continued to turn
against the Cairo-backed side. In total, Egyptian expected costs remained
high during this period.

In Israel, the prospects of a renewed blockade, at a time when terrorism was increasing and diplomatic support from their allies was falling,
created a pessimistic view of the future. Israeli economic growth slowed in
1964 and 1965 and was marginal in 1966 (Brecher 1974, 326). At the same
time, Syria recommenced using Palestinian refugees to fight Israel, and positioning artillery on the Golan Heights. Syria also trained the members of
the new and highly militant al-Fatah faction. This group, led by Yasser
Arafat, who was a relative of the Mufti of Jerusalem, used bases in Jordan
and Syria to launch ambushes on the Israeli side of the border. These attacks became frequent after 1966. As tensions with Syria mounted, Nasser
sent 20,000 troops into the Sinai and began ordering the UN to withdrawal
from the Gaza Strip and Sharm al-Sheikh.

As Israel's enemies seemed to be increasingly active, her allies in the
United States, Britain, France, and Germany were characterized by inactiv-
ity. As a threat from Egypt mounted in May 1967, neither the United States
nor Britain attempted to arbitrate an agreement. In meetings in Paris, London, and Washington, Abba Eban, the Israeli minister of foreign affairs,
was told that Israel was in no danger and warned that the Jerusalem government would forfeit help if it acted first (Shlaim 2001, 239–40; Brecher
1974, 322–24) Although the U.S. position changed by the end of June,
high-level American diplomats continued to tell Israel that they would
win any confrontation with Egypt without U.S. help and offered little to
no aid.

However, the biggest shock to Israeli expectations about the future
came on May 19–21. It was during this time that Nasser reoccupied Sharm
al-Sheikh, which guards the Straits of Tiran, and then sent a destroyer, two
submarines, and four missile boats through the Suez Canal to blockade the
Gulf of Aqaba. Simultaneously, Nasser broadcasted a message claiming the
Straits and barring any ship calling on Israel from passing. Although it had
little immediate economic impact, the blockade would have proven lethal
to the Israeli economy. By 1967, the port of Eilat and the Straits provided

Israel with its most important trade routes to Africa and Asia. Eilat was also the port from which over 30 percent of Israeli mineral exports were transported and was the principal Israeli oil port. It was only after these developments that Israeli expected costs were high. The status quo, even with al-Fatah's attacks, would have been only moderately detrimental to the Israeli economy or security position, but the blockade would have the long-term consequence of stripping Israel of its economic might if unchecked (Sachar 1981, 123–45; Brecher 1974, 318–31; Laqueur 1968, 39–71).

Domestic Rivalry Outbidding Environment

The domestic political environment in both countries became ripe for rivalry outbidding during this period. In Egypt, Nasser continued his tirades against Israel in both speeches and in the state-controlled press. More pressure was placed on Nasser as Syria and Jordan criticized Nasser for not taking a hard enough line against Israel. There is little doubt that both the domestic and regional mobilization of public opinion against Israeli "imperialism" weighed on Nasser's decisions. Tensions between Nasser and King Feisal and King Hussein ran so high that Nasser accused the other Arab leaders of planning to take over Egypt (Hasou 1985, 39). Looking weak in the face of Israeli moves that were explained as "aggressive" in official propaganda would only increase the protests and demonstrations in Egypt. Therefore, Nasser continued to divert attention from domestic ills by playing the Israel card and continuing to inflate the Israeli threat (Shlaim 2001, 237; Sachar 1981, 144–46). For example, Nasser stated, "If [the Israelis] want to try war, then I say again today: Welcome" (Sachar 1981, 144). Nasser went to such rhetorical extremes in criticizing Israel, and his speeches were so popular in the region, that even Feisal and Hussein were forced to step up their own condemnation of Israel to keep pace (Hasou 1985, 39–40; El-Gamasy 1993, 33–35).

In Israel, the increasing violence from Syria and al-Fatah again mobilized support behind the Israeli hard-liners. Through control of information, Israel blamed the artillery shelling on Syria, even when there was some evidence that Israeli commanders instigated the fighting. On May 12, 1967, chief of staff Yitzhak Rabin explicitly threatened to overthrow the Syrian regime, which was harboring and training the new al-Fatah guerrilla force. Even Eshkol, the next day, stated that Israel "may have to teach Syria a sharper lesson" (quoted in Shlaim 2001, 237). One by one, politicians began calling for escalation. The new Rafi coalition, which Ben-Gurion came out of retirement to lead, was the vituperative critic of Eshkol's policies. As Shlaim notes, the coalition "tried to make political capital out of the crisis by drawing attention persistently to Eshkol's shortcomings" (2001, 238). These included a relatively late and unorganized mobilization and poor leadership during the crisis. By late May, there were calls for immediate military action following the closure of the Straits of Tiran and Egyptian moves in the Sinai (Brecher 1974, 327–30).

Opportunity for Escalation

The perceived military balance between Israel and Egypt during this period has been analyzed by a number of observers (El-Gamasy 1993, 36; Laqueur 1968, 65–70). It is clear that the objective balance of weapons and technology favored Israel, which both Nasser and Eshkol knew as late as 1966. Nevertheless, there are a number of intervening factors that are less transparent. First, the Soviet Union had given Nasser a pledge in 1966 to support a military buildup to confront Israel and the United States. Also, Nasser had American assurances that it would not support Israel if Eshkol fired first (Nutting 1972, 408). Finally, there is evidence that Nasser received false information from General Amer on the readiness of his troops, many of which were still bogged down in Yemen (El-Gamasy 1993, 37–40). Misleading intelligence was also passed on to Egypt by the Soviet Union, stating that Israel was preparing to invade Syria (Shlaim 2001, 237).

Despite the capability distribution, Egypt did have an opportunity to take back the Gaza Strip and Sharm al-Sheikh, and with Russian support Nasser believed he could hold these territories. This point is supported by his orders to the army to construct defensive positions only, while rejecting General Amer's strategy of a preemptive strike (Nutting 1972, 410–11).

Throughout the crisis, Israel remained confident that it could win any conflict with the Arab states, short of direct Soviet intervention. The Israeli air force and paratroop divisions, as events would show, were both highly trained and effective weapons against both Egypt and the other Arab states. The only disagreement among the Israeli cabinet concerned how to defeat the Arab states, rather than whether a victory was possible (see Brecher and Geist 1980, 96–100; Leng 2000, 152).

Summary and Analysis

Egypt's initial bellicose policy was motivated both by future considerations and by domestic calculations. Nasser was assured of Soviet assistance, which came in the form of a global arms shipment program from the communist bloc that by 1969 had replaced all the war matériel lost in 1967. In addition, the Suez would allow Nasser to fight a trench battle with his new mass of artillery, pinning Israel down on the eastern banks and serving to deter Israel's highly effective land assaults. This situation was a unique opportunity for escalation. It was widely recognized that Egypt had more men and a growing supply of arms to throw into a "war of attrition." Israel, on the other hand, with its more limited population, would be at a comparable disadvantage in this type of battle.

The general timing of the Israeli response is also explained by the elevated expected future costs after the Straits were closed. Before that decision, Israel would have been able to maintain the rivalry and not suffer serious losses. For example, Israel was holding off Syria, and the IDF was more than able to exact retribution on al-Fatah. But once the Straits of Tiran were sealed and guarded by Egyptian forces at Sharm al-Sheikh, the future looked bleak for Israel. The loss of jobs and increased public scrutiny would surely have had long-term electoral consequences for Eshkol and the Labor party, which was already splintered by Rafi. This explains why Israeli escalation was more likely after mid-May.

1970–1973

Rivalry History

To some extent, relations between Egypt and Israel relaxed from 1970 to 1972. Both parties accepted a second Rogers Plan in 1970, leading to a cease-fire and an end to the war of attrition. When Nasser died on September 28, 1970, the Israeli leadership believed that peace was possible. The influential editor Mohamed Heikal wrote about accepting Israel as a neighbor, and Anwar al-Sadat, the new Egyptian leader, began sending signals that he was ready for dialogue (see Meital 1997, 79–80; Shlaim 2001, 300–304). On February 4, 1971, Sadat proposed the reopening of the Suez Canal and a partial withdrawal of the Israeli troops from the eastern bank.

These years saw a flurry of diplomatic exchange, both public and private, between these two states. Sadat and Meir both supported secret high-level talks. Yet neither was willing to concede much to the other. In fact, Israel showed a complete lack of willingness even to discuss the future status of the West Bank, while Sadat insisted that any discussions include mention of the occupied Palestinian areas. Meir and Dayan continued to support the consolidation of the formally Egyptian-occupied territory, rather than preparing the Gaza Strip and Sinai to be handed over to Egypt. Although Sadat initially sought an agreement with Israel over the Sinai, his hope foundered as neither the leadership in Jerusalem, nor in Washington, was willing to compromise (Shlaim 2001, 315–19; Gazit 1995, 115).

After asking for more arms and being rejected by Brezhnev, Sadat evicted the Soviet advisors from Egypt. This move turned out to be very popular, as it was viewed as terminating a socialist imperialism. The expulsion yielded Sadat full control over new combat aircraft and SAM missile sites that had previously been under the direction of Moscow. Sadat believed that no war could be fought while the Soviets were in Egypt. This move was misperceived in Washington and Jerusalem as a sign of increasing weakness. Therefore, Israel moved to an even less compromising bargaining position, feeling increasingly secure without a Soviet presence next door.

Sadat proposed a joint Egyptian-Syrian attack in March 1973, and October 6 was set as the date for the offensive. Jordan pledged to feign an attack to draw Israeli troops, and King Feisal of Iraq offered cash to keep the Egyptian economy afloat. Israel at the time was more worried about terrorism than interstate war, and thus was very slow to react to both Egyptian and Syrian deployments. Even after the Egyptian crossing of the canal had begun, Israel remained on "warning" rather than on the higher status of "alert."

The first-move advantage and Israel's late mobilization allowed Egypt to win a number of swift early victories. Although Egypt expected 10,000 casualties, they lost only 180 troops in the initial crossing and were able to capture the east bank of the canal and the Bar-Lev fortifications. The tide of the battle soon turned, as Israel was able to subdue Syria and then establish a beachhead on the west bank of the Canal in Egyptian territory. However, Egypt held the east bank of the canal to the north, despite its Third Army division being completely encircled to the south. The initial success of the campaign as well as the seizure of the northeast bank, allowed Sadat to bargain from a position of relative strength, especially compared to the Egyptian position following the 1948, 1956, and 1967 wars.

The subtleties of this period can be observed in figure 16. After 1970, cooperation increases toward the pre-1967 level, but then it quickly degenerates into increased conflict by 1974 for both rivals. Some of Sadat's signals for cooperation show up as upward spikes in 1971. Further, the Egyptian escalation and increased threats are apparent in the top graph. By 1974, the long strokes of escalation are again apparent.

Conventional Explanations

The failure of peace and the initiation of war in the early 1970s is an example of asymmetrical reciprocity, rather than a stable international action-reaction sequence. Egypt made a number of lukewarm overtures toward compromise that were unreciprocated by Israel. After negotiations failed, Sadat moved to launch a surprise attack. The interesting questions during this period are not explained by reciprocity, but instead are related to the very absence of reciprocation.

Domestic politics goes some way in explaining the bilateral imbalance in conflict and cooperation during this time. Both leaders were relatively constrained by domestic opinion that would only allow limited compromise. Had domestic circumstance been different, and more open to compromise and sacrifices for peace, the October war might have been avoided. However, these highly mobilized political environments were present during the relative peace of the early 1950s and early 1960s. Therefore, domestic politics may explain why cooperation was truncated in the 1970s but does little to elucidate why Egypt chose escalation over lower-level conflict.

Another perspective on the 1973 war highlights the rampant misperceptions during this period (see Gross Stein 1985). For example, Israel did not anticipate the Egyptian assault, and moreover did not foresee the comparative strength of the Egyptian army. Also, Israeli and American elites mistook the expulsion of Russian personnel from Egypt as decreasing the probability of Egyptian escalation. While there is little doubt that Israeli overconfidence helped to supply Sadat with important advantages in the fighting, misperceptions related to the balance of forces does not clarify

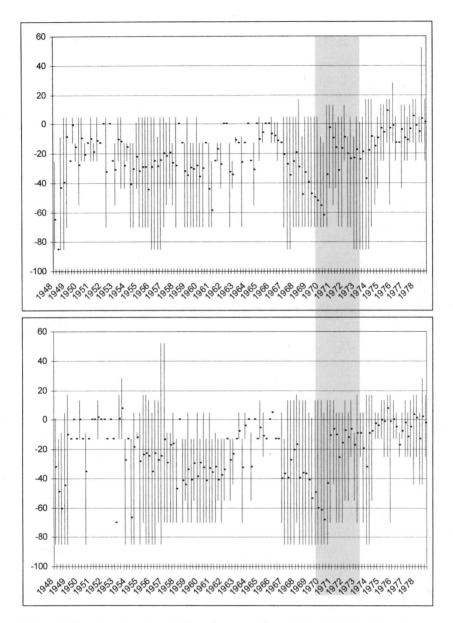

Figure 16. Egyptian-Israeli conflict and cooperation, 1970–1973. *Top:* Egyptian-to-Israeli events; *bottom:* Israeli-to-Egyptian events. COPDAB scale -100 to 60. Smaller numbers represent more conflict, 1970–1973 in frame.

why Sadat first chose to attempt negotiations with Israel. More important, there had been incorrect assessments of the rivalry many times in the past. In 1948, the Arab states had underestimated Israeli strength at independence. In the early 1950s, Israel inaccurately accused Nasser of supporting terrorist raids based in Gaza. These erroneous expectations occurred in peacetime and during war. Misperceptions were important factors in the outcome of the battle and the way in which it was fought in 1973, but a more comprehensive framework is needed to understand what perceptions are important and whether they will reinforce peace or increase the probability of war.

Dynamic Two-Level Pressures

The rivalry interactions during this time are consistent with the shifting dynamic two-level pressures in the early 1970s. Israel did not expect high future costs, while Egypt did, as the occupied territories were consolidated and fortifications built. Therefore, Egypt should have been the first to seek some way out of its current rivalry trajectory. Clearly, Sadat explored a number of possibilities for negotiating with Israel, both through secret direct channels and with the Americans. Nevertheless, the outbidding environment in Egypt would not allow Sadat to recognize Israel or end the state of general bellicosity between the two states without substantial territorial gains. Because Israel perceived that its bargaining situation would only improve in the future, substantial territorial concessions to Egypt were eliminated at the start of all negotiations (see Shlaim 2001, 318; Meital 1997 chap. 5). Hence, de-escalation became unlikely, as Israeli intransigence blocked Sadat's path toward compromise.[2] Escalation was also unlikely until 1973 because Sadat did not have an opportunity to escalate the dispute, especially with the Soviet Union controlling the sophisticated SAM sites. Rivalry maintenance was therefore the most probable path for each state, as Israel attempted to support the status quo and Egypt lacked an opportunity to change its rivalry trajectory. It was only after the Soviets

2. One may point out that Sadat could have "compromised" and given up the occupied territories, but that move would have almost certainly cost him his position, as even the more moderate terms of the Camp David Accords later gave him cause for concern. Thus, the outbidding environment made this development unlikely.

were expelled and Sadat completed his reorganization of the military that Egypt found a potential military opening out of the status quo.

Future Expectations

Having won a decisive victory in 1967 and holding on to its new territory in the ensuing years, Israel remained optimistic about its future. The United States, while pushing for a cease-fire, had agreed to sell Israel its new Phantom fighters. When Israel signed the cease-fire in 1970, and Egyptian missiles were found in the demilitarized zone, Washington promised even more military support to ensure Israeli strength.

The future Israeli security situation in the region also looked manageable. The Jordanian civil war in 1970 signaled the deep divisions between the Arab countries, most notably Jordan and Syria, and lowered the probability of a unified Arab attack. In the event of an attack from Egypt, the Bar-Lev fortification lines were viewed as more than ample defense measures. Finally, the leadership in Jerusalem perceived Egypt as an embarrassed and militarily inferior bargaining partner and saw little reason to compromise (Sachar 1981, 173–75). Kissinger summed up Prime Minister Meir's perceptions at the time by noting that because "she considered Israel militarily impregnable, there was, strictly speaking, no need for any change" (Kissinger 1982, 218–19).

In Egypt, expectations grew continually more pessimistic. The defeats of the previous five years had weighed heavily on the Egyptian economy. None of Nasser's plans for industrialization had come to fruition, and increased spending on Soviet arms for the war of attrition only exacerbated the problem. Between 1968 and 1973, Egyptian defense spending reached 26 percent of its total budget (Whetten 1974, 164). When Nasser died before completing negotiations to end the civil war, the task fell to Anwar Sadat to rebuild Egyptian morale. Yet in this task he had little help. The Soviet Union continued to be a useful ally for arms but was worth far less as an economic trading partner. Thirty-eight percent of all Egyptian exports went to the Soviet bloc, and 92 percent of nonagrarian imports came from communist countries. Most of these goods were of low quality. Thus, there was little diversification in trade, and the Egyptian economy continued its stagnancy. In addition, 400,000 refugees continued to tax the government, as did the loss of Suez tolls, which amounted to $6 billion by 1971.

The loss of the Sinai also represented a $3 billion loss in production (Sachar 1981, 176–77; Meital 1997, 100–105).

Even as the Soviet Union continued to supply large quantities of arms to Egypt, the quality of the weapons continued to fall short of the sophisticated war matériel that would be needed to push Israel out of the Sinai (Heikal 1975, 165–67). The situation only looked to get worse in the future. Israel, under the direction of Dayan, was considering a plan to build a deep-water port at Yamit, which would cut off the Gaza Strip from Egypt proper. In response, Sadat stated, "Every word spoken about Yamit is a knife pointing at me" (quoted in Heikal 1975, 205). Yamit and the Bar-Lev lines of fortification were some of the higher-profile means by which Israel was consolidating its position at Egypt's expense. As Meital writes about Egypt, "the feeling [was] that the status quo was intolerable" (1997, 103).

Domestic Rivalry Outbidding Environment

The outbidding environment in Israel became increasingly mobilized against Egypt. In 1968, Rafi and the Alignment Party had reformed Mapai, with Golda Meir taking over as prime minister in 1969. At the same time, the threats emanating from the War of Attrition and Syria increased the political clout of right-wing groups such as Gahal, who increased their representation to twenty-three seats. Even the stronger Mapai party was pulled into the war of words against Egypt, winning the election under the slogan "Sharm al-Sheikh without peace is better than peace without Sharm al-Sheik." The years of secrecy associated with the Dimona reactor, the Lavon Affair, and retaliatory raids allowed Israeli politicians from Gahal, but also Dayan, to trumpet the external threat Israel faced. As such, the Israeli public continued to be suspicious of the Arab world because of continued terrorism, the Munich Olympic massacre, and the previous wars (Shlaim and Tanter 1978; Meital 1997, 37–38; Shlaim 2001, 290–310).

Dayan led the Alignment Party toward an expansionist policy, calling for both a port at Yamit and increased defenses and consolidation in the occupied territories. Not wanting to appear weak, with the Soviet Union continuing to feed Egypt weapons, other leaders supported Dayan's plans. Shlaim notes that, "[Sadat] watched parties and candidates outbidding each other in their plans for taking over conquered Arab territory" (2001, 317). The situation was inflamed by the fact that there was no leader that matched the political clout Ben-Gurion held during his prime. There were a number of Mapai ministers who thought they could lead the party, including Eban, Dayan, and Meir. The slightest mistake, for example appearing too weak, could ruin a career (see Shlaim 2001, 316–20; Rafael 1981, 211). As Sachar averred, Meir and the Labor alignment did not "permit itself to be outbid in its stance of intransigence on defense issues" (1981, 190). Mapai members Eban and Pinhas Sapir both aborted their stillborn attempts to support compromise with Egypt.

In Egypt, two opposing forces were at work, at once mobilizing and demobilizing public perceptions of Israel. As Sadat took control of the government, he began to loosen the government's control on propaganda. He first allowed increased press freedoms, along with encouraging general discussion of government policies. In addition, Sadat banned arrests without warrants and closed the detention centers that Nasser had used as a shrewd political tool. This process engendered a "demythologization" of Nasser's previous policies (Sachar 1981, 192; Meital 1997, 6). The public was allowed to hear opposing views on both domestic and foreign policy and even to form a more complex view of the Israeli problem. All of this worked against potential rivalry outbidders, such as Ali Sabry, as a freer press made threat inflation more difficult.

Yet Israeli intransigence proved to be a powerful countervailing force. At each turn, Israel was unwilling to compromise on the occupied territory. Thus, the information people were receiving was not conducive to supporting de-escalation. Israeli proposals for peace never spelled out reparations to refugees or a schedule for withdrawal. The failure of the Jarring mission peace talks, coupled with the construction of the Bar-Lev fortifications, further inflamed public opinion. Just as Sadat was lowering the probability of threat inflation, Israel itself was supplying a more tangible threat to react against (Meital 1997, 103).

In this environment, Sadat had to contend with his main rival, Ali Sabri. Sabri was chairman of the Arab Socialist Union and wanted a more militant pro-Soviet stance. Sadat and Sabri sparred over the confederation with Libya and Syria in April 1971, and Sadat dismissed and imprisoned Sabri after information was discovered pointing to a coup. In fact, during this time, Sadat worried about being deposed by a number of his critics in the Egyptian National Assemby (Heikal 1975, 210). The Egyptian leader continued to make public speeches supporting the Palestinian cause, stating, "We shall not be the generation that gave up the Palestinian people's rights" (Sachar 1981, 183). But he also attempted to explore compromise solutions with Israel. By 1972, students began protesting for a change in policy, chanting, "wage war or conclude peace." However, the terms Israel set out for peace would not allow Sadat to stay in power if he accepted them, even with Sabri in prison (Meital 1997, 103–6). As Gazit (1995, 115) points out, Sadat's advisors continually reiterated the need to press Egyptian claims and the potential costs of conciliation with Egypt.

Opportunity for Escalation

It is clear that Egypt did not have an opportunity to escalate the conflict before 1973. On December 28, 1971, Sadat told the Arab Socialist Union that "without additional Soviet help," Egypt could not win a conflict with Israel (quoted in Sachar 1981, 185). While Egypt could eventually mobilize more troops than Israel, its more sophisticated weapons, including the important SAM sites, were under Russian direction. As Russia wanted to continue détente with the United States, these systems would not be available for use in an offensive. Sadat also doubted that Syria or Iraq would open an eastern front to pressure Israeli forces in 1972 (Meital 1997, 100).

An opportunity did open, however slightly, in mid-1973. In Egypt, the Soviet Union had continued to impede Sadat's plans to escalate toward Israel. First, as noted, the Soviet Union controlled the most advanced anti-aircraft batteries in Egypt. These weapons would prove invaluable in any conflict with the Jewish state as a defense against Israeli air power. Second, Moscow controlled the reconnaissance base at Garabalis, as well as twelve other airstrips in Egypt, and did not allow the Egyptian army access to any of these resources. After two letters reminding Brezhnev of the terms of their military aid agreement received unproductive replies, Sadat evicted the 15,000 Soviet personnel from Egypt on May 29, 1973. Suddenly, Sadat controlled an additional 150 combat aircraft, 30 SAM sites, and additional airfields (Sachar 1981, 188). Sadat later explained the decision by noting that "no war could be fought while Soviet experts worked in Egypt" (quoted in Sachar 1981, 188–89).

In addition to this new war matériel, Sadat had improved the efficiency of his force. Most important, the Egyptian army had been training for an amphibious landing across the canal and the retaking of positions on the east bank for several months prior to planned operation. Also, Sadat had completed his reorganization of the military, which included more efficient communication and leadership. Finally, in the days leading up to the operation, Sadat learned that only 2,000 Israeli soldiers manned the Bar-Lev bunkers, half of the listed peacetime strength (Sachar 1981, 198). When Syria agreed to coordinate a surprise attack against Israel, an opportunity to change the status quo militarily, although a risky one, was present.

Summary and Analysis

The deviations in international reciprocity can be explained by the specific interaction between international and domestic variables over time. Looking at the dynamic two-level pressures in 1973, the final piece of the escalation puzzle fell into place, and Sadat initiated war with Israel. With extremely high expected costs and an opening for escalation, some change in rivalry trajectory was probable. Furthermore, the Egyptian domestic outbidding environment was mobilized against Israel, as a result of continued Israeli threats and inflexibility. The same pressures were at work in Israel, but in a different direction. Low expected costs of future rivalry maintenance made both compromise and escalation unlikely from the Israeli side. Neither escalation nor de-escalation was perceived in Jerusalem as more beneficial than the status quo. Israel felt little pressure to reciprocate Egyptian cooperation, however limited.

1974–1979

Rivalry History

After the war, the disengagement treaty of 1974 mirrored similar short-term and shallow diplomatic activity after the other Arab-Israeli wars. However, the Sinai II treaty, including its promises of long-term agreements and Israeli flexibility on the Sinai, was an unprecedented step toward cooperation. In 1976, a potential flashpoint, with escalation in the civil war in Lebanon, passed without a significant crisis between Egypt and Israel. By September 1977, Dayan was sent to meet with King Hassan of Morocco to arrange a meeting with the Egyptian representative Tuhami.

The first of what would be three secret meetings between Dayan and Tuhami took place on September 16, 1977, in Morocco.

Sadat's initiative for peace picked up its pace in November when he announced, "I am prepared to go to the ends of the earth for peace, even to the Knesset itself" (quoted in Shlaim 2001, 359). After his speech, Begin and Sadat agreed to: (1) renounce the use of war against each other; (2) formally restore sovereignty over the Sinai to Egypt; and (3) demilitarize most of the Sinai and limit Egyptian forces at the Suez Canal and the Mitla and Gidi passes (Shlaim 2001, 361). In December 1977, Begin met with Sadat at Ismailia, and the Knesset approved a compromise plan on the Sinai and the West Bank. While it took almost two years for these principles to be set down in a treaty and ratified, the level of tension between the two states was considerably lower in 1976 than in 1972, or at any previous time in the thirty years of rivalry. This de-escalation is graphically recorded in figure 17 as conflict is significantly bounded, and the mean cooperation scores increase. After difficult negotiations at Camp David, and United States security guarantees, Egypt and Israel signed a peace treaty in Washington on March 26, 1979.

Conventional Explanations

The quick turn from war to peace and significant de-escalation is unique in the rivalry. Escalation in 1948, 1956, and 1967 through 1970 bred only continued conflict, if at a lower level. Conventional single-level explanations of rivalry behavior fail to account for the different outcomes of these crises. Why did a virtuous if at times sputtering spiral of reciprocated cooperation grow in 1974 and not before? Similar negotiations had been offered by both parties previously but failed to pick up momentum. Surely without the willingness of both rivals to compromise as evidenced in the Sinai II agreements and at Camp David, de-escalation would have been improbable. However, the initial motivations for peace remain to be explained. Equally, changes in the democracy levels of both countries fail to account for the increasing cooperation beginning in 1974. To be sure, the Peace Now movement and other constituencies for peace benefited from the democratic institutions in Israel, such as the free press, but Egypt made only small incremental steps away from autocracy during this time. What forces explain this shift from war to peace?

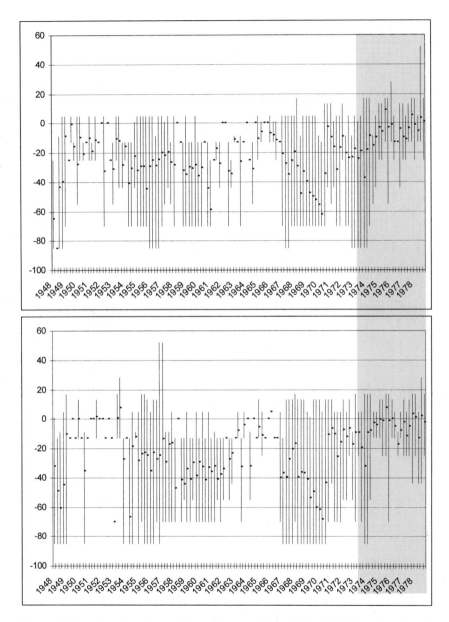

Figure 17. Egyptian-Israeli conflict and cooperation, 1974–1979. *Top:* Egyptian-to-Israeli events, *bottom:* Israeli-to-Egyptian events. COPDAB scale -100 to 60. Smaller numbers represent more conflict, 1974–1979 in frame.

Dynamic-Two-Level Pressures

Dynamic two-level pressures help to accentuate important differences between the 1974 to 1979 period and the other phases of continued rivalry conflict. After the 1973 war, the respectable showing of the Egyptian army in the October campaign set off two important changes. First, the high Israeli casualties, especially in the initial stage of the war, shocked expectations about the future in Jerusalem. Prior to 1973, the Israeli leadership and Meir believed that time was on their side. By maintaining the rivalry, the occupied territories could be consolidated. Further, any Arab attempt to alter the status quo was expected to fail, given the particular strength of the Israeli air force. After 1973, continued consolidation and inflexibility might mean a costly war of attrition that, in the long run, the small isolated Jewish nation would not win. Second, the running of the Bar-Lev line supplied Sadat with a flood of domestic support.

The Egyptian leader could now bargain both internationally and domestically from a position of relative strength. Sadat could take certain risks for peace that would have been highly dangerous under different domestic situations. The visit to the Knesset, for example, would almost surely have been viewed as treasonable in 1970. Yet in 1977 the move was generally perceived as a step toward diplomatic equality with Israel (Meital 1997, 138–39). Finally, the United States pressured Israel to de-escalate, while it also maintained a security guarantee, aiding the progress toward peace.

Future Expectations

The most important change in expectations occurred in Israeli thinking after the October War. Sachar notes that "for the under-populated Zionist republic, with its numerically small army, the demographic implications of a possible future shift to large scale infantry warfare was unsettling" (1981, 221). Unlike the previous wars in 1948, 1956, and 1967, the October war was fought mainly with tanks and infantry, as SAM missiles neutralized the Israeli air force. Moreover, the Israeli method of overrunning infantry with a quick tank assault, proved ineffective against the new Sagger antitank missiles in the Egyptian arsenal. Maintaining and escalating the rivalry in the future would be costly for Israel, as more people, a relatively scarce commodity for Israel as compared to Egypt and Syria, would have to be thrown into battle. Israel had spent $7 billion on the October campaign, which was equal to the total GNP of the country the previous year. To Israel, the "era of quick cheap victories were a thing of the past" (Sachar 1981, 226).

The severe costs of mobilization, as well as the possibility of a new and more costly war of attrition, eclipsed Israeli optimism from the prewar years. Also, the United States used the postwar settlement to press for an intermediate peace agreement, threatening Israeli arms shipments if peace was not pursued. U.S. pressure stepped up considerably when President Carter took office. He was the first U.S. president to call for Israeli withdrawal to the pre-1967 borders, and the creation of a Palestinian homeland. In addition, Turkey, France, West Germany, and Britain all communicated their preferences for peace in the Middle East (Shlaim 2001, 320–50; Sachar 1981, 227; Meital 1997, 140–45; Eisenberg and Caplan 1998).

In Egypt, the leadership felt vindicated, but this conviction came at a high price. Egypt had spent $8 billion on the war, and while the perceived victory of breaking through the Bar-Lev line increased Sadat's prestige, economic and social progress was still sputtering. Although the Soviet Union had supplied weapons to Egypt, Sadat did not see economic help in a continued alliance with the communist bloc. Continued conflict would only push Egypt closer to the Soviet Union, and away from what Sadat perceived as Western progress and industrialization (Meital 1997, 149–51). Continued high unemployment rates, low GDP growth, and war debts supported the expectations of high future rivalry costs.

Domestic Rivalry Outbidding Environment

The central changes in domestic political relations occurred in Cairo. The Egyptian army's ability to place high costs on Israel, as well as the pride the country felt at the capture of the Bar-Lev lines, decreased internal pressure on Sadat (Meital 1997, 137–38, Telhami 1992). Editors and scholars noted that Egypt could now bargain from a position of strength, relative to its prewar bargaining power. Influential editor Mahfouz and politician Boutros Boutros-Ghali both argued for peace in order to help the economy. Even Heikal, who was critical of Sadat's policies during this time, did not dispute the ends of peace, only the timing of Sadat's initiatives. Sadat's strategy of limited war and closer ties with the United States seemed to have paid off in Israeli cooperation. As the threats from Israel decreased, so did the strength of the anti-Israeli lobby in Cairo. Although other Arab states, especially Syria and Libya, excoriated Sadat and eventually voted to expel Egypt from the Arab League, public opinion in Egypt seemed to support diplomatic engagement with Israel (Meital 1997, 136–39). Support from the United States allayed Egyptian fears of an Israeli attack.

Lower information asymmetries, as a result of Sadat's relaxed censorship power, also aided the building of a more complex image of Israelis and Israel in the mind of the average Egyptian (Meital 1997, 138). Even if domestic institutions remained constant, the increased cooperation from Israel eased the pressure placed on Sadat to continue the conflict. Although Sadat would have two foreign ministers resign over his compromises to Israel and would face severe regional reactions, the eventual peace treaty was popular. Protests by the Muslim Brotherhood failed to derail the diplomatic efforts (Eban 1979, 1).

In Israel, public opinion conditionally favored peace, rather than continued conflict. Rabin was able to pass the immediate and intermediate peace proposal in the cabinet and Knesset rather easily despite having the narrowest of parliamentary majorities. Even the hawks in Likud, such as Begin, were forced to withdraw claims on the Sinai and support taking steps toward de-escalation with Egypt. Rabin felt pressure to keep the West Bank because of terrorist threats that had emanated from there, as well as for religious and historic reasons. Conversely, the Sinai and Suez Canal areas were open to negotiation and compromise. Therefore, the military disengagement treaty between Egypt and Israel was signed on January 18, 1974, and the Sinai II intermediate agreement in 1975, setting the stage for a future territorial compromise (Shlaim 2001, 336–40).

When Likud gained power in 1977, it was not the result of threat inflation and vituperative anti-Egyptian language, but Labor party scandals and infighting between Peres and Rabin (Shlaim 2001, 348). In fact, Likud only increased its representation by four votes, while the Labor Alignment lost nineteen. As Begin gained the prime ministry, he supported the intermediate peace treaty with Egypt and continued negotiations. He believed the true threat to Israel came from a Palestinian state, not from Egypt. The winning Likud party platform in 1977 read that "any plan that involves surrendering parts of Western Eretz Israel . . . [would] threaten the security of the civilian population, endanger the existence of the State of Israel, and defeat all prospects for peace" (quoted in Shlaim 2001, 353). Although the Likud platform, and Begin's personal beliefs, prevented him from acceding any of the Eretz Israel territory to an Arab state, that did not include the Sinai. In a meeting with President Carter, Begin agreed to withdraw a significant portion of Israeli forces from the Sinai area (Shlaim 2001, 356; Eisenberg and Caplan 1998, 28–40).

Moreover, there was a large constituency for peace in Israel. When Sadat came to speak at the Knesset, Begin's inflexibility in negotiations drew criticism. In 1978, as it appeared that Begin was backing off a peace initiative, a group of 350 reservist officers signed a letter calling for the prime minister to trade land for peace. The Peace Now organization was founded and received public support from thirty Knesset ministers from six different parties. Peace Now organized demonstrations to press the government toward compromise with Egypt. The day before the Camp David summit, 100,000 people demonstrated for peace in the Tel Aviv central square, marking the largest demonstration in Israeli history. The Israeli cabinet voted in favor of the peace treaty eleven to two with one abstention, and the Knesset ratified the agreement by an eighty-four to nineteen vote with seventeen abstentions. Opinion polls at the time found 82 percent of the Israeli public in favor of the peace treaty. Even the hard-liner Sharon supported the return of the Sinai to Egypt in return for peace guarantees. While the eventual signing of the Camp David Accords brought some criticism from the right, including a group of Likud members waiting for Begin at the gates of Jerusalem with black umbrellas shouting "Chamberlain," this was the minority view (Shlaim 2001, 371–73; Meital 1997, 168–72.

Opportunity for Escalation

During the 1974 to 1979 period, neither state had a clear opportunity to escalate the dispute and improve its immediate position in the rivalry. Both states had proven their ability to inflict high costs on the other. But this ability sprang from external superpower support in the 1973 war. As Egypt had distanced itself from the Soviet Union for economic reasons, escalation became less likely in the present context. The United States made it clear that it would not support another Israeli escalation. Although Israel did have a higher potential for domestic arms production, Israeli power had been neutralized to a large extent by the SAM sites and the loss of an inordinate amount of officers in the 1973 fighting. Further, a war of attrition would be more costly to Israel then to Egypt. With both states economically exhausted from the past war, only external aid would allow either state to escalate. Therefore, the U.S. policy of encouraging détente and peace in the area was decisive in depriving either state of a war option.

Summary and Analysis

As seen during the Israeli-Egyptian rivalry, as well as in the other case studies, wars serve as expectational shocks. Winners and losers alike are often faced with new realities after the fighting stops. In the Israeli-Egyptian case, the changes after the three previous wars were not conducive to peace. Israel's clear victories in 1956 and 1967 and optimistic expectations in their wake decreased the likelihood of compromise. Similarly, Egyptian losses and regional outbidding made retreat politically intolerable because of domestic and regional outbidding. After the 1973 war, in contrast, Israeli casualties and the probability of more bloody losses in the future served to shock Israeli status quo evaluations downward, while Sadat's respectable showing increased his bargaining position. Reciprocated compromise was both desired and probable in Egypt and Israel because both states saw the status quo as untenable and compromise as politically viable.

Conclusion

Complex shifts in rivalry behavior, which are blurred when only one level is analyzed in isolation, come into focus when both international and domestic variables are synthesized in a dynamic two-level pressure explanation. Table 2 compares the different periods of rivalry based on the dynamic two-level pressures present at the time. As noted in the narrative, the 1948, 1967, and 1973 wars were all preceded by high expected future costs and a mobilized outbidding environment in Egypt. In 1948, Egypt could not stand by and watch King Abdullah control Palestine, and Farouk stirred domestic opposition to Israel in order to outbid the Wafd party. By 1967, Nasser was under extreme pressure both at home and abroad to take

Table 2

Egyptian and Israeli dynamic two-level pressures

Years	Costs	Outbidding	Opportunity	Prediction	Observed
Egypt					
1948–49	High	High	High	Escalate	War
1949–54	Medium	Medium	Low	Maintain	LC
1955–56	Low	High	Medium	Maintain	LC/War
1957–65	Medium	High	Low	Maintain	LC
1966–70	High	High	Medium	Escalate	War
1970–73	High	High	Medium	Escalate	War
1974–79	High	Low	Low	De-escalate	CO
Israel					
1948–49	High	Medium	Low	Maintain	LC/War
1949–54	Low	Medium	Low	Maintain	LC
1955–56	High	High	High	Escalate	War
1957–65	Low	Medium	High	Maintain	LC
1966–70	High	High	High	Escalate	War
1970–73	Low	High	High	Maintain	LC/War
1974–79	High	Low	Low	De-escalate	CO

LC: Limited conflict/limited cooperation
CO: Cooperation

back Gaza and Sharm al-Sheikh, and in 1973, Sadat faced similar pressures. In all three cases, threat inflation stirred popular and elite opinion toward conflict rather than reconciliation. Therefore, when the status quo became uncomfortable, and an opportunity for escalation arose, pressure toward war had already gained momentum.

Similarly, Israel faced these same dynamic two-level pressures in 1956 and 1967. By 1956, the blockade and boycott of Israeli goods and shipping, as well as the influx of immigrants, strained the Jewish state's economy. Also, the prospect of facing a stronger Egypt in the future loomed on the horizon. Continued terrorist attacks and raids inflamed Israeli public opinion against any measure that might deteriorate security. When France and Britain supplied an opportunity for escalation, in the form of a coordinated raid and intervention, Ben-Gurion was assured of domestic support for war, but not for compromise. In 1967, the blockade of the Straits of Tiran would have proven costly, and thus dynamic two-level pressures were built into the attacks on Sharm al-Sheikh and the Sinai.

Conversely, both Egypt and Israel expected high future costs, and a less-mobilized domestic environment after 1974. In this context, de-escalation was the most probable path, as maintenance became costly to both states, and domestic support for compromise outstripped the counterpressure toward escalation. In Egypt, Sadat's initiative to increase openness decreased the information asymmetries that had supported threat inflation and rivalry outbidding under Nasser. Yet the relaxing of Israeli intransigence was also necessary to demobilize distrust and support for a hard line against the Jewish state. Similarly, after 1974 there arose a constituency for peace in Israel, finding voice in the Peace Now movement and in opinion polls finding robust support for a land-for-peace deal and compromise with Egypt. Likewise, the prospect of a expensive war of attrition in the future, where the more populated Egypt would have an advantage, created a sober mood among hawks in Israel. Both Rabin and Begin saw the domestic opening for peace to be ratified, as well as the international exigency for a relaxing of tensions with Egypt. These motivations led to the disengagement agreement in 1974, Sinai II in 1975, and the Camp David accords in 1979. It is only with the dual focus on international and domestic politics, and the interaction between the two, that rivalry interactions can be accurately explained and analyzed.

6 Climbing the Wall
The Sino-American Rivalry

THE RIVALRY between China and the United States provides a variety of questions to investigate. What explains China's choice to challenge U.S. forces in Korea, and correspondingly, why did the United States continue toward the Yalu, ostensibly threatening Chinese forces? Why did China initiate international crises in 1955 and 1958, but stop short of war? What precipitated the U.S. decision not to reciprocate Chinese attempts at negotiation and cooperation in 1956 and 1957? What motivated Beijing to support North Vietnamese forces but not to intervene directly in the Vietnam War, despite the similarities between that crisis and Korea fifteen years earlier? Possibly the most important question is how both countries came to embrace de-escalation in the early 1970s.

From the Korean War to the Shanghai communiqué, the Sino-American rivalry had a number of ups and downs, hits, misses, and near misses. This chapter analyzes how a dynamic two-level pressure explanation of rivalry behavior fits Chinese-American major power rivalry. Although the previous chapters explored minor power rivalry interactions with strong territorial stakes at issue, this section extends the case study analysis to stronger states with greater capability reach and positional overtones. The territory of Taiwan remained at issue throughout the rivalry and indeed continues to color relations between the two states as this chapter is being written, but Washington and Beijing also jostled over American forces and prestige in Asia. As noted previously, both minor and major power rivalries are expected to react to dynamic two-level pressures. Although the ability of great powers such as the United States to pay the costs of rivalry may be greater, they also face stronger external threats. Great powers have more chips, but the games are usually played with

157

higher stakes. Similarly, leaders in larger states also desire to remain in power. Thus, domestic pressure to maintain or escalate a rivalry should remain salient irrespective of the positional context.

Background

Throughout the early twentieth century, the growing power of the United States in Asia contrasted sharply with China's perception of itself as the "Middle Kingdom." While Russian and then Japanese forces occupied Chinese territory, American forces populated bases in the Philippines and then Japan. In addition, external threats were mixed with internal dissension.

Beginning with the successful anticommunist coup in 1927, led by Jiang Jieshi and his nationalist supports, tensions mounted between the nationalist (Guomindang or GMD) and communist (CCP) parties in China. Jiang's rule through the "Nanjing decade" saw the central government wrestle power away from local warlords and press their battle to control the CCP. When the Japanese invaded Manchuria and then northern China in 1931, Jiang was faced with a choice of how to prioritize his enemies. The communists, led by Mao Zedong, had continued to fight the nationalist government throughout the late 1920s and early 1930s. Initially, Jiang decided to deal with the communists first and then turn to the Japanese. The nationalist leader rationalized this policy by stating, "the Japanese were the disease of the skin, and the communists were the threat to the heart" (Chen 2001, 20). Therefore, the nationalist forces pressed their military advantage against Mao's forces. By 1936, the communists were compelled to abandon their base at Jiangxi to find safer havens. During this "long march," the communist army lost 90 percent of its strength. Some sources suggest that the Red Army could not have survived another large-scale GMD assault (Esherick 1995, 53).

The tide of battle shifted decisively in September 1936, as two of Jiang's top generals continued to worry about the Japanese threat, which was being ignored to deal with Mao's forces. Generals Zhang Xueliang and Yang Fucheng kidnapped Jiang in Xi'an to "convince" the nationalist leader to unite his forces with the communists to face the Japanese. Happy to have this reprieve, the communist forces agreed to form a "united front" with the nationalists.

As the head of this "united front," Jiang gained significant international attention. Both Washington and London recognized him as one of the "Big Four" leaders during the later stages of World War II. Mao gained prestige, too, as a result of the struggle with the Japanese. The communist leader positioned his troops behind the Japanese forces and fought a guerrilla campaign. Although Mao's main goal remained developing his own forces for an eventual showdown with Jiang, there was a general perception in China that Mao was leading a dangerous and important battle against the invaders (Chen 2001, 21; Eastman 1974).

The wartime alliance between Jiang and Mao only partially obscured the continued competition between the two parties. In early 1941, the New Fourth Army, a CCP unit, was attacked and "wiped out" by nationalist troops in Wannan. This visible fissure in the "united front" sounded alarms in Washington and Moscow. Both the American and the Soviet leaderships had a strategic interest in the ability of the Chinese to fight and tie down significant numbers of Japanese forces. After the Wannan incident, President Franklin Roosevelt sent an envoy to meet Jiang and other leaders to convince them to avoid a civil war. Georgi Dimitrov, the Soviet party head, sent a telegram to Mao containing a similar message.

As the war wound down in 1944, the United States was forced to choose sides in the impending civil war. Since 1943, Jiang's nationalist forces had suffered several high profile defeats, and his reign was marked by growing corruption in the military. In contrast, the CCP now claimed a force of almost one million troops and over one million party members. Therefore the balance of forces, hearts, and minds in 1944 China seemed to be favoring the communists. With this growing support, Mao decided to pursue closer diplomatic ties with Washington. This initiative stemmed in part from the recognition that Washington now wanted landing bases in China, and thus Mao would have some bargaining leverage. Mao also realized that the United States would be an important player in the ensuing contest for control of China.

The communist party began a campaign to convince the U.S. leadership of Jiang's corruption and antidemocratic principles. In July 1944, a group of American military observers visited CCP leaders at Yan'an. This "Dixie Mission" constituted the first direct official contact between the United States government and the communist party. Later, Roosevelt sent Patrick Hurley to negotiate with the CCP in an attempt to diffuse tensions in China. At almost the same time, frictions erupted between Jiang and

Roosevelt over control of the Chinese military forces, sparking hope in the CCP for more support from Washington.

But cooperation between the CCP and Washington was fleeting. Hurley had agreed to a five-point plan with the communists calling for a coalition government. When Jiang summarily rejected the plan, and the Americans supported an abridged three-point plan that failed to guarantee the CCP legal status as a party, Mao and other communist leaders felt betrayed by Hurley and Washington. This perceived betrayal sparked a trans-Pacific war of words. The growing power of the Soviet Union was also pulling the Chinese away from deeper relations with the United States. In 1945, Moscow was ready to take on a greater role in the Pacific and communicated this to the CCP. To Mao, this information meant that a new and potentially more attractive suitor was available. When Moscow abrogated the Soviet-Japanese Neutrality treaty in April 1945, Mao ordered his military commanders to coordinate with the Soviets (Westad 1993, chap. 1). Potential cooperation between the nationalists and Moscow also faltered until Jiang was willing to give up substantial territory for Soviet help (see Chen 2001, 26; Kusnitz 1984, chap. 3).

As expected, when the war ended and perfunctory negotiations failed, civil war broke out in China. Although Stalin had initially recognized Jiang as the legitimate leader of China in return for a substantial amount of Chinese territory, he supported Mao's forces in Manchuria. In a twist of history, Stalin protected Mao's bases and resupplied the CCP troops on land that was given to the Soviet Union by Jiang. Conversely, Washington backed Jiang, transporting nationalist troops to northern China to fight the CCP. U.S. Marines landed at several points in the north to support the nationalists and record the movements of Mao's forces.

In the civil war, domestic rivalry became nested in superpower politics. The CCP grew closer to Moscow, and the nationalists increasingly turned to Washington for aid. These overlapping conflicts reinforced each other and incubated the rivalry between China and the United States. Both Moscow and Washington viewed China as an important theater in the first stages of the cold war. For Moscow, U.S. control of Japan necessitated a communist counterbalance. For Washington, a communist-controlled China would threaten U.S. interests in the region. Yet these overlapping dynamics were not unilinear. Not only did Washington support Jiang, but the United States also dissuaded the nationalists from compromising with

Moscow. When Jiang was on the verge of signing an economic agreement with the Soviet Union, the United States leadership released the Yalta agreement whereby Stalin claimed Manchuria and other Chinese territory. This act was sufficient to scuttle the agreement.

Issues under Contention

When the CCP finally emerged victorious in 1949, the leadership was distrustful of the United States. This distrust stemmed not only from the previous backing of the nationalists, but also from perceived goal incompatibilities. Mao wanted to return China to the "Middle Kingdom," or at least to being a major player in the region. The U.S. hegemony in Asia challenged this goal. As Jiang and his followers retreated to Taiwan and several other offshore islands, American aid and military support were viewed as "imperialism" and an attempt to block Chinese growth (Chen 2001, 31, 46–48; Kusnitz 1984, 25–36). Mao's goals were to reunify Taiwan and China and to avoid being subordinate to the superpowers. Both of these goals came into conflict with the American objectives of combating communism and remaining an Asian power. Therefore, the rivalry involved both territory (Taiwan) and positional prestige considerations in Asia.

1949–1953

Rivalry History

Until the Korean War, both states followed a cautious and moderately conflictual course toward the other. The United States signaled its hostility toward China in the 1949 White Paper and PPS 39, a document prepared by the Policy Planning Staff that same year, in which Mao and China were listed as primary enemies. The United States also terminated economic aid to the CCP-dominated areas in early 1949 (Chang 1990, 12–14, 19). China harassed U.S. consul general Angus Ward in 1948, limiting the movements of the people who worked in his office and attempting to confiscate his radio transmitter. But in 1949, neither the United States nor China wanted war with the other party (Accinelli 1996, chap. 2; Chang 1990, 19, 62–63; Chen 2001, 39, 52).

Although neither side marched toward war in 1949, both states also avoided compromise. The Huang-Stuart contacts were the only evidence of cooperation in 1949. John Leighton Stuart, the U.S. ambassador to China, and Huang Hua, the director of the Foreign Affairs office under the communist Nanjing Municipal Military Control Commission, extensively discussed their respective governments' positions without any relaxation in tensions. In fact, in 1949, when Stuart offered over $10 million in unauthorized U.S. aid to China, contingent on Mao moving away from an alliance with Stalin, Huang was insulted at the attempt to "buy" the Chinese people (Chang 1990, 41). Secret meetings between Stuart and Chen Ming-Shu, a pro-communist figure, reached a similar impasse. The crux of the impasse was that Mao would only compromise with the United States if Washington reversed its policy toward the GMD and agreed to treat China as an equal world power. These demands were unlikely to be met by Washington (Accinelli 1996, 13–15; Chen 2001, 41–42; Kusnitz 1984, 25–27).

It was only after the Inchon landing that Mao was compelled to enter the Korean War (Chen 2001, 57–58; Lowe 1986, 182–83). Mao had allowed a number of ethnically Korean People's Liberation Army (PLA) soldiers to fight for the North, but that was under the assumption that Washington would not become involved in the conflict. Although much still remains to be learned about Mao's decision making, the Chinese revolutionary leader noted that he did not want the United States to become more involved in the region. In May 1950, during a meeting with Kim Il Sung, Mao said that he did not want North Korea to launch its assault on the South until China had liberated Taiwan. From the beginning of Kim's offensive until September 14, Mao did not offer any additional Chinese troops to aid the North. Even after President Harry Truman announced that the United States would intervene to support Syngman Rhee's regime, Mao only announced the creation of the Northeastern Border Defense Army (NEBDA). Even while the NEBDA was being mobilized, its assigned task was limited to preparing for the possibility that the North would begin losing the war. As the U.S. and South Korean forces began to push north, Mao only pressed toward intervention when he received firm confirmation of Moscow's military backing. By this time, the Chinese leader had decided that he could not stand on the sideline allowing the North to falter (Chen 2001, 54–56; Lowe 1986, chap. 7; see also Chen 1994).

A similar calculus was at work in Washington. Truman and Dean Acheson perceived that losing Korea would continue what they saw as a grow-ing string of previous communist victories. Domestic pressure from the China lobby and McCarthyism decreased the probability of cooperation toward China, and the strong presence of the Seventh Fleet in Asia gave Washington an opportunity to escalate and support the Korean regime. A pictorial view of the conflict-cooperation during the rivalry illustrates the high level of conflict and volatility during this period (figure 18). As iden-tified in the narrative, neither country showed much cooperation with the other, while threats of force and military confrontations became frequent.

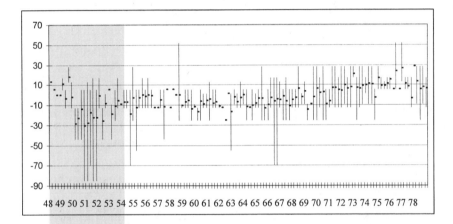

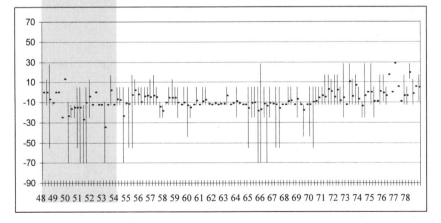

Figure 18. U.S.-Chinese event data scores, 1948–1953. Quarterly highs, lows, and means. COPDAB series. 1948–1953 in frame. Lower scores equal more conflict. *Top:* U.S. actions toward China; *bottom:* Chinese actions toward U.S.

Conventional Explanations

Conventional theories of rivalry escalation supply only partial explanations for the events of this period. For example, a focus on reciprocity would suggest that the United States was only matching aggression from the north, and China in turn was responding to U.S. pressure. Of course, this view fails to explain the limited Chinese support for the initial North Korean invasion. In addition, a reciprocity perspective does not explain why Mao continued to wait for Soviet military support before joining the fray. There is an interesting pattern of reciprocity during this period, but it involves domestic rather than purely international factors.

Domestic constituencies in both China and the United States amplified and reciprocated threats from the other side. The Chinese used the U.S. White Paper to support their anti-U.S. propaganda campaign, while the anti-China lobby in Washington utilized Chinese statements to underscore their interpretation of the bellicosity and danger inherent in the Beijing government. These threat inflation dynamics were bounced back and forth, as verbal threats and public mobilizations in each state spurred similar movements in the other. Eventually, this mutual threat inflation made compromise unlikely in both domestic contexts, as neither Mao nor Truman wanted to appear weak or as an "appeaser."

A focus solely on domestic politics and coalition building also misses the crucial aspects of the Korean War. The United States was the more democratic member of the rival dyad but significantly escalated the conflict. The joint UN/U.S. force not only matched North Korean aggression, but further threatened to, and nearly succeeded in, unifying Korea under the rule of the Southern leadership. As China was mobilized toward escalation by the propaganda issued by well-placed elites, so was the United States, by McCarthyism and anticommunist sentiments. In fact, it is hard to understand the Chinese decision to enter Korea without recourse to U.S. threats and the potential future Beijing faced if the North was totally defeated.

Finally, a popular explanation of the Korean War is that it occurred because of a deterrence failure (see Whiting 1960). The announcement of the U.S. defense perimeter in 1949 ignored Korea, supporting both Stalin's and Mao's expectations that Washington would not intervene in Korea. If Washington had clearly signaled its intention to support the South, a priori, would it have made a difference? Although this question is difficult to answer, new evidence suggests that Kim was going to launch his offensive regardless (see Chen 1994, 87–90). The Soviets, not the Chinese gave the green light to Kim, both in a secret April meeting with the North Korean leader in Moscow and by sending aid and advisors to organize the offensive from June 12 to June 23 (Weathersby 1995/96, 31). Also, the Soviets, in contrast to Mao's position, saw it as possible, if not probable, that the United States would intervene (Lowe 1986, 156–57). If we take as given that Kim started the Korean War with Moscow's backing, then Chinese and American actions still would probably have proceeded as history has recorded them. The United States would support the South, and China still could not see the North totally defeated (see Cumings 1983, 39).[1]

Dynamic Two-Level Pressures

A better explanation of the Chinese-U.S. involvement in Korea comes from dynamic two-level pressures. Most important, this perspective helps to explain the immediate U.S. intervention in Korea, as well as the timing of Chinese involvement across the Yalu. Both states had high expected future costs, mobilized domestic outbidding environments, and opportunities for escalation in 1950. Therefore, escalation was likely from both sides, although at slightly different intervals.

Future Expectations

For China, the future costs of rivalry were manageable until the Inchon landing. As Mao was declaring the formal creation of the People's Republic of China, the country was in dire economic straits. Throughout China, industrial output was negligible, and the production centers of the state had been destroyed in almost fifteen years of continual war (Chen 1994, 11). Strategically, the continued threat from the nationalists, as they retreated to Taiwan (Formosa), promised to further strain the limited resources under the communist leadership's control. Further, Mao worried openly

---

1. It is possible that if the United States had stopped its counteroffensive before threatening China, leaving the North intact, China might not have intervened (because Mao would still have a friendly neighbor across the Yalu).

about U.S. intervention on the side of the nationalists (Accinelli 1996, 3–13, 37).

The bleak economic and strategic picture in China was brightened by overtures from the Soviet Union. In 1949, Stalin promised aid to China during two secret diplomatic missions. By mid-August, ninety-six Russian experts were assisting China's military buildup and economic reconstruction, and from December 1949 to February 1950, Mao visited Stalin and cemented a strategic alliance with Moscow. On February 14, 1950, the Soviet Union formally agreed to provide military aid and to build air defense installations on the Chinese coasts. In return, the Soviet Union gained continued use of the northeast and Xinjiang (Chen 2001, 52; Goncharov, Lewis, and Xue 1993, chap. 4; Zubok and Pleshakov 1996, 56–61).

The crucial event affecting Chinese expectations about the future involved Korea. Mao placed high priority on having a friendly government across the Yalu River in Korea and avoiding Western encirclement. As late as December 16, 1949, Mao told Stalin, "China needs a period of 3–5 years of peace, which would be used to bring the economy back to pre-war levels" *(Cold War* 1995, 5). The first months of the Korean War, which broke out on June 25, seemed to favor the North, and Mao showed at least tacit support for the invasion by allowing "volunteers" in China to fight in Korea. In addition, on July 13, Mao organized the NEBDA but did not deploy it. At this point, Chinese expectations for the future were not pessimistic because the war seemed to be progressing to their satisfaction (Lowe 1986, 157). However, the tide of battle turned decisively on September 15, with the U.S. landing at Inchon. As the combined U.S.–South Korean force moved into the North, Mao was faced with the possibility of a North Korean defeat and, eventually, another anticommunist neighbor, as well as a possible U.S. invasion of Chinese territory. The U.S. victory at Inchon, and quick offensive into the North, significantly raised the costs Mao and the Chinese leadership expected to bear if they did not intervene in the Korean conflict (Chen 2001, 55; Zubok and Pleshakov 1996, 62–64).

A number of successive events led the leadership in Washington to perceive high prospective costs for rivalry in 1950. The Berlin blockade in 1948–49, the communist coup in Czechoslovakia, the victory of the CCP in China, and the successful Soviet test of a nuclear device signaled to Washington that the communist bloc was simultaneously gaining strength and global reach. China grew closer to the Soviet Union, just as the Soviet Union was perceived by the U.S. leadership as stronger because of its newly acquired nuclear potential, and more belligerent because of the Berlin crisis (Chang 1990, 19; Accinelli 1996, 11).

Projecting into the future, high-level government policy makers believed that the Chinese-Soviet alliance would remain strong; as a CIA report read, "the grasp of the USSR upon China and of the Chinese Communists on the Chinese people will grow more firm for the foreseeable future" (quoted in Chang 1990, 39). Secretary of State Dean Acheson viewed the Korean War as part of the greater struggle of the cold war. He stated that "there can be little doubt that Communism, with Chicoms [Chinese communists] as one spearhead, has now embarked upon an assault against Asia, with immediate objectives in Korea, Indo-China, Burma, the Philippines and Malaya, and with medium-range objectives in Hong Kong, Indonesia, Siam, India, and Japan" (quoted in Chang 1990, 76). Therefore, as the North invaded the South in Korea, the administration viewed the potential loss of Korea against not only the loss of Eastern Europe, but the potential for greater future losses in Southeast and Central Asia as well (Lowe 1986, 153–54).

Domestic Rivalry Outbidding Environment

The domestic political landscape in China became increasingly skewed against the United States during this period. Beginning on June 25, 1949, Mao launched a large-scale anti-American propaganda campaign. He accused Consul General Angus Ward and the U.S. consul staff of espionage and plotting against China and broadcasted a message to the public that the United States might land at any moment and mount an attack. Mao made this speech knowing that an attack was not forthcoming. Mao also wrote five articles directly criticizing the United States and singling out Washington as his most "dangerous enemy." The U.S. White Paper on China, articulating American support for the nationalists, spurred Mao's animosity and supported the CCP hard-liners' position that Washington was anti-Mao and pro-nationalist (Chen 2001 43, 300nn. 47, 52). Once the Korean War began, Mao instigated the "Great Movement to Resist America and Assist Korea." The main slogan of the propaganda was, "beating American arrogance." As Chen states, "The party used every means available to stir the 'hatred of the US imperialists' among common Chinese, emphasizing that the United States had long engaged in political and economic aggression against China" (2001, 59). The propaganda was particularly successful given the well-known role the United States played in the Chinese Civil War.

The United States domestic arena also became markedly more polarized against cooperation with China from the late 1940s to the early 1950s. Truman was pressured toward conflict with the Chinese communists as conservatives in the government preemptively equated cooperation with China with "selling out" the nationalists. In 1949, there was a short-lived countervailing liberal voice for compromise and accommodation (Chang 1990, 21). For example, John M. Cabot, the consul general in Shanghai, and O. Edmund Clubb, the consul general in Beijing, supported cooperation with China as a way to split the USSR-CCP alliance.

On the other hand, backing for continued conflict with the CCP and support for Jiang's nationalists came from Henry Luce, the head of Time-Life and Roy Howard of Scripps Howard, as well as congressmen Walter Judd, William Knowland, Kenneth Wherry, and Senator Styles Bridges. In April 1949, Bridges called for hearings to investigate the administration's "capitulation to communists" in China. By 1950, Joseph McCarthy had begun his witch-hunt in the State Department, attempting to undermine the careers of anyone who might appear to support cooperation with China and Russia. Chang notes that the fear of appearing to be weak on communism "tainted the American political landscape" (1990, 24). Along with McCarthy, the most vociferous outbidder was Congressman Richard M. Nixon, who stated, "apologists for the Chinese Communists in the United States, both in and out of the State department [were guided by] the fallacious theory that Chinese Communists somehow are different from Communists in other countries" (quoted in Chang 1990, 26). Therefore, in the United States, China was to be treated as part of the "evil" communist monolith emanating from Moscow (Chang 1990, 26; Accinelli 1996, 13, 17; Young 1968, 3–23). In fact, by 1951, one poll showed 80 percent of the public thought of China as a "puppet" of Moscow (Kusnitz 1984, 53).

In the 1952 presidential election, Eisenhower had threatened to "unleash Chiang Kai-shek" in order to end the Korean War in victory, hinting that Truman had not done enough to challenge communism in Asia (Chang 1990, 82; Brown 1968, 86–98). As Mao, Zhou Enlai, and Lui Shaoqi were labeling the United States the principal enemy of China, Acheson began a public campaign to mobilize support against China. After Angus Ward was released, Acheson told Truman that the former consul general should have "ample opportunity to give his story to the American people" (quoted in Chang 1990, 67). Acheson believed that the administration would be able to use Ward's incarceration to increase public support for anti-Chinese and pro-Jiang policies. Further, Acheson decried the Sino-Soviet alliance as "an evil omen of imperialistic domination" (quoted in Chang 1990, 71). Threat inflation reached such a high pitch that General Omar Bradley suggested that the Chinese might be able to stir up an armed struggle in the United States. As public opinion became increasingly mobilized against China, because of both the work of the administration and the rhetoric of Mao and Zhou Enlai, the pro-Taiwan faction of the government gained the upper hand. Even Clubb changed his position and supported taking a hard line on China (Chang 1990, 71; Accinelli 1996, 17–19; Brown 1968, 86–98)

Opportunity for Escalation

Both states had an opportunity to use military means to alter the status quo. Not only did the United States have a preponderant naval force in the area, but it had a growing land presence as well. Bases in the Philippines and Japan could serve as a headquarters for direct U.S. intervention in China, while growing involvement in South Korea also provided local bases. Washington also had the support of UN forces in Korea. Before the war, the United States, despite rapid demobilization in the wake of World War II, possessed a military force of 1,461,000 men, 48 air force wings, and 671 ships (Brown 1968, 53).

As figure 19 illustrates, the United States had a large aggregate capability advantage, but these data neglect several important contextual factors. Although Mao could not have attacked the continental United States, U.S. troops in Asia were within reach. The most important component of Chinese war planning was Soviet support. Stalin had promised air cover and stepped up military aid if China entered the Korean War (Chen 2001, 55; Lowe 1986, 156–57). Despite this offer, Mao twice delayed deploying the People's Volunteer forces between October 7 and October 18 because he wanted to make sure Stalin would send the necessary aid. With air cover and Soviet matériel support, along with the proximity of the fighting in

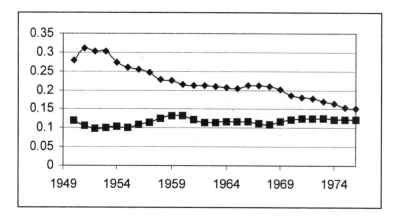

Figure 19. Comparison of Chinese and American capabilities. Diamond = U.S. capabilities; squares = Chinese capabilities. From Correlates of War Project.

North Korea to China proper, Mao's forces possessed a localized chance to engage American forces, with a high probability of aiding the North Korean cause.

Mao did not have an opening to move against Taiwan in 1949. He failed to take the Jinmen and Dengbu islands in October and November because of lack of equipment. China's opportunity to take back Taiwan further decreased as the Korean War broke out and the United States moved the seventh fleet into the Taiwan straits. The GMD also broke up a high-level spy ring in 1950 that severely decreased Beijing's military intelligence on Taiwan (Chen 2001, 165).

Summary and Analysis

The timing of both states' escalation is explained by the sequence of successive shocks to the rivals' expectations. Even before 1950, both states possessed mobilized outbidding environments and opportunities for escalation, although the Korean War accelerated outbidding in both capitals. Yet it was the North's invasion of the South that ratcheted up Washington's assessment of its future rivalry costs with China, making escalation and intervention likely. Meanwhile, in Beijing, the North Korean invasion did not increase Chinese expected rivalry costs. Not even American intervention threatened Mao's China, as long as the North continued to press south. It was the landing at Inchon and Washington's push into the North that significantly clouded Mao's expectations about the future. Similarly, domestic pressure in both states made cooperation and compromise unlikely. Thus, it was only after the triple pressures of future losses, domestic outbidding, and an escalation opportunity were present that war broke out.

1954–1959

Rivalry History

Neither state chose to escalate or de-escalate the rivalry substantially during this period. By 1954, the United States had issued NSC 166/1 that spelled out the U.S. goals toward China as "weakening or at least retarding the growth of Chinese Communist power in China," and "impairing Sino-Soviet relations" (Chang 1990, 91; Kusnitz 1984, 63–65). This policy called for the United States to continue to pressure China and avoid cooperation that might enrich and empower Beijing, but also to avoid war or a direct push to overthrow the regime there. Dulles did everything in his power at Geneva to illustrate Washington's tough and uncompromising stand toward China and the communist world. This effort included the now infamous anecdote in which Dulles refused to shake hands with Zhou Enlai. The policy adopted by the administration was described by Nixon, the vice president at the time, as "tough coexistence," which he described as "an area of action in between war and appeasement" (Chang 1990, 112). The language calling for a "rollback" in China was dropped from NSC 5429 (Young 1968, 91–116, 199–220).

Washington's stalling policy continued after the 1955 crisis with Beijing. Even as Zhou Enlai offered an opportunity to discuss the major issues underlying the Sino-American rivalry, the United States did not reciprocate. As Chang asked about this time period, "Why should the United States take the heat off [China] now?" (1990, 169). Dulles asserted that a "policy of pressure," ruling out conciliation, and stopping short of military conflict, was Washington's best strategy. NSC 5612/1 articulated Washington's impression that China was a threatening nation and that South Vietnam needed to be defended against aggression from Beijing. In 1957,

Eisenhower welcomed Ngo Dinh Diem, the leader of South Vietnam, to Washington and agreed to provide more aid for the South Vietnamese cause (Chang 1990, 165–69, Zhang 1992, 225–49).

The American pattern of maintaining the rivalry is best exemplified in the Sino-American ambassadorial talks that opened in Geneva in 1955 (Chen 2001, 191; Young 1968, 163). Washington agreed only to discuss the return of civilians held in each country, but China wanted to negotiate over trade and a future meeting of foreign ministers. Dulles's goals for the meeting were "to settle repatriation of U.S. civilians and other practical problems," and "to maintain a talking relationship which would make it less likely that the PRC would attack in the [Taiwan] area" (Chang 1990, 155–56). But Dulles refused to compromise on all other fronts, including formal recognition. The U.S. leadership emphasized that they wanted to talk, mainly to influence world public opinion, but did not want to compromise.

At the same time, Eisenhower and Dulles made sure that the situation in the Taiwan Straits did not boil over. Dulles made it clear to the Taiwanese leadership that the United States would not support a military effort to overthrow the Beijing government. However, Washington did agree to continue supplying Taipei with military equipment. Between 1951 and 1957, the United States gave approximately $1.5 billion to Taiwan, constituting 63 percent of the total military budget of the country (Eisenhower 1963, 520; Chang 1990, 160–61).

Even during the 1955 and 1958 crises the United States refused to back down, while simultaneously avoiding attacking China. The U.S. navy helped in the 1955 Taiwanese retreat from the northern offshore islands but refused to defend the small nationalist enclaves. Washington also neglected to guarantee the protection of Dachen and Yijiang in the defense treaty signed with Taipei in December 1954 (Chen 2001, 168–69). American ships were placed in harm's way, especially during the 1958 crisis, but they never fired on China. Although contingency plans were drawn up for a full-scale war with China, they were never carried out. Instead of escalating tensions militarily, Washington signed a mutual defense treaty with Taiwan. At the same time, Eisenhower and Dulles prodded Jiang into giving up the Dachens and desisting from initiating future unauthorized military combat with the Chinese (Chang 1990, 121). The leadership in

Washington was almost unanimous in not wanting war in 1955 and 1958, especially over the Dachens (Zhang 1992, 279).[2]

A similar pattern is illustrated in Chinese actions toward the United States during this time. In 1954 and 1955, Mao wanted to "highlight" the Chinese communist claims, not just on the Chinese mainland but also on the offshore islands controlled by the nationalists. He first set out to attack Dachen and Yijiangshan islands, rather than Jinmen and Mazu, because of the better military infrastructure in the adjoining Zhejiang province, as compared to the Fujian province. To accommodate the military buildup, Beijing created a headquarters for joint naval, air, and land operations in the Zhejiang area. The final attack included the shelling of Jinmen both to make the attack more dramatic and to distract Taipei from Dachen and Yijiang. Mao's goal was to send a signal to the United States that China would continue to compete for Taiwan (Chen 2001, 166–68). Yet Mao did not want the crisis to escalate to war (Chang and Di 1993). In fact, the U.S. National Security Council (NSC) agreed that Mao was only making a limited strike and was not even aiming for Jinmen (Accinelli 1996, 158–60). The general in charge of the military action, Ye Fei, describes the crisis as limited and "normal" in his memoirs, and the CIA reported that Chinese activity was "not unusual" (Chang and Di 1993, 1507). The shelling began at Jinmen on September 3 and resumed on September 22. By February 1955, the Chinese PLA took over not only the Yijiangshan islands but also all of the Dashen islands, and ceased operations on Jinmen.

After the 1955 crisis, China seemed willing to negotiate. In March 1955, Zhou Enlai announced in Bandung that Beijing was willing to talk with the United States to "reduce the tension in the Far East" (quoted in Chen 2001, 169–70). The following year, Zhou Enlai publicized China's

2. It should be noted that if China started a war in Taiwan, the United States was willing to intervene. In fact, several steps such as a U.S. naval blockade of China and the mining of the Taiwan Straits were planned to both deter Chinese aggression and increase the probability that Washington would prevail in an ensuing war (Chang 1990, 140–42). A Chinese invasion would have significantly altered future expectations in Washington. At home, a president who was seen as selling out Jiang would face serious elite opposition. Internationally, this eventuality would seem to fit a pattern of continuing communist advances in Asia. Therefore, like Israeli decisions in 1967, maintenance would no longer have been an attractive policy trajectory.

offer of visas to fifteen newsmen who had requested a visit to China. After Washington rejected the offer, China offered an exchange of press the next year (Chang 1990, 161–62). But as noted above, Mao was still very skeptical of the United States and was not in a hurry to normalize relations. He stated to the CCP in 1957 that "it is preferable to put off the establishment of diplomatic relations with the United States for some years. This will be more to our advantage" (Chang 1990, 170). Mao also criticized Moscow for moving too quickly toward détente with the United States (Zubok and Pleshakov 1996, 220–22; Chen 2001, 168; Zhang 1992, 254–56).

The talks in Geneva, and then in Warsaw, illustrated the limited nature of Zhou's peace initiative. Although the Chinese offered to publicly support a peaceful solution to the Taiwan issue, and to negotiate with the Taiwanese leadership, they did not budge on the issue of U.S. support to Taiwan. Chinese diplomat Wang Bingnan reiterated Beijing's position that Taiwan was an internal matter and that Washington would have to stop all arms and military aid transfers to Taipei. Both parties knew at the time that this was not going to happen (Chang 1990, 156–57). Therefore while the tone and pitch of Beijing's foreign policy changed in 1955, its contents remained firm.

With the talks in Warsaw stalled in 1957 and neither side willing to compromise, Mao cut short the new pacific tone in Chinese foreign policy. In late 1957 and early 1958, the rhetoric from Beijing became much more militant. Further, Mao began to move the air force to Fujian province and completed a railway from Xiamen into Fujian (Chen 2001, 171). Mao stated, "to have an enemy in front of us, to have tension, is to our advantage" (Chen 2001, 180). Mao's "tension" was analogous to Dulles's "pressure," as both sides continued to compete with each other, following their current policy trajectories. For Mao, this policy included probing Washington's intentions toward Jinmen and other offshore islands. Thus, China initiated another bombardment of Jinmen on August 23, 1958.

As in the 1955 crisis, Mao maneuvered to pressure the United States, while avoiding war. To avoid a general war once the firing started, Mao ordered planes (if called upon) not to protrude over Jinmen or Mazu airspace. Mao also decided to reduce the size of the attack, limiting the shelling to Jinmen rather than both Jinmen and Mazu (Chen 2001, 180). Finally, when the United States began escorting Taiwanese supply boats, the Chinese gunners were ordered not to hit the U.S. vessels. Mao stated, "although we have fired dozens of thousands of rounds on Jinmen, we only mean to probe" (Chen 2001, 183; Zhang 1992, 254–55; Tyler 2000, 10)

The 1958 shelling ended on October 6 as both the United States and the Soviet Union pressured their respective allies to settle the issue short of war. Dulles told Jiang on September 30 that the United States would not help him retake the mainland and criticized him for massing troops on Jinmen and Mazu in the first place. Likewise, on October 5, Khrushchev was quoted in the Soviet press as stating that Moscow would only help China if the United States invaded the mainland (Chang 1990, 196–97; Zhang 1992, 255; Young 1968, 199).

Despite provoking two high-profile crises and one peace initiative, China never substantially deviated from its course of limited competition with the United States. Both Mao and the CCP leadership tended to put off a final "reckoning" with the United States, as the future was apt to provide a better context for reunifying Taiwan. As figure 20 shows, after 1954, the variance in conflict decreases for both states. Both cooperation and conflict were bounded in each graph, rarely reaching beyond either verbal threats or verbal agreements. The only substantial deviation was in 1959, with the Sino-U.S. agreement to release prisoners. This event shows up as a spike in late 1958.

Conventional Explanations

A focus on purely international reciprocity fails to account for a number of important events during this period, including the failed Chinese peace overtures. Why did the United States stall during the Geneva talks and not reciprocate even the limited nature of Zhou's initiative? Similarly, Mao's shelling of Taiwan did not lead to return artillery fire from the U.S. navy, but instead resulted in strong pressure from Eisenhower to convince Jiang to give up a number of his offshore islands. Washington's intransigence resulted from domestic variables related to the China lobby and their optimistic time horizon given détente with the Soviets. In this case, they did not need to reciprocate.

Likewise, a domestic-centric focus on coalition-building might suggest that the United States, as the democracy in the pair, should have been

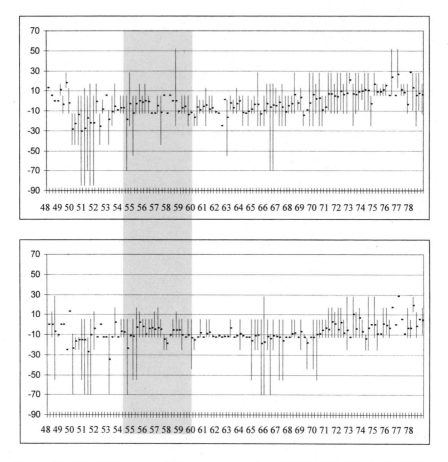

Figure 20. U.S.-Chinese conflict and cooperation, 1954–1959. Quarterly highs, lows, and means. COPDAB series. 1954–1959 in frame. Lower scores equal more conflict. *Top:* U.S. actions toward China; *bottom:* Chinese actions toward U.S.

more likely to initiate a peace conference and to offer a compromise to re-solve the underlying conflict. Instead, the more autocratic Chinese regime was the initiator. Although it might be pointed out that Mao's regime also instigated two crises and conquered several islands during this time, the dominant pattern in Chinese-American relations during this time was lim-ited competition. Despite disparate institutions, both Beijing and Wash-ington acted to contain their rivalry during this time, although with important deviations.

Dynamic Two-Level Pressures

A dual focus on both international and domestic variables over time, as offered by an analysis of dynamic two-level pressures, goes some way to explaining the motivations and rationales behind this pattern of rivalry
maintenance. Neither Beijing nor Washington felt that time was working
against them. Détente with the Soviet Union lessened the threat burden
Washington faced, while Mao was more secure with friendly regimes in
North Korea and Vietnam. Domestic outbidding and threat inflation also
continued in each state, making compromise unattractive. Therefore, continued but limited conflict was the most likely rivalry path.

Future Expectations

Expectations remained positive in both capitals during this period. After
the Korean War ended in stalemate, the Sino-Soviet alliance remained
strong, as economic and military aid continued to flow from Moscow to
Beijing. During a visit to China in 1954, Khrushchev signed a series of documents giving Luchen (Port Arthur) back to China, transferring ownership
of four large companies to China (they had shared ownership previously),
and offering to finance and consult on 156 separate industrial projects
(Chen 2001, 61). Moscow and Beijing carefully coordinated diplomatic
policy position on the Geneva conference negotiations and the creation of
the Warsaw Pact. Chen (2001, 62) notes that "the 1954–1955 period
shined as a golden age of the Sino-Soviet alliance."

A small split started in February 1956 with Khrushchev's policy of
de-Stalinization, with which Mao disagreed (Chen 2001, 64; Zubok and
Pleshakov 1996, 210–15). The Chinese leader only supported the Soviets in
the Hungarian and Polish crises in 1956 after considerable deliberations
and complaints about "big power chauvinism." Despite these protests,
Moscow still continued to provide China with substantial military and
economic aid. A larger disagreement erupted over the Soviet idea of creating a joint Sino-Soviet naval and air force in East Asia. This suggestion
piqued Mao's sensitivity to being dominated by Moscow. The Chinese
viewed the auxiliary Soviet plan to jointly build a communication station
in China as a way for Moscow to keep tabs on Beijing. Although this dis-

agreement was resolved a short time later, Mao continued to worry about the level of intervention from Moscow (Chen 2001, 73–74; Chang 1990, 204). Moscow's criticism of the Great Leap Forward in 1958 reinforced Beijing's wariness of becoming too close to the Russians (Chen 2001, 68–70, 82; Chang 1990, 208; Zubok and Pleshakov 1996, 215–17).

There were two outstanding security concerns for Beijing after the Korean War. First, nationalists on the Zhejiang offshore islands threatened Chinese trade from Shanghai and the coast. Since 1949, Jiang had used his bases on Yijiangshan and Dachen to harass Chinese shipping lanes through this strategic area. Second, the evolving role of the United States in Taiwan challenged Mao's plans to reunify China eventually. After 1955 and the "liberation" of the Zhejiang islands, the first concern was ameliorated, at the direct cost of exacerbating the second problem. The Chinese shelling of Jinmen during the 1955 crisis eventually drove the United States to sign a defense pact with Taipei. Therefore, Beijing planned for continued conflict with the United States. A CCP telegram to Zhou stated, "after the armistices in Korea and Indochina, the Americans will not be willing to accept their failure at the Geneva conference, and will inevitably carry out policies designated to create international tension . . . to expand military bases and prepare for fighting a future war, and to remain hostile towards our country" (Chen 2001, 167–70; Zhang 1992, 225–28).

Optimism for the future was fueled by both domestic and international events. The creation of the first five-year plan, the successful completion of the agricultural cooperatives, and the planning of the socialization of urban industry pointed toward increased Chinese development and power in the future. "[We are] now preparing to make a revolution in the technological fields, that [we may] overtake Britain in fifteen or more years," was Mao's articulation of his expectations (Chen 2001, 72). China was also more secure after the French surrendered at Dien Bien Phu on May 7, 1954 (Chang 1990, 101–2; Chen 2001, 66). Therefore, continued Soviet aid, a secure Korean border, and an improving situation in Vietnam led to an optimistic projection of the future in Beijing.

The United States viewed the failure in Vietnam as a harbinger of greater communist gains and conflict. The Fleet Report, a pessimistic analysis of the early trend in cold war relations and named after its principal investigator, General James Van Fleet, suggested that the United States was losing ground to the Soviets and Chinese. Further, in a report ordered by President Eisenhower, named Project Solarium, George Kennan wrote that the United States had "lost prestige in Asia, vis-à-vis the Chinese Communists as a result of the Korean war," and that the outlook in the future was pessimistic. Moreover, conflict with China would be costly to the United States because allies, especially Britain, supported a much more cooperative policy toward Beijing than Washington was following at the time (Chang 1990, 90–103, 121; Accinelli 1996, 18, 165–68; Project Solarium Reports 1953).

Washington was also facing a heavier burden in Vietnam and Taiwan. In April 1956, the French disbanded their High Command in Vietnam, leaving the United States to train and outfit the South Vietnamese army. At the same time that Zhou was attempting to negotiate with Washington, the United States was pouring more aid and equipment into Taiwan. By the end of 1957, this assistance included the installation of Matador missiles in Taiwan, which were capable of delivering nuclear warheads. Jiang also had moved 100,000 troops to the offshore islands and had continued a guerrilla campaign designed to disrupt trade to China (Chang 1990, 161–65, 183–84; Accinelli 1996, 190–98).

A major cause for optimism in Washington was the prospect for détente with the Soviet Union. These hopes were on the rise in 1955, as Khrushchev and Nikolai Bulganin visited the U.S. embassy on the July 4 holiday. Khrushchev's "secret speech" denouncing Stalin in 1956 also was interpreted by Washington as a sign that Moscow was embracing détente. At the Geneva summit in mid-July 1955, the two superpowers agreed on general terms to keep peace in Asia, although no specifics were worked out. Further, Eisenhower emerged from the meeting very optimistic about making progress to further de-escalate tensions with the Soviets (Chang 1990, 155–57; Zubok and Pleshakov 1996, 188–202). A tangible outcome of the slowly emerging cooperation between Washington and Moscow was Eisenhower's decision to suspend the reconnaissance overflights of the Soviet Union (Chang 1990, 159).

Superpower cooperation continued into 1958. The day before the shelling of Jinmen recommenced, Eisenhower issued a public invitation to the Soviets and other nuclear states to meet and discuss a ban on atomic weapons testing. Khrushchev accepted the invitation on August 29. On September 10, representatives from Moscow and Washington signed an agreement to exchange cultural exhibitions, one of which eventually culminated in Vice President Nixon's visiting Moscow (Chang 1990, 192–93). Therefore, the future costs of rivalry with China were only moderate for the United States. The relaxation of tensions with the Soviet Union easily made up for the incremental increase in tensions in the Asian theater (Zubok and Pleshakov 1996, 199–200).

Domestic Rivalry Outbidding Environment

The Chinese leadership continued to warn the public about severe threats from the United States. Mao wanted a "world revolution" and rapid economic growth to combat the "American Imperialists." Other leaders, such as Zhou Enlai and Chen Yun, supported a less radical growth program. The policy-faction debate during this time ebbed and flowed with the events of the day.

After the Jinmen bombardment and retaking of the northern offshore islands, the CCP moved toward supporting a limited compromise with Washington. Owing to the "victory" in the 1955 Taiwan crisis, as well as in the Korean War, Mao and other leaders believed that China could bargain from a position of strength. Bargaining would not appear weak domestically, and political attacks to the contrary could be parried with the past foreign policy successes. Therefore, Zhou was given the green light to signal Chinese intentions to seek some unspecified agreement with Washington. In July 1955, Zhou stated, "there are two ways for the Chinese people to liberate Taiwan, one military and one peaceful way. If possible, the Chinese people are willing to [try] the peaceful way" (Chen 2001, 170). Diplomatic talks began in Warsaw that year. To Zhou's personal disappointment, this cooperative attitude was short-lived. Illuminating the shallowness of the peace overtures, U.S. intervention in Lebanon was used to fuel anti-American propaganda. Even more shocking to Beijing was the fact that the United States continued to increase its aid to Taiwan during the Warsaw talks. In fact, the Washington delegation purposely stalled negotiations on all issues except the return of CIA personnel being held in China (Chen 2001, 173; Zhang 1992, 225–28).

Mao seized on Washington's lack of reciprocation to censure Zhou Enlai and other party members who supported slowing down Chinese industrial growth. Mao criticized Zhou Enlai for supporting peace and promoting a weak foreign policy that allowed China's enemies to gain strength. In response to Washington's failure to reciprocate, the Chinese chairman began a new propaganda campaign against both the United States and Zhou, coupled with a program to consolidate his own rule. Mao's plans for "radical" growth culminated in the 1958 Great Leap Forward. Zhou Enlai was forced to admit publicly that he was wrong in opposing the "rash advance of the Chinese economy" and supporting détente with the "imperialists" (Chen 2001, 73). Those party officials who supported Zhou's limited peace initiative in 1956 called for his "self-criticism" and apology in 1957 (Chen 2001, 66–77; Westad 1995/96, 164–69). Mao's popularity and standing within the party soared from 1956 to 1958 as a direct result of his tough stance on confronting the United States. A CCP politburo member remarked at one point, "it is alright to worship Chairman Mao to the extent of having blind faith in him" (quoted in Chen 2001, 67).

During the mid-1950s, the domestic political context in the United States remained tilted against cooperation with China. The China lobby accused Dulles of not doing enough to control China and the communists. Senate majority leader Knowland threatened to resign and to campaign to end U.S. membership in international organizations if China was admitted to the United Nations. Many hard-liners seized on the report by General James Van Fleet that stated that U.S. leadership in Asia had "fallen far short of the need," and that the U.S. position vis-à-vis China was "rapidly deteriorating." The report also stated that China was a "greater menace to the free world than the Soviet Union itself" (Chang 1990, 102–103).

There were many people in the United States who disagreed with the Fleet Report and favored a "soft" policy toward China. Even within the Policy Planning Staff (PPS), Robert Bowie and Louis L. Halle challenged the "closed door" policy toward China and proposed using trade and economic incentives to pry Beijing away from Moscow. However, Bowie and Halle, as well as the relative doves in the State Department, were attacked as "pro-Red China apologists" (Chang 1990, 103, 107; Ridgway 1956, 279). When the Jinmen crisis broke out on September 3, 1954, the differences in opinion among the foreign policy leadership were highlighted. Admiral Arthur Radford and the majority of the Joint Chiefs (JCS) supported all-out defense of the islands, including the use of nuclear weapons in response to a major Chinese offensive. The chairman of the JCS argued that the United States would be much worse off in the future if it did not escalate. Secretary of Defense Charles Wilson argued against direct intervention because of the costs of escalation and the low strategic value of the islands (Chang 1990, 119–21; Young 1968, 20–22).

There were also various academic and private meetings to analyze U.S. policy toward China in the late 1950s, sponsored by the Council on Foreign Relations and the Rockefeller Brothers Fund. Although no elite consensus emerged from the meetings, there was significant support for a softer line on China, specifically with respect to trade and formal recognition (Chang 1990, 178–82; Zagoria 1962, 200–217). The foreign policy doves both in and out of government stressed that in 1955, public opinion polls showed that 70 percent of Americans surveyed agreed that the United States should pursue bilateral talks with the Chinese, and 66 percent favored including China in a summit (Chang 1990, 164; Page and Shapiro 1992, 242–57).

Eventually, both the 1955 and 1958 crises served to increase the threat the United States perceived from China. This threat perception was amplified in public statements by Dulles and other government officials calling for a hard line and uncompromising position concerning China. Dulles said that China was attempting to push, "U.S. influence away from the entire offshore island chain, from the Aleutians to New Zealand, and [to become] themselves dominant in that part of the world." He continued to express the opinion publicly that China was more belligerent than the Soviet Union, and that the 22 million Chinese living abroad could be used as a fifth column in a future conflict (Chang 1990, 149–50; Zhang 1992, chap. 7–8; Chang and Di 1993). In the Senate, opponents of the Taiwan defense treaty complained of being pressured and even bullied against speaking against the resolution (Briggs 1991, 95, 100–101). After the crises, public opinion was overwhelmingly against compromise with China, and Beijing's entry into the United Nations (Kusnitz 1984, 67).

Domestic pressure to avoid compromise with China strengthened as cooperation with Moscow continued. Eisenhower and Dulles worked in 1955 and 1956 to demobilize public distrust of the Soviet Union, simultaneously warning about the dangers of China. Dulles called Khrushchev's speech a "new look," and "highly significant," suggesting that "we can really hopefully look forward to a transformation of the international scene." Eisenhower stated that the Soviets "have gone into a totally different attitude." The secretary of state estimated that "the risk was greater [from China] than from Soviet Russia and we could not assume that fighting might not break out in any one of three danger spots—Taiwan, Vietnam, or Korea," and that the United States and China were locked in a "virtual state of war." (Chang 1990, 159–61). Eisenhower and Dulles both used the now-infamous "domino" metaphor to explain the Chinese danger in Vietnam, suggesting that after Vietnam, other countries would fall quickly into communist hands. Anti-Beijing sentiments were politically popular, and both party platforms in the 1956 presidential election called for a tough stance on China (Chang 1990, 162–66; Christensen 1996; Brown 1968, 65–70).

Opportunity for Escalation

Although the United States continued to have a strong position in Asia, Mao had access to limited escalation opportunities during this period. American force strength rose steadily during the Korean War. The manpower of the army more than doubled, as did the number of air force wings. The ability to project this military force also increased as the total number of U.S. ships increased to over 1100 by the end of the war (Brown 1968, 53). As U.S. strength continued to support South Korea, the only significant improvement in China's military machine was improved infrastructure. With a new air force base and railway in Fujian province, it was easier for China to pressure Taiwan, and specifically the offshore islands close to the mainland, directly. Mao still did not possess the amphibious landing equipment necessary to project Chinese power outside of the mainland, but he did add heavy artillery from the Soviets (Zubok and Pleshakov 1996, 220–22).

Summary and Analysis

In both states, dynamic two-level pressures made rivalry maintenance the most probable strategy. In Washington, growing cooperation with the Soviet Union meant that American bargaining power might be greater in the future. There was no imperative to invade China or to change policy trajectories. Similarly, the domestic outbidding environment in Washington made de-escalation unlikely. The powerful China lobby and the residual uncertainty from McCarthyism pressured Eisenhower and the policy elite away from making any concessions to Beijing, including diplomatic recognition. Likewise, in China, the enduring Sino-Soviet alliance, coupled with the "victory" in the Korean War and early stages of the Vietnamese conflict, increased Mao's optimism that Chinese goals could be achieved without a major war and without major concessions. Thus, dynamic two-level pressures explain the bounding of both cooperation and conflict during this time, as neither leader had an incentive to alter their rivalry paths.

1959–1965

Rivalry History

Upon entering office, President John F. Kennedy ordered a review of the Sino-Soviet split. His policy staff, including Dean Rusk as secretary of state, Chester Bowles as undersecretary of state, and Adlai Stevenson and George Kennan as advisors, agreed that the United States should pursue a two-China policy, whereby Washington would recognize both governments, Taipei and Beijing. However, this policy change was not motivated by a new spirit to negotiate or cooperate. Instead, Kennedy's foreign policy group believed that future diplomatic struggles with China were inevitable and that formal diplomatic communication could help to avoid an unwanted war (Chang 1990, 219–21; Kusnitz 1984, 95–98).

In Taipei, Jiang wanted war in 1962, viewing the Sino-Soviet split as possibly his last chance to regain the mainland. The leader-in-exile even sent small teams of men into China to try to stir up a revolt against Mao, and he asked Washington to support a much larger operation. When Beijing answered with a half-million-man mobilization near Taiwan, the United States announced, to Jiang's disappointment, that it would not support a nationalist escalation or invasion (Chang 1990, 223). This message was transmitted to Taipei, Beijing, and Moscow.

After 1964, the United States and China faced "another Korea," as Washington intervened in a communist revolution in a country bordering Chinese territory. Yet in Vietnam, in contrast to Korea, neither the United States nor the Chinese wanted their rivalry to escalate to war. While the United States risked escalation by intervening, they were careful to avoid a pretext for a Chinese assault. Walt Rostow and other high-ranking foreign-policy advisors discussed the prospects of creating a buffer zone near the

Chinese border, hoping to avert any accidental provocations. Even more obviously, the Chinese did not want to fight a war against U.S. forces in Vietnam. As Mao succinctly told Le Duan, the Vietnamese Communist Party first secretary, "It seems that the Americans do not want to fight a war . . . and we do not necessarily want to fight a war" (Chen 2001, 213).

Although Beijing continued to prepare for "the worst-case scenario," that the United States would invade the North and then China, Mao was not going to take the first step. Instead, Mao communicated through multiple channels to Washington that there would only be a Sino-American war if U.S. forces invaded the North. Even after the U.S. Rolling Thunder action in Vietnam, Mao did not intervene directly in that conflict. Instead, Mao sent engineers, antiaircraft artillery troops, and material military aid to the North (Chen 2001, 206–36; Kim 1975, 61). In 1965 the chairman told Edgar Snow, a sympathetic U.S. journalist, that China had no plans to intervene directly in Vietnam unless its border was directly threatened (Chang 1990, 270n. 35). Unlike in Korea, Chinese expectations about the future were never pessimistic enough to trigger intervention and a direct war with the United States. Similarly, President Lyndon B. Johnson felt pressure to maintain the struggle against communism in Asia but wanted to avoid a war with China.

Another "near miss" involved Washington's decision not to launch a preemptive strike on China's nuclear facilities. A U.S. government report called for "radical steps, in cooperation with the Soviet Union, to prevent the further proliferation of nuclear capabilities" (U.S. Defense Dept. 1963). One option that was discussed in Washington was a joint U.S.-Soviet strike on the Lop Nor nuclear facilities in Western China. There were high-level discussion in early 1964 as to whether the United States should destroy China's nuclear weapons production capabilities. However, several realities decreased the attractiveness of this option. First, the Soviets were not receptive to the idea, fearing backlash from other communist states. Second, if the United States alone attacked the Lop Nor facilities, both China and the Soviet Union might denounce the strike, reinvigorating the Moscow-Beijing alliance against the United States. Finally, the United States did not want to strike before testing began. National security advisor McGeorge Bundy reported that "we would prefer to have a Chinese test take place than to initiate action now." There would be time to take Chinese nuclear weapons offline in the event of future hostilities (Chang 1988; Tyler 2000, 64–72).

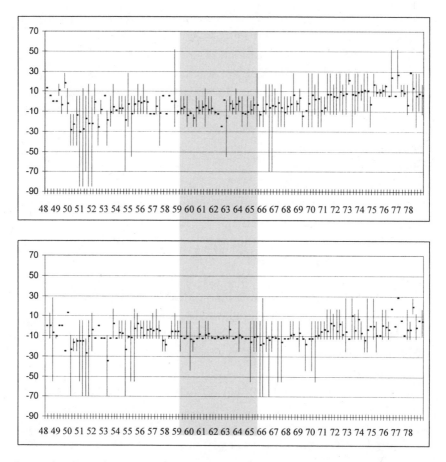

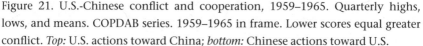

Figure 21. U.S.-Chinese conflict and cooperation, 1959–1965. Quarterly highs, lows, and means. COPDAB series. 1959–1965 in frame. Lower scores equal greater conflict. *Top:* U.S. actions toward China; *bottom:* Chinese actions toward U.S.

Again, quantitative event data (fig. 21) illustrate a stable pattern of rivalry maintenance. The variance is truncated for both states and represents the period of least volatility, both in conflict and cooperation, for the entire rivalry. No U.S. actions toward China in this period are more cooperative than a simple verbal message, and only in one quarter, in 1962 was a threat of force made. Chinese-to-U.S. events show a remarkably similar picture.

Conventional Explanations

It is clear that the Sino-American interaction discussed above cannot solely be explained by the culmination of international reactions and reciprocity, or by a perverse autocratic system in China. Chinese restraint during the 1962 Taiwan crisis was not matched by U.S. restraint in Vietnam. Further, Mao did not match Johnson's escalation in 1965. There is little doubt that each rival's action created a reaction in the other's decision-making circle, but that reaction was neither opposite nor equal. Had the United States crossed a certain threshold in Vietnam, by invading the North and threatening China, Mao would have reciprocated, and invasion would have been met with invasion. Below the threshold, the reciprocity did not hold. The United States sent bombers to the North in 1965; China sent engineers. In addition, this asymmetrical pattern of rivalry maintenance cannot be explained by a domestic coalition-building argument. In Vietnam, the democratic state was the intervener, and it was the United States that contemplated preemptively striking Chinese nuclear facilities. The more cartelized and autocratic Chinese state showed restraint in 1962 and in the Vietnam conflict.

Dynamic Two-level Pressures

Neither domestic nor international theoretical layers solely explain rivalry interactions. Instead, a more convincing argument appears when both levels are collated, forming a picture of the international-domestic interactions over time. The avoidance of war during the early to mid-1960s, as in the late 1950s as discussed in the previous section, stemmed from the lack of pessimism over the future, and the moderate domestic outbidding environments. Likewise, compromise and diplomatic activity was curtailed for similar reasons.

Future Expectations

The Chinese leadership's expectations were mixed in the early 1960s. By 1960, the negative effects of the Great Leap Forward were evident in China's economy. Economic output throughout the country did not increase, as Mao had expected. Also, in July 1960, Khrushchev withdrew all Soviet advisors from China, further degrading China's ability to deal with the economic turmoil (Chen 2001, 82). Although China had made great strides during the last decade, creating industrial centers in Manchuria and increasing domestic production by 400 percent from 1950 to 1960, the economic outlook was uncertain.

The biggest shock to Chinese expectations of the future came from growing antagonism with Moscow. The Sino-Soviet rift opened as a result of three outstanding issues. First, Mao and the Chinese leadership disagreed over Moscow's "capitulation" to the West, especially regarding nonproliferation. When Khrushchev visited Beijing in 1959, the growing disagreement between the two communist nations consumed most of the discussion. Khrushchev reportedly accused China of "craving for war like a cock for a fight." When Chinese foreign minister Chen Yi rebutted Khrushchev the next day, the Soviet leader returned to Moscow early (Chang 1990, 212–13). The closer Moscow appeared to cooperating with Washington, the more China felt betrayed (Zubok and Pleshakov 1996, 220–30).

Second, Moscow's criticism of the Great Leap Forward reminded Mao of the Soviet Union's "big power chauvinism" of the 1950s. The CCP consistently worried about being dominated by the Soviet Union. This fear led to the third rift, related to differences in communist ideals. As Chang (1990) details, Mao doubted Khrushchev's revolutionary dedication, viewing Moscow as more imperialist then communist. Mao's criticism of Russia's road toward "imperialism" would eventually lead to his push for the Cultural Revolution. The sum of this divide was that China could no longer count on Russian support. In addition, before Khrushchev's visit to the United States, he reneged on supporting China's nuclear weapons program (Chang 1990, 213; Zagoria 1960; Prozumenschikov 1996).

While the Sino-Soviet alliance crumbled, tension began rising in Vietnam. Beijing had given substantial aid to the North Vietnamese government and guerrilla forces between 1956 and 1963. When Hanoi increased its military attacks on the South in 1959, despite China's reservations, Beijing was forced to anticipate Washington's reaction. As American forces arrived to reinforce the South, the situation was similar to Korea fourteen years earlier. In the short term, American involvement in the crisis was promoted in public as an opportunity for China because it held the possibility that Washington's strength would be overstretched.

The obvious downside to U.S. intervention in Vietnam, for Beijing, was the possibility that the South could invade the North and unify the country in "imperialist" hands. Short of this eventuality, Beijing did not view the simmering conflict as overly threatening. The future only would look bleak in Mao's eyes if the United States invaded the North and then Chinese territory. Chinese military aid to Hanoi increased in 1963 and then again after the American bombing campaign in March 1965 (Chen 2001, 206–34). Even after the Gulf of Tonkin incident brought more U.S. troops to Vietnam, the Chinese were quite confident of victory without the need for direct Chinese intervention. In January 1965, Zhou Enlai told a Vietnamese military delegation that continued resilience in the North would result in a quick victory, "even sooner than our original expectation" (Westad 1998, 75; Kim 1975, 5).

In addition to expecting a victory in Vietnam, a number of diplomatic victories increased Chinese prestige internationally. In January 1964, France, despite desperate U.S. objections, recognized China and broke off relations with Taiwan. This defection was only the highest profile one from the Taiwan camp. During the mid-1960s, Chinese trade with Japan, as well as with Canada, Australia, and Britain, increased. Also in 1964, Zhou Enlai and Foreign Minister Chen Yi completed a tour of Africa, where Ethiopia, Somalia, Tunisia, Ghana, Mali, and Guinea all offered recognition and diplomatic ties. Even U.S. national security advisor McGeorge Bundy saw that it was a "virtual certainty" that China would soon join the United Nations (Chang 1990, 261; Kim 1975, 35–36).

Intermittent détente with the Soviet Union remained Washington's largest concern. The de-escalating trend of the cold war in the late 1950s gave the outgoing Eisenhower and incoming Kennedy administrations hope that America's external threat burden could be lightened by mutual cooperation with the Soviet Union. Eisenhower, Kennedy, and most of the policy leadership were optimistic that relations would be even better with the Soviet Union in the future (Chang 1990, 213; Kim 1975, 36–44). Specifically, the policy leadership saw some strategic ground for compromise with the Soviets. Although the United States was still militarily stronger than the Soviet Union, the U.S. administration perceived that as Moscow gained strength, both states would be able to destroy each other in a surprise attack. This approaching unstable state of the world proved unsettling to both leaders and instigated the planning of the test-ban meetings, as well as a special session on surprise attacks. Allen Dulles also suggested in a meeting with the Council on Foreign Relations that a Sino-Soviet spit might be developing, as Moscow worried about Beijing's growing power and prestige (Chang 1990, 200–201; Kusnitz 1984, 98–107). Khrushchev visited the United States on September 26–27 in 1959, marking the growing superpower cooperation. As long as the United States avoided facing a united Sino-Soviet front, prospects for the future were optimistic.

Against the backdrop of superpower diplomacy, Washington continued to worry about future crises over Jinmen and Mazu, and attempted to convince Jiang that he should withdraw a substantial number of troops. To Kennedy's relief, Jiang seemed to be backing away from his desire to use military means to harass the Chinese. The United States leadership knew that China would soon join the nuclear club. In January 1961, high-level army sources were predicting that Beijing would detonate a nuclear test device in 1962, and by 1965 would have a small atomic stockpile. This news was a great shock to Kennedy, who reportedly said that "the biggest event of the 1960s may well be the Chinese explosion of a nuclear weapon." The Kennedy administration also perceived that China would be a bigger threat to the Soviet Union than to the United States because of their proximity and historical border disputes. As the Sino-Soviet rift was growing, and Chinese nuclear capabilities were strengthening, Kennedy and his advisors believed that Khrushchev would be interested in arms control to ease his security burden (Chang 1990, 198, 229–30).

The optimism in Washington was curtailed in 1961 and 1962. Khrushchev and Kennedy met in Vienna in 1961, but the meetings were not productive, with no agreement being reached on nuclear arms control or on how to restrain China. Following Vienna, the Berlin Wall went up in August 1961, further worrying the administration. The Soviet Union also recommended atmospheric testing of nuclear weapons in 1961, with the United States following suit in 1962. In that year, the trilateral meetings between Britain, the United States, and the Soviet Union, which had begun in 1960, broke off. Still, Kennedy wanted to push for a nuclear test ban treaty with the Soviet Union. (Chang 1990, 233; Kusnitz 1984, 109–12). However, a comprehensive ban on nuclear testing, and a more limited treaty banning only testing in the atmosphere, in space, and underwater, were rejected by the Soviets in 1962.

This ominous trend in cold war relations between the United States and the Soviet Union in the early 1960s peaked and then reversed course with the Cuban missile crisis. The highly dramatic standoff had two important indirect effects on U.S.-Chinese relations. First, the Chinese were highly critical of Moscow's handling of the crisis, publicly attacking both the original decision to place the missiles in Cuba and the subsequent weakness of backing down. In response, Moscow failed to support China in its border dispute with India in November. Tensions on the USSR-China border flared, drawing Moscow into closer cooperation with Washington. In August 1963, the Soviets accepted virtually the same limited test ban treaty that they had rejected in 1961 before the Cuban missile crisis. This acceptance had the effect of greatly buoying Kennedy's hopes for a comprehensive test ban in the future and decreasing the expectation of war between the United States and the Soviet Union. Second, the Sino-Soviet split meant that Khrushchev, even if he wanted to, could not pressure China into abandoning its nuclear program. Mao condemned the limited test ban treaty openly and recalled his delegation from talks in Moscow. Therefore, while tensions subsided between Moscow and Washington, the threat from Beijing mounted, as Khrushchev could no longer be used as a lever to turn off the Chinese nuclear program (Chang 1990, 233–45; Kim 1975, 36–44; Briggs 1991, 148–50).

This tradeoff, of course, was not an equal one. The Soviet Union, with its proximity to Europe and growing atomic arsenal, was a much greater threat to the United States than was the nuclear novice China. If continued competition with China was the price of détente with the Soviets, it was a bargain. Also, Moscow's cooperation with Washington was prying apart the Sino-Soviet alliance, drawing on Beijing's fears of "superpower imperialism." In direct contrast to improved relations between Moscow and Washington, the Soviet leadership was verbally attacking Beijing daily. Public statements accused Mao and the Chinese of being drug dealers, expansionists, and even racists (Chang 1990, 259). Thus, Washington would not have to face a monolithic communist bloc, and although China would become a nuclear player, there would still be time to strike Beijing's atomic facilities preemptively in the event of a future crisis (Kim 1975, 33–55). Johnson, the CIA, and high-level elites such as Walt Rostow all agreed that future relations with the Soviet Union would hold more op-portunities for cooperation, and that this deflation in Soviet threat out-weighed any increase in China's threat during this period (Chang 1990, 259; Kusnitz 1984, 109).

Domestic Rivalry Outbidding Environment

In China, Mao was in the process of orchestrating a propaganda about-face. The CCP decided in 1960 to make the Soviet Union the scapegoat for the Great Leap debacle. This policy of singling out the Soviet Union as a target for negative propaganda served to legitimize the purge of a number of pro-Soviet politburo members as Mao saw his domestic prestige chal-lenged. Chen suggests that "the Chairman found in the conflict with the Soviets a long-term weapon he badly needed to enhance the much weak-ened momentum of his continuous revolution" (2001, 82).

For the first time in a decade, owing to the failed Great Leap Forward, an opposition voice was standing up. Wang Jiaxing, head of the CCP's In-ternational Liaison Department, argued that China should focus on do-mestic economic growth, rather than conflicts with Russia and India. He stated, "it is necessary to carry out a foreign policy aimed at easing inter-national tension, and not exacerbating [it]" (quoted in Chen 2001, 83). Mao answered that he wanted to fight and grow at the same time. The chairman used the propaganda tools at his disposal to trumpet the Soviet threat to China and the need for a firm international position (Chen 2001, 83). The broad-based public support to regain Taiwan was used to justify this bellicose international policy. Economic growth without military might would not accelerate the cause of unification.

In April 1960, the CCP issued a number of essays rejecting "modern re-visionism" and defending Lenin's doctrine. Although Khrushchev was not named in the documents, it was clear that Beijing was accusing Moscow of selling out the international communist movement for détente with the West. The thinly veiled attacks on Soviet foreign policy were openly broad-cast to the public (Chang 1990, 213–14; Kim 1975, 5–7, 36–44).

The Vietnam conflict was also useful to Mao in outbidding Wang. There were relatively close ties between the North Vietnamese leadership and China. Ho Chi Minh, the leader of the Vietnamese revolution, lived in China for a time, and many of the North Vietnamese communists had been supported by Mao in the 1930s (Chang 1990, 254–55). Mao began a "Resist America and Assist Vietnam Movement" in 1964, stating in harsh terms that the United States was a threat to both Vietnam and China. While Wang argued against fighting the Americans in China, Mao publicly excoriated the budding opposition leader for "conciliations" to the enemy. Despite the public debate between Mao and Wang, Mao in private agreed that China should avoid a confrontation with the United States (Chen 2001, 210). But this conviction did not stop Mao from inflating the external threats from Moscow and Washington to humiliate Wang. Eventually, Wang's side lost, and Mao continued to attack Moscow and the United States publicly (Chen 2001, 84). It is clear that domestic opinion in China was not unilaterally mobilized against the United States during this time. Domestic pressure on Mao, to a large extent created by his own rhetoric, was directed at continuing support to the Vietnamese, but this aid did not have to take the form of direct escalation (Chen 2001, 209–11; Kim 1975, 61; Young 1968, 247–75).

In the United States, Kennedy appeared to be more open to accommodation with China, having written that the Eisenhower administration was being overly militant in its relations with Beijing. But many in the Kennedy government saw China as more threatening than Moscow. Chester Bowles wrote a vituperative speech in 1960 criticizing China and warning of its danger to the United States. He compared Mao to Hitler, extending the metaphor to compare the CCP to the Nazis. Bowles stated publicly in 1961 that the Beijing government could be "far more dangerous, in some ways, than even the Committee of One-Million would have us think." Zbigniew Brzezinski suggested that continuing to ostracize China and further strain Moscow was the best U.S. policy (Chang 1990, 217–23, 229).

There were other elites that argued against the continuation of hostility toward China. Roger Hilsman argued that China had shown restraint in the 1962 Taiwan Strait crisis and that the testing of nuclear weapons would not alter the balance of power in the region. General Maxwell Taylor also counseled against striking at Chinese nuclear facilities, stating that Beijing would not act recklessly and would not change the status quo in the region (Chang 1990, 351).

The positions of Hilsman and Taylor were supported by Chinese overtures from Wang Bingnan to U.S. diplomat John Cabot. Wang noted that

China was interested in exchanging "friendly gestures" and improving relations with the United States. While it was doubtful that a peace treaty would have sprung from these sentiments, it did signal a decrease in hostility from Beijing, as compared to the 1955 and 1958 Taiwan crises (Chang 1990, 251).

In the final analysis, both Kennedy and Johnson felt strong pressure to maintain a firm line against China and communist movements in Asia. Vietnam became a lightning rod for political pressure to maintain the rivalry with communism in Asia, and in China specifically. After ascending to the presidency, Johnson was quoted as saying, "I am not going to lose Vietnam" (Chang 1990, 254). Further, the U.S. leadership had stated throughout the 1950s that it would not allow Chinese communist values to diffuse into Vietnam (Kim 1975, 57–75). This sentiment was supported and reinforced by the Nationalist China lobby. In the 1964 election, China policy and communism became an issue, although both Johnson and Barry Goldwater, the Republican nominee, spoke about the communist threat and the importance of actively combating China's "aggressive attitudes" (Chang 1990, 262). Therefore, as Vietnam became a theater for the maintenance of Washington's conflict with China and communism, it also became a campaign issue. A president who was seen as allowing communism to push through Vietnam would have faced considerable opposition in the early 1960s. In 1964, almost 70 percent of citizens polled supported American involvement in Vietnam (Page and Shapiro 1992, 232).

Opportunity for Escalation

During this period, the United States maintained a two-to-one aggregate capability ratio over China.[3] While this was smaller than the three-to-one advantage Washington enjoyed in 1953, Beijing no longer had the firm backing of Soviet military support. As this inter–communist bloc feud escalated in rhetoric, especially after the Great Leap Forward, Beijing's hopes for gaining Soviet nuclear as well as advanced conventional weapons dimmed. The Soviet Union failed to back China against India in 1962 and warned Mao that it would not support an attack on Taiwan (Zubok and

3. This figure is calculated using capabilities data from Singer (1987).

Pleshakov 1996, chap. 7; Young 1968, 223–25). Counterbalancing the loss of confidence in military aid from Moscow was the fact that U.S. forces were now massing in Vietnam. Taiwan and Korea remained out of reach, but with the help of Hanoi, Mao could have intervened in Vietnam. Therefore, both states had an opportunity to escalate.

Summary and Analysis

A dynamic two-level pressure explanation predicts that neither state would deviate substantially from a process of rivalry maintenance during this period. The future costs were only moderate for each, and the domestic situation remained conducive to threat inflation. The evidence from this period supports the maintenance view, as both China and the United States did not escalate tensions in the 1962 Taiwan Strait crisis, China did not intervene directly in Vietnam, and the United States did not choose to strike Chinese nuclear facilities preemptively. The avoidance of war during the early to mid-1960s, as in the late 1950s, stemmed from confidence in the future and the moderate domestic outbidding environments.

1966–1973

Rivalry History

The events of the 1966–73 period illustrate a trend toward de-escalation in both states. In 1966, the United States for the first time began referring to the capital of China as Beijing, which meant "northern capital," rather than the nationalist phrase that had been used, "Peiping," or "northern peace." In apparent response, Mao communicated to Washington that it would not become directly involved in Vietnam, as long as the United States did not invade China or North Vietnam, or bomb the North's Red River dikes. President Johnson acquiesced quickly to this deal. Also, the United States did not support Soviet strikes in 1968 on Chinese nuclear facilities (Chang 1990, 286; Tyler 2000, 65–70). By November 1968, the United States had offered to resume the Sino-American ambassadorial talks in Warsaw, to which Beijing responded positively. On July 21, 1969, Washington relaxed restrictions on Americans traveling to China. Less than a week later, a letter from Senator Mike Mansfield arrived in Beijing, asking for a visit to China to seek a compromise between the United States and China (Chen 2001, 247; Tyler 2000, 63).

Because there were no formal diplomatic channels between Washington and Beijing in 1969, Nixon used his meeting with other leaders to convey his desire for détente with China to Mao. Nixon asked both Pakistani president Mohammad Yahya Khan and Romanian leader Nicolae Ceausescu to relay to Mao his intention to move toward cooperation with Beijing. Nixon met again with Yahya Khan in 1970, asking for a higher-level meeting between representatives from the rival states. Washington renewed the offer for a new round of Warsaw talks in December 1969. In October and November 1970, Nixon continued to communicate through the Pakistani and Romanian channels to Beijing that he wanted to send a high-level representative to China. Eventually, these signals were answered positively by Mao (Tyler 2000, 64).

Beijing reciprocated and offered to add momentum to de-escalation. Two months after Washington asked for new ambassadorial talks, in a subtle move, Mao personally ordered the publication of Nixon's inaugural speech in the *Renmin Ribao* (People's daily) and *Nongqi* (The red flag) (Chen 2001, 238, 245). Mao also organized a group of four military marshals to study Chinese international affairs. This group returned several documents, most cautiously toeing the party line. One interesting interaction between Mao and the group occurred in mid-May 1969. The previous month, the CCP's Ninth National Congress had culminated in a speech by defense minister Lin Biao that gave no sign that Beijing was looking to cooperate with the United States (Tyler 2000, 71–73). After the meeting, Mao instructed the group to reanalyze the party position toward the United States. Zhou told the marshals that the international situation was "too complicated" for Lin Biao's view of the world, and that the new report should not be "restricted by any established framework." This incident illustrates a new flexibility in both Mao's and Zhou's thinking about a strategic compromise with the United States. The ensuing policy evaluation highlighted the increasing threat the superpowers faced with each other.

After the Zhenbao Island and Xinjiang incidents, the marshals supported using negotiation with the United States to lighten China's external threat burden (Chen 2001, 246–47). Mao is quoted as saying,

> We have the Soviet Union to the north and the west, India to the south, and Japan to the east. If all our enemies were to unite, attacking us from

the north, south, east, and west, what do you think we should do? . . . Beyond Japan is the United States. Didn't our ancestors counsel negotiating with faraway countries while fighting with those that are near? (Chen 2001, 249)

Some change in behavior was needed for Beijing, and increased cooperation with the United States provided an opening because both were menaced by the Soviet Union (Kim 1975, 145).

Mao and Zhou both agreed to reopen the Warsaw talks in December 1969. As an additional measure, both leaders agreed to free two Americans who had been held in China when their boat strayed into Chinese waters in February. Chinese diplomat Lei Yang and U.S. ambassador Walter Stoessel met "informally" on December 11, 1969, and January 8, 1970. On January 20, 1970, the ambassadorial meetings reconvened officially (Chen 2001, 249–52).

By August 1970, Mao had decided to use journalist Edgar Snow, whom he knew from Snow's time covering the civil war, as both a symbol of détente and a go-between to Washington. In that month, Snow was told by Huang Zhen, the Chinese ambassador to France, that he should apply for a visa to China. Snow told Huang that he had been turned down numerous times by Beijing. In response, Huang reportedly revealed to Snow that the invitation "comes from the top." On October 1, 1970, Snow reviewed the National Day parade with Mao, and a picture of the meeting was published on the front page of the major Chinese newspapers. Mao meant the gesture for both domestic and international consumption. It was supposed to tell Washington that Beijing was ready again to negotiate[4] and the Chinese people that the United States was now a potential ally against the Soviets. If that was not enough, Mao told Snow that he would like Nixon to visit China, saying he would be "happy to meet Nixon, either as president or tourist" (Chen 2001, 255–56; Tyler 2000, 81–87).

There were several bumps on the road to cooperation. In February 1969, Laio Heshu, a Chinese diplomat in the Netherlands, defected to the West and was granted asylum in the United States. In response, Mao canceled the ambassadorial talks. By March 1970, the Chinese had allowed Prince Norodom Sihanouk to set up a Cambodian government in exile in

---

4. Kissinger reports that he did not get the message (Kissinger 1979).

China, in response to the coup by American-backed general Lon Nol. The next month, Jiang Jingguo, Jiang Jieshi's son, was scheduled to fly to the United States. Both Washington and Beijing decided to postpone the Warsaw meetings at this point. Nixon's cross-border raids into Cambodia further delayed Sino-American negotiations. Despite this backsliding, Nixon continued to express his willingness to compromise with China, and in July 1970 Beijing released American bishop James Walsh, who had been held on espionage charges since 1958 (Chen 2001, 245, 252–53).

After Mao invited the American Ping-Pong team to China in 1971, the Chinese and Americans began to expand their communication channels beyond the use of Pakistan as an intermediary. By May 21, Nixon had agreed to visit Beijing and had offered to send Kissinger on a secret visit to arrange the details (Chen 2001, 262–63). Kissinger visited Beijing on July 9–11. The most noteworthy discussions of the seventeen hours of meeting between American and Chinese representative during the trip involved American compromises on Taiwan. Kissinger stated that Washington would not support an independent Taiwan or pursue a two-Chinas policy. He also agreed to withdraw two-thirds of American forces from Taiwan after the Vietnam War, promising additional withdrawals as Sino-American cooperation increased. This agreement was a clear break with a State Department report in early 1971 that stated the Taiwan issue was "unsettled" (Chen 2001, 266; Tyler 2000).

Mao convened a series of meetings attended by regional governors and party cadre members to sell the idea of Sino-American détente. Zhou told the attendees that representatives from Washington were coming to Beijing because they needed peace with China. Further, Zhou stressed that China was coming to the bargaining table as an equal. Mao's avowed policy goal was to "improve Sino-American relations" (Chen 2001, 266).

After hearing that the United States was willing to pull back most of its forces from Taiwan, Mao agreed to drop his long-held demand that it be done immediately (Chen 2001, 267). When the drafting of the joint report of the secret meetings in China was completed, Kissinger sent a one-word cable to Washington that read, "Eureka" (Chen 2001, 266). The Kissinger visit paved the way for Nixon's trip to China in spring 1972. Nixon's visit ultimately produced the Shanghai communiqué, signed by both parties on February 28, 1973. In this document, Nixon formally agreed to remove U.S. troops from Taiwan and Mao stated his willingness to use peaceful means to reunify Taiwan with the mainland (Chen 2001, 274–75; Kim 1975, 237–47). By 1973 Sino-American tensions had been reduced substantially.

The event data in figure 22 show an increasing pattern of cooperation beginning in 1968 for the United States and in 1970 for China. From 1970 to 1974, U.S. actions toward China reach at least ten in eighteen of the twenty quarters. Similarly, Chinese actions toward the United States cross that threshold twelve out of the twenty quarters. In 1973, the mean cooperation scores for each state were the highest they had ever been, and they intermittently increased thereafter.

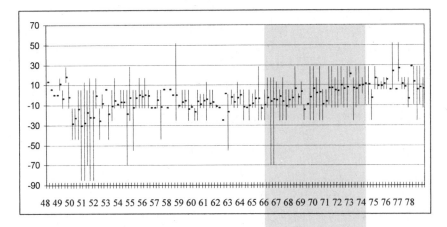

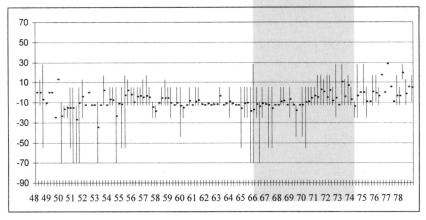

Figure 22. U.S.-Chinese conflict and cooperation, 1966–1973. Quarterly highs, lows, and means. COPDAB series. 1966–1974 in frame. *Top:* U.S. actions toward China; *bottom:* Chinese actions toward U.S.

Conventional Explanations

Other explanations of international conflict-cooperation only explain part of this picture. For example, reciprocity did reinforce cooperation in each state. Washington's offer to open the Warsaw talks was agreed to by Beijing and eventually matched by the release of several Americans being held in China. Further down the line, American proposals to pull out a substantial number of its troops from Taiwan corresponded to Mao's agreement to renounce the use of force to annex Taiwan. It is indeed unlikely that de-escalation would have occurred had either state refused to reciprocate during the whole period under investigation in this section. Yet what is missing from an explanation that relies on the ping-pong action-reaction sequence of international events is that states have to be willing to play the game.

There were important triangular pressures on both states forcing them to consider altering their rivalry trajectories, and eventually initiating and reciprocating cooperation. Soviet behavior and the expected outcome of the Vietnam War served as catalysts for change in the rivalry. In addition, domestic pressure helps to explain some of the subtleties of the process. Kissinger's trip to China in 1971 was "secret" to avoid domestic backlash from the right, which had been a powerful force in the China lobby. And in China, the death of Lin Biao eliminated a potential outbidder who might have attempted to block Sino-American cooperation. Similarly, a realpolitik look at the global situation may have suggested that China and America cooperate against the Soviets, to balance "threat," if not power. Yet the process of de-escalation did not come to fruition until 1972 with Nixon's trip or 1973 with the Shanghai communiqué. The international imperatives for de-escalation were present from at the latest 1968. Domestic pressure helps to explain this lag.

A unilevel domestic analysis of the Sino-American rivalry may also miss several important aspects of de-escalation. Chinese behavior does not correlate with domestic changes. Although a new constitution was under consideration during this time, the main institutions of government remained undemocratic. If anything, the Cultural Revolution increased the cartelization of government. Therefore, a coalition-building theory would not have predicted de-escalation. Although it could be argued that democratic institutions in the United States made Nixon more likely to de-escalate tensions with China, these same institutions had been a constant throughout the previous periods of rivalry. Instead of relying on one level or the other, international or domestic, the interaction between both arenas illuminates a more complete picture of rivalry dynamics.

Dynamic Two-Level Pressures

A closer look at the expected future costs of rivalry and changes in domestic outbidding environments in both states clarifies the motivation for increased cooperation. China was confronting an impractical threat burden by taking on the United States and the Soviet Union. In the future, if any crisis were to erupt, China would be left vulnerable on at least one flank. Domestically, the decade of growing public antipathy between China and the Soviet Union promoted Moscow, rather than the United States, as public enemy number one, thus opening space for negotiations with Washington. Similarly, the domestic outbidding environment was considerably demobilized toward China in the United States, and by 1973 a large majority of Americans supported Nixon's trip to Beijing.

Future Expectations

The expected costs of rivalry increased rapidly for both China and the United States after 1966. In China, the escalation of the Vietnam War further exacerbated the Sino-Soviet fracture. Both countries gave considerable aid to Hanoi but continued to compete over the leadership of the communist bloc. As an example of this continued struggle, it was reported that the Chinese blocked Soviet aid to the North, while accusing Moscow of collaborating with Washington. In 1966, for various reasons (see Chen 2001, chap. 8), the North Vietnamese leadership moved away from China and toward the Soviet Union (Chang 1990, 278). This move angered Beijing and raised the possibility of Soviet domination in Asia. Tensions between Moscow and Beijing continued to rise with the 1968 Soviet invasion of Czechoslovakia. The rolling of Soviet tanks into Prague was taken by Beijing as a blatant illustration of Moscow's "big power chauvinism" and its desire to dominate the other communist states. After this incident, China publicly promoted Moscow over the United States as its principal enemy, even though the CIA had suggested that this was the case in 1967 also (Chang 1990, 277; Kim 1975, 152).

The Sino-Soviet rift began to turn into a volcano in 1968 and 1969. The historical border dispute in Manchuria and Mongolia between the two communist powers had remained dormant since the beginning of the communist alliance. Yet in the winter of 1968, hundreds of thousands of troops were massed on each side of the Sino-Soviet border. In January 1969, Chinese and Soviet soldiers fought around Zhenbao Island in the Ussuri River. This clash was followed by the large-scale mobilization of forces on each side of the former allies' border (Chang 1990, 277). Chinese and Russian troops clashed again in March, leaving thirty Soviet soldiers dead and fourteen wounded in one incident on March 2. By March 15, Russian forces were launching heavy artillery shells into Chinese territory (Tyler 2000, 48–60). A larger military clash between Soviet and Chinese forces occurred in Xinjiang on August 13, when a Chinese brigade was routed (Chen 2001, 248; Ostermann 1994/95). The Zhenbao Island and Xinjiang incidents were merely the loudest and latest military eruptions around Chinese territory. With the Vietnam War still raging, and military clashes with the Soviets brewing, continued conflict involving China's other competitors, including South Korea, Taiwan, India, and Japan looked to be increasingly costly in the future (Ross 1995, 23–29). Mao worried about a general war with the Soviet Union and noted, "all under the heaven is in great chaos" (Chen 2001, 240–45).

Pessimistic expectations about the future also entered Washington's policy planning. Most notably, U.S.-Soviet relations became increasingly strained after 1968, with the enunciation of the "Brezhnev doctrine" and its military illustration in Prague (Chang 1990, 278–79; Kim 1975, 152–57). Moscow seemed to shift away from Khrushchev's policy of détente and toward a strategy of continued conflict with the West. This change was highlighted by Soviet aid to Vietnam, as well as by cagey responses to Washington's overtures for increased limitations on nuclear testing (Tyler 2000, 51–52, 64). A potential crisis also arose over the Soviets' stationing nuclear submarines at Cienfuegos in Cuba. Furthermore, the Nixon administration was worried about the growing production of Soviet SS9 ICBMs, which were being deployed in the Soviet Union at a rate of 250 or more per year from 1969 to 1971, and the growing possibility that Moscow would reach qualitative military parity with the United States sooner than was previously expected (Ross 1995, 19). Likewise, continued conflict with China was perceived as costly as Chinese and American capabilities trended toward equality (see fig. 19).

Even more shocking for Washington was the Tet offensive in 1968. The surprise North Vietnamese attack caught Washington's and Saigon's forces off guard and signaled to the American leadership that not only could the war not be won with the current troop deployment and strategy, but that the U.S.-backed forces had not imposed enough costs on Hanoi to reach an "honorable" compromise (Briggs 1991, 175–76). Domestic turmoil in the United States over the Vietnam War, including the riots at Kent State in 1970, led to further pessimism in Washington (Ross 1995, 20–21).

Domestic Rivalry Outbidding Environment

Chinese propaganda increasingly attacked Moscow. The government reported in the *Renmin Ribao* newspaper that Moscow had singled out Beijing as its "principal enemy," instead of the United States, and had forsaken the communist cause (Chang 1990, 268; Kim 1975, 152–54). In 1966 and 1967, with the Cultural Revolution, Mao attempted to erase Soviet influence in the Chinese Communist Party. Mao's plan was to avoid "Khrushchev-style revisionism," which he believed would lead to the forsaking of the Marxist-Leninist ideals that supported communism. Toward this end, the Chinese leader purged foreign and domestic elites, promoting younger and more militant protégés. Mao made no secret of his distaste for Moscow's policies of the last decade, entitling one part of a multivolume attack on the Soviet Union, "On Khrushchev's Phony Communism and Its Historical Lessons for the World." The Chinese public became increasingly polarized against Moscow. In January 1967, spurred by the government, tens of thousands of protesters plastered the Soviet embassy with placards reading "Shoot Brezhnev" and "Fry Kosygin" (Chang 1990, 276–77). Until 1966, a number of CCP members had supported an eventual reconciliation with Moscow. But Mao's purging of pro-Soviet elites, and the public's active support of anti-Soviet policies, undercut any chance or incentive for accommodation with Moscow (Chang 1990, 276–77; Kim 1975, 147–76; Tyler 2000, 84).

The United States was also derided as imperialist, and in 1966 Lin Biao, the Chinese defense minister, published his essay "Long Live the Victory of People's War!" calling for the destruction of North America and Europe. In the United States, Dean Rusk and others compared Lin Biao's ideas to Hitler's. What Rusk and Johnson did not note in public was that Lin Biao's essay was a statement calling on Vietnam and other states to fight their own battles, without direct Chinese troop support (Chang 1990, 269–70; Kim 1975, 119–22).

As Mao contemplated the "international situation" facing China, a coalition led by Lin Biao and other leftists opposed reconciliation with the United States. Mao publicly signaled his support for détente with Washington by standing next to the American author Edgar Snow on a reviewing platform for China's national day celebration in 1970 and by inviting Nixon to visit China. Yet these accommodative hints led to increasing pressure on Mao from the Lin Biao faction. At the Ninth National Congress in April 1969, Lin and Mao verbally sparred over domestic policies. This dispute between Mao and his handpicked successor escalated at a plenary session of the Central Committee at Lushan in 1970. At this meeting, Lin and his followers, who included Wu Faxian, the commander of the air force, gained nearly equal political footing with Mao's supporters (Chen 2001, 253).

The row with the Lin Biao faction continued into 1971, when Mao investigated "conspiracy activities" in the opposition. On a tour of southern China in August 1971, Mao harshly criticized Lin. In response, Lin Liguo, Lin Biao's son, reportedly organized a squadron of troops loyal to his father with the goal of killing Mao. When this plan failed, Lin's family attempted to flee to Russia, but the plane crashed in Mongolia. It had been unclear until the death of Lin, whether détente would threaten Mao's domestic position (Chang 1990, 287–88). After Lin's faction was broken, a large political obstacle to Sino-American détente was lifted. Further, Lin's death increased the political clout of Zhou Enlai, a strong proponent of Sino-American cooperation (Tyler 2000, 110–12). Zhou still had enemies, including Jiang Qing, Mao's wife, who continued to lobby against compromise with Washington, but conciliation was now less of a threat to both Mao's and Zhou's domestic positions (Tyler 2000, 97).[5]

5. It is important to note that at least one source disagrees with the historical account that Lin Biao wanted to challenge Mao for leadership. Jin Qiu, the daughter of General Wu Faxian, one of Lin's followers, argues that Lin Liguo never executed his plan to murder Mao and that Lin Biao never challenged Mao's authority. What Jin Qui does

In the United States, hawkish positions on China were becoming less politically stable. By 1966, when China had illustrated that it would not directly confront the United States in Vietnam, William Bundy directly contradicted Rusk's China-Nazi metaphor by stating in a speech that "Chinese leaders have not wished to seek a confrontation of military power with us," and that Mao was not "another Hitler" (Chang 1990, 272). There remained considerable domestic pressure on Johnson to support the South Vietnamese cause. Johnson himself made reference to the idea that the Vietnam War was a test of his administration's toughness on communism. Republicans claimed that the Democrats had lost China in the late 1940s by not fully supporting Jiang, and that this pattern was being repeated in Vietnam (Kim 1975, 83–98).

As China surprised some hard-liners by not becoming immediately involved in Vietnam and by refraining from sending troops into the fray, academics and Congress began taking a closer look at Sino-American relations. The Senate Foreign Relations committee, chaired by J. William Fulbright, began hearings on U.S. policy toward China in March 1966. Commentators such as A. Doak Barnett, Benjamin Schwartz, Hans Morgenthau, and others testified in this public setting. With only a few dissenters, almost all of the experts proposed a softer approach toward China. While the spotlight was still on the issue, two hundred Asian specialists took out an advertisement in the New York Times calling for the United States to discuss the establishment of formal relations with Beijing. That same year, the Council on Foreign Relations published a study of Sino-American relations that generally promoted a more flexible China policy in Washington (Chang 1990, 273–74; Kim 1975, 104–11).

A high-profile coalition of elites continued to see Moscow as the most menacing threat to U.S. interests. Thus, this group began to espouse a more moderate line toward China in order to place more pressure on the Soviets. General Van Fleet, after his retirement, called China "our future friends," against the Soviets, an opinion contrasting sharply with his previous policy evaluations for Asia. Edwin O. Reischauer, the U.S. ambassador to Japan, supported Van Fleet's revised viewpoint (Chang 1990, 263).

---

not argue against is that both Mao and Zhou Enlai expected that Lin would attempt to use the reconciliation with Washington to gain more political power in the party (see Chen 2001, 270n. 145).

Additionally, Roger Hilsman and James Thomson continued to be active in promoting a more moderate stand on China (Chang 1990, 271; Tyler 2000, 58–60). In fact, by 1969, Democrats such as Edward Kennedy were attempting to "trump" Nixon on rapprochement with China. Senator Kennedy argued that perpetuating conflict with China was counterproductive, and that there was now "a new opportunity to rectify the errors of the past" (Tyler 2000, 59).

All of these forces reduced the political pressure Nixon faced from the China lobby when he agreed to go to Beijing. Although Walter Judd personally wrote to Nixon chastising the president for his "sharp reversal" in policy, the China lobby proved to be weaker than expected. When Judd formed the Committee for a Free China to mobilize elite and public opinions against Nixon's trip to Beijing, he found only limited support. Even Admiral Radford, who had previously supported an attack on mainland China, described Nixon's trip as a "valuable discussion [that might lead to] a more peaceful world" (quoted in Chang 1990, 290). Chang notes that "the usual anti–Chinese Communist shock troops did not jump to rally to the former missionary's call, as in the days of old" (1990, 290). Nixon, himself a high-profile anti-Chinese outbidder in the 1940s and 1950s, espoused a flexible line on China going back to 1967. In his *Foreign Affairs* article that year, the future president called for the eventual recognition of China as a part of the "family of nations" (Nixon 1967). After the Shanghai communiqué was drafted, there was vociferous criticism from the conservative right, including Patrick Buchanan, whom Nixon took to Beijing as a speech writer. But the major news coverage and general public reaction was overwhelmingly positive (Tyler 2000, 143–44; Chang 1990, 290).

Opportunity for Escalation

Both countries had significant obstacles blocking an obvious opportunity to escalate the rivalry during this period. Beijing was directly threatened by the Soviet nuclear rockets and military units arrayed along its border. Any direct attack on Taiwan, or in Vietnam, would have weakened the northern front. China had developed atomic weapons, showing off its new firepower decisively in two tests at the height of Sino-Soviet tensions in 1969, but possessed only limited stocks and delivery systems. The United States was recoiling from Vietnam and was unlikely to muster the domestic resources to launch another operation in Asia. Washington's attention was also focused on the Middle East and conflict between the oil-producing states there and Israel (Ross 1995, 18–22). Therefore, both countries had only moderate opportunities to escalate the rivalry.

Summary and Analysis

The two-pronged threat from the Soviet Union, especially after 1968, increased the expected costs of future Sino-American rivalry in both capitals. China was faced with the prospect of fighting both the Americans and Soviets, a combined force that not only dwarfed Beijing's conventional technology and fighting capacity, but also its nuclear capabilities. After the Tet offensive, Washington needed to find a way out of the Vietnam War. Also, the Brezhnev doctrine led American decision makers to plan for rising conflict with the Soviet Union and an increased external threat burden (Tyler 2000, 42, 56; Ross 1995, chap. 1).

The growing threat from the Soviet Union was used by both states to demobilize public opinion against the other. There was considerably less pressure on Nixon to maintain American strength toward China than there had been on Johnson, Kennedy, and especially Eisenhower. Similarly, Mao began in the mid-1960s to promote Moscow as the Chinese people's principal threat. By the early 1970s, Mao and Zhou were able to convince a majority of Chinese elites that peace with the United States would improve China's position vis-à-vis the West and vis-à-vis the Soviet Union. Therefore, dynamic two-level pressures in the Sino-American rivalry were pushing toward de-escalation. High expected future costs of rivalry maintenance, mixed with demobilized domestic outbidding environments, opened a window of opportunity for peace. While China continued to have an opportunity to escalate conflict with Washington, either in Vietnam or Taiwan, escalation would have been unduly costly, especially in exposing the Chinese northern territories to Soviet threats and expansion.

Conclusion

As the previous narrative suggests, the major changes and continuities in the Sino-American rivalry followed the ebb and flow of dynamic two-level pressures. Table 3 lists the configuration of dynamic two-level pressures for the rivalries. The highest levels of escalation, in the Korean War, were

Table 3

Chinese and U.S. dynamic two-level pressures

Years	Costs	Outbidding	Opportunity	Prediction	Observed
China					
1949–53	High	High	High	Escalate	War
1954–59	Low	High	Low	Maintain	LC
1959–65	Low	Medium	Low	Maintain	LC
1966–73	High	Low	Low	De-escalate	CO
United States					
1949–53	High	High	High	Escalate	War
1954–59	Low	Medium	Medium	Maintain	LC
1959–65	Low	Medium	Medium	Maintain	LC
1966–73	High	Low	Medium	De-escalate	CO

LC: Limited conflict/limited cooperation
CO: Cooperation

marked by expectations of high future costs and severely mobilized domestic outbidding environments. Throughout the next decade and a half,
domestic pressure remained moderate to high, and the costs of rivalry were
perceived to be manageable. Therefore, both countries continued to compete with each other, bounding both cooperation and conflict. These periods of rivalry maintenance are evidenced in figure 18 by the narrowing
variance in cooperation and conflict.

It was not until after 1966, and especially 1969, that severe international changes affected the rivalry status quo. For both states, the growing
Soviet threat, felt most acutely by Beijing, provided a path toward de-escalation. Increasing triangular conflict raised the costs of future rivalry for
both parties. Moreover, the shared threat that both countries faced could
be used domestically to legitimize compromises. In China, Mao rationalized de-escalation with Washington as a way to deal with Moscow. For
Nixon, the Soviet threat helped appease and split the right-wing Republicans. Those hawks that promoted Moscow as the state most threatening to
U.S. interests were now allied with relative doves and those who had approved of increased cooperation with China.

7 Zooming Out

Evidence from Fifty-six Rivalries

THUS FAR, I have explored the ramifications of dynamic two-level pressures in three contexts. Although it would be optimal to have in-depth case-study evidence from all rivalries throughout time, this approach would be unnecessarily time-consuming. Instead, we can create summary measures of the related concepts and analyze how they are related to rivalry interactions across many different rivalries and time periods. In the following sections, I describe the various libraries of conflict behavior and dynamic two-level pressures as well as the relational techniques I use to analyze all rivalries in the world between 1950 and 1990.

Research Design

To systematically test the effect of dynamic two-level pressures on rivalry interaction, I employ a cross-sectional time-series design, using information from many places over many years. This type of analysis has several important benefits as compared to a time-series analysis of one rivalry or a cross-sectional analysis of many rivalries in just one time period. First, by using more than one case, the evidence and theory can be applied to a large grouping of cases and will improve external validity. Therefore, the test is less vulnerable to criticism that it only applies in one place. A solely cross-sectional analysis would suffer from a similar weakness, that the explanatory power of the theory may not apply outside of the limited time frame. Moreover, since the present analysis is dynamic and attempts to analyze changes in expectations over time, it is unlikely that a solely cross-sectional analysis could provide an adequate test.

One downside of any large-n analysis involves measurement considerations. As discussed below, measuring costs, expectations, rivalry outbidding, and other concepts related to dynamic two-level pressures requires case-specific knowledge of beliefs, perceptions, and rhetoric. Therefore, while the large-n statistical analysis will help to enervate criticism related to external validity, it does leave open the question of internal validity. Specifically, is the analysis actually testing the related dynamic two-level concepts? These measurement difficulties are dealt with further in the case studies. By magnifying the details in the Somalia-Ethiopia, Egypt-Israel, and United States–China cases, measurement can be more precise, and the process of rivalry outbidding and escalation/de-escalation can be examined in depth. Therefore, the use of multiple methods, statistical analysis, and case studies can increase our confidence in the findings.

Measuring Conflict and Cooperation

For the cross-sectional time-series design, I create a time-series of rivalry behavior for each rivalry that was ongoing in 1948. I include two measures of escalation and de-escalation for the period 1948 to 1990. The first is scaled event data that were created by splicing together data from the Conflict and Peace Database (COPDAB) and the World Events Interaction Survey (WEIS) following the methods of Reuveny and Kang (1996). This procedure consists of:

1. Scaling the events in COPDAB (using the method of Azar and Havener 1976) and WEIS (using the method of Goldstein 1992) separately.

2. Aggregating the events to quarterly averages.

3. Regressing the WEIS scores on the COPDAB scores for the years that they overlap, 1966–1978, for each directed dyad.

4. Analyzing the output from each regression to see if COPDAB is a significant predictor of WEIS, as is shown by a positive and significant regression coefficient.

5. When the regression was successful for a particular directed dyad, the COPDAB events from 1948 to 1966 are transformed into WEIS-like events. This calculation is done by multiplying each COPDAB quarterly score by the estimated coefficient, and adding the estimated intercept.

6. When the regression was unsuccessful for a particular directed dyad, only the WEIS scores from 1966 to the present were used.

This process provides a continuous scale of conflict and cooperation from 1948 to 1990 for each directed dyad.[1]

There are several sources of event data on international relations. COPDAB and WEIS are the most widespread because they include events from most states in 1948–78 and 1966–90, respectively. Other event data systems include the Global Event Data System (GEDS), various Kansas Event Data System (KEDS) datasets, the Protocol for the Assessment of Nonviolent Direct Action (PANDA), and the Virtual Research Associates (VRA) Reader collection. As compared to COPDAB and WEIS, these alternative sources of international events include data over a limited time span, or narrow the number of cases. For example, PANDA includes data only after 1984, GEDS only after 1999, and KEDS datasets cover only particular dyads or regions, mostly after 1979. The superior spatial and temporal coverage of COPDAB and WEIS make them the best choices for the present analysis.

Despite the drawback of not having one uniform data source from 1948 to the 1990s, event data are the most relevant measures for the theory. Event data have the benefit of picking up cooperative and conflictual events that would be missed when only measuring alliances, treaties, or disputes. Specifically, cooperative events and agreements usually fly under the radar of MID (militarized interstate dispute) catalogs and other data collections, and thus avoid explicit measurement by other means.

Some authors criticize the use of event data in international relations. The main issues revolve around measurement error and bias. A number of authors argue that there is considerable error in event data (see Azar and Havener 1976; Vincent 1983). Some actual events remain uncoded, while coded events may be misleading. Although any measurement error is troubling, event data are the best available measure for the present study. Likewise, Vincent (1983) has found that WEIS overreports events on major powers, while COPDAB overreports events on minor powers. Both datasets contain a paucity of events for most African countries. Therefore, even in event data, there are blind spots that complicate measurement. Luckily, the different sources used by each coding scheme—COPDAB uses many

---

1. A table listing the coefficients, intercepts, and significance levels for each directed dyad is available from the author upon request.

sources and WEIS uses the *New York Times* exclusively—allow for cross-validation of the hypotheses. If major power overreporting causes false positives to be found, this bias should affect WEIS and not COPDAB. Further, by also controlling for major power status we can minimize the inferential damage. If a minor power bias causes false positives to be found, this bias should affect COPDAB and not WEIS. As noted below, the fact that the findings are consistent across event measures decreases the odds that any results are only artifacts of inconsistent reporting.

The second dependent variable is a measure of the initiation of a militarized dispute against the rival. This information is taken from the MID dataset 2.1 (Jones, Bremer, and Singer 1996). A large proportion of quantitative international-relations research has used militarized interstate disputes. Thus, to ensure that this study's conclusions can be compared to past research on the causes of war and peace, the use of militarized dispute data seems appropriate. MID data cover the entire world, including Africa, and allow the inclusion of some cases that are left out of the event data analysis. The downside to using MIDs to operationalize escalation is that there is no similar measure for de-escalation. Some may argue that the end of MID is a "de-escalation," but it neither ends the underlying tensions in most cases, nor does it mean that cooperation is increasing. Despite this shortcoming, dynamic two-level pressures should apply to the initiation of MIDs.

Measuring Dynamic Two-Level Pressures

For the quantitative analysis, the observable implications of dynamic two-level pressures can be tested. First, the interaction between high costs and high information asymmetries/rivalry outbidding should lead to escalation, while low information asymmetries/rivalry outbidding and high costs should increase the chances of de-escalation. Therefore, I code an interaction variable measuring when costs are high and outbidding/information asymmetries are present.

There are a number of complications in operationalizing expectations and rivalry outbidding. One could attempt to measure expectations of rivalry costs by tracking the change in all rivalry costs over time. These costs involve dips in gross domestic product (GDP) and increases in external threats. But, the quantities of each are not transferable. How can you weigh a 2 percent drop in GDP against a rising international threat? Likewise, a measure of elite positions on issues and quarterly public opinion polls of international perceptions would be helpful in gauging the use of information asymmetries and the level of rivalry outbidding. However, these do not exist for a majority of the times and countries in this analysis.

Instead of attempting an ad hoc aggregate measure of costs, I create a variable that marks significant changes in any of the costs of rivalry. One of the problems with an additive operationalization of rivalry expenses is that the costs are substitutable. High rivalry costs can come in the form of falling domestic production, rising external threats, or a loss of alliance support. If any of these three indicators show costs increasing over a period of time, the expected future costs should be coded as rising. In a competitive environment, both economic and political security is needed to induce optimism.

I first construct a GDP measure that uses the previous five years of gross domestic production to make a linear prediction of the next year's GDP. Economic growth is measured from the Penn World Tables (Summers and Heston 1991). If GDP is projected to fall (when the projection is lower than the current total) in constant dollars, costs are coded as high. Similarly, I construct an external threat measure that sums up the capabilities of a state's international rivals from the past five years using Thompson's (2001) dataset, creating a linear prediction for the next year. If the projected threat level is rising, the costs variable is coded as high. I create a third variable that measures the sum of a state's allies' distance-discounted capabilities. If this projection is lower than the current level, costs are again coded as high. The alliance data are taken from the EUGene program (Bennett and Stam 2000).

Of course, other information will affect the expectations of decision makers, for example knowledge about new technological developments, but no factor is more important in forming a picture of the future than past performance. For example, Young (1998) builds evolutionary models with the assumption that future expectations are directly influenced by past actions. Empirically, May (1973), Neustadt and May (1986), and Khong (1992) all find that decision makers use the past as an model for future expectations. Thus, while this measure will not correlate perfectly with actual projections, it is a close approximation.

Although direct information on rivalry outbidding is unavailable, I use information centralization mechanisms to measure the domestic pressures on elite decisions. Pervasive information centralization mechanisms widen knowledge asymmetries between elites and the relevant public. It is these resulting information gaps that provide fertile ground for threat inflation. The uncertainty and fear generated by threat inflation, potentially spurred on by the rival's bellicosity, lead to greater rivalry outbidding and cut off opportunities for de-escalation. Specifically, I operationalize information centralization mechanisms by taking into account the press freedoms, the level of power concentration, and the intragovernmental oppression (purges) in specific countries.

A freedom to exchange information and participate in civil discourse can serve as a check on the information elites might propagate to the masses. As Van Belle (2000b) argues, a free press greatly increases the information available to the public and decreases the ability of elites to "dehumanize" a potential enemy. I measure this factor using the press freedom index from Van Belle (2000a). If a country is coded as not free, it counts as one information-centralization mechanism.[2]

I include the level of government concentration from the Polity III database (Jaggers and Gurr 1995) as an additional information-centralization mechanism. The more a leader concentrates power, especially if external threat is used as the dominant rationale, the greater the (dis)incentive to (de)escalate the rivalry. As power is concentrated in the hands of a few elites, information is likely to be concentrated also. Thus if a state scores at least a 6 on the Polity III concentration score, an additional centralization mechanism is coded (Jaggers and Gurr 1995). Finally, I include a measure of whether or not the government has killed any dissidents or purged members of government in a year to assess the amount of intragovernment repression (Banks 2000). If opposition forces do not feel physically safe criticizing the government, outbidding is more likely. The resulting count of information-centralization mechanisms ranges from 0 to 3. This measure is similar to the transparency index created by Finel and

---

2. I also used alternative measures of press freedom taken from Freedom House and Bollen (2001). These other measures offer a much more limited time frame (post-1978 for the Freedom House scores) and geospatial scope (the Bollen data include numerous missing values). Despite these drawbacks, the results were substantively similar to those reported below.

Lord (2000, 140–42). Although the Finel and Lord study only creates the index for six cases, it includes the same emphasis on open debate and free opposition. The current dynamic two-level pressure index has the benefit of being applied to a wide range of cases (in theory all rivalries) over a number of years. Moreover, the new measures include information on both expectations and information centralizations, rather than on just the latter.[3]

Reciprocity and Past Behavior

The model presented earlier also suggests that past behavior and actions by the rival will affect decisions to escalate/de-escalate. In the event-data analysis, past behavior is controlled for by including the conflict/cooperation value for the previous year. A positive relationship is expected, whereby past conflict makes conflict more likely, and past cooperation makes cooperation more likely. Similarly, the actions of the rival are included in the estimation. I expect significant reciprocity to be present, meaning that conflict from the rival should be mirrored with more conflict, while cooperation from the rival should increase the opportunities for de-escalation. Of course, as discussed earlier, this reciprocity component should not fully determine the extent or intensity of rivalry interactions.

In addition, de-escalation is more likely if the states share a strong external threat. For example, Rock (1989) hypothesizes that a rising German threat led to Anglo-French détente after Fashoda. Therefore, if both states face the same rival in any year, the capability of that shared rival is coded as the shared threat. The threat is then divided by the sum of the two initial adversaries' capabilities following Bennett (1997). Table 4 summarizes the variables included in the analysis.

---

3. The information-centralization mechanisms are measured as counts rather than substitutes because each component (centralization, press freedom, and purges) incrementally increases information. These mechanisms are not substitutes. A free press does not produce the same information or outbidding context as a decentralized government institution does. Further, to create an extreme rivalry outbidding environment, all three would be necessary. The executive would have sole access to most information, no instigative press would be available to broadcast any leaks, and anyone that did leak information could be purged. Taking one mechanism away at a time decreases the probability of information asymmetries, threat inflation, and outbidding.

Table 4
Dynamic two-level pressure index and constituent parts

Concept	Constituent Parts	Equation (values)
Expectations (EX)	Predicted Economic Growth (EG)	
	Predicted External Threat (ET)	
	Predicted External Assistance (EA)	= 1 if (EG < 0 I ET > 0 I EA < 0) (0,1)
Rivalry Outbidding (RO)	Press Freedom (PF)[a]	
	Concentration (CN)[b]	
	Purges (PR)[c]	= PF + CN + PR (0–3)
Dynamic Two-Level Pressures	Expectations * Rivalry Outbidding	EX * RO (0–3)

[a] 1 = Not free; 0 = other
[b] 1 = High concentration; 0 = other
[c] 1 = Any purges;, 0 = other

Measuring Rivalry and Control Variables

The population of interest for the quantitative study will be all international rivalries that were ongoing as of 1948 or after. The observations are directional, so there will be two observations for each rivalry in each year. Rivalries are operationalized using Thompson's (2001) list of strategic rivalries. While Goertz and Diehl (1995) and Bennett (1998) propose alternative measures of international rivalry, their use of militarized interstate disputes conflates the concepts of rivalry with the dependent variables of interest (escalation and de-escalation). By their measures, a certain number of militarized interstate disputes and escalations are necessary for international rivalry. This requirement induces explicit selection bias into the case inclusion rule because rivalries had to escalate a certain number of times. Any state that somehow avoided escalation but was still intensely competitive with an adversary, where that adversary reciprocated the perception of competition, would not be included in the analysis. Thompson's perceptual measure of rivalry avoids this censoring problem to a large extent. The number of rivalries included in the analysis is seventy-eight. I also include four control variables: the democracy level of the actor, whether a formal alliance is present between the actor and the target, the capability ratio between the actor and target, and whether or not the rivals are contiguous by land.

Statistical Estimation

The two dependent variables, conflict/cooperation and MIDs, call for distinct statistical techniques. The conflict/cooperation event data are continuous in nature and thus can be estimated with variations of ordinary least squares (OLS). To account for dyad-by-dyad differences, I estimate models that account for unit-specific effects for each directed dyad. As Green, Kim, and Yoon (2001) suggest, several dyad-specific traits, if uncorrected for, can cause misleading results. Specifically, statistical significance may be overestimated (see also King 2001). These models allow each rivalry to have its own mean conflict level. Theoretically, the inclusion of unit-specific effects is supported by the work of Azar and Sloan (1975) and Diehl and Goertz (2000), who suggest that rivalries have a "baseline rivalry level" (BRL). Although many variables may affect this BRL, it is quite possible that unmeasured concepts and heterogeneity increase or decrease conflict levels. The initiation of a militarized interstate dispute, conversely, is not a continuous variable. The discrete nature of an initiation of a dispute calls for alternative specifications (see Long 1997). Estimating an OLS model with a discrete dependent variable can lead to inefficiency and inconsistency, as well as nonsense predictions (such as negative probabilities). I estimate both semiparametric and parametric hazard models to account for time-dependence. These techniques allow for complex interactions between the "risk" or likelihood of an event and time. Empirically, the MID dataset includes multiple conflicts for some directed dyads. These data insinuate that the event outcomes are not independent (see Box-Steffensmeier and Zorn 2000). Specifically, Colaresi and Thompson (2002) supply evidence that past conflict and subsequent outbreaks of violence are related over time. To relax the independence assumption built into the hazard models, I stratify the baseline hazard by the previous number of conflicts following the methods of Prentice, Williams, and Peterson (1981).

Selection Effects

Political scientists have become acutely aware of the possible selection bias in observable data. Studies by Huth (1998), Reed (2000), and Lemke and Reed (2001) each use a censored probit model to account for the possibility that the observed data are not representative of the phenomena of interest. Why would this be? Achen (1986) notes that in social data, when people select themselves into or out of a particular dataset, one may only be observing one part of reality. Take for instance the question of whether a dispute escalates to war. If we gather information on all the disputes that occurred, and then estimate the effect of a matrix of independent variables on the propensity to escalate, inferences may be biased. Incorrect inference occurs because some states may not even initiate a dispute for fear that it will escalate. One state may have a significant disagreement with another state but may also be much weaker. Because of this weakness, that state may avoid a crisis for fear of being on the losing end of any escalation. Thus, asymmetric dyads may not find themselves in crisis because they want to avoid escalation (see Reed 2000).

Any attempt to measure the effect of capability balance on crisis escalation using only crisis events cannot account for the decision of the weaker state to avoid a crisis altogether. Moreover, any asymmetric dyad that does find itself in crisis may be atypical. For example, the weaker state may have a strong patron for military support. Thus, the estimated effect of capabilities on escalation may be picking up something else, like explicit alliance commitments. This problem can be dealt with by explicitly modeling the selection process and estimating the probability of escalation and crisis initiation. This adjustment allows the estimates to be partially corrected for selection bias (see Heckman 1976).

Selection bias could pose problems for inference in the present study. When attempting to analyze the predictors of rivalry escalation and de-escalation, I initially analyze only states that find themselves involved in rivalry, which is a problem if some states will avoid becoming embroiled in rivalry because of the fear of escalation. For example, the leadership in Britain was angered by the U.S. decision to cut funding for the Skybolt joint missile program in 1962. Britain could have reciprocated by kicking U.S. personnel out of England, possibly initiating a rivalry. While there were many reasons that did not happen, including the "special relationship" between the two countries, one possibility is that Britain feared what an escalation in tensions between the two countries would mean. Likewise, at the turn of the century, France had to decide whether Britain or Germany was its principal threat. Although there were rivalries between both states, the rivalry between Britain and France ended to a large extent because the Fashoda crisis made the dangers of escalation apparent to both. An escalation of tensions within their rivalry would improve the German position. Therefore, it is plausible that in certain situations, rivalries are not initiated or maintained because of the fear of escalation. In fact, dynamic two-level pressures explicitly assume that states form expectations about future escalation and de-escalation costs. If the same factors affect whether or not we observe a rivalry as they do whether or not the rivalry escalates, the present analysis may be biased.

To correct for this problem, I estimate a version of the Heckman two-step selection model for the conflict-cooperation scale, and a two-step censored hazard model for the MIDs analysis (Heckman 1976). In both cases, I include all directed dyads in the system as the comparison group.[4] In the

4. I also randomly selected 250 directed dyads for the selection equation, with similar results. Alliance membership is included in the selection equation but not in the rivalry analysis, satisfying the exclusion restriction imposed by Heckman (1976), along

selection equation, I control for whether or not the dyad is democratic, the capability ratio between the actor and target, formal defense alliance ties, contiguity, and the number of years the states have jointly been a member of the international system. Following the work of Hensel, Goertz, and Diehl (2000), dual democracy is hypothesized to decrease the chance of observing a rivalry. Similarly, it is expected that states that are allied and of unequal capabilities (see Vasquez 1996) are less likely to be rivals. It is also likely that contiguous states are more likely to be rivals. Finally, it is possible that the length of time the dyad has spent in the international system may affect the propensity for rivalry (see Maoz 1996).

Complex Correlation and Nonindependence of Observations

In addition to problems with selection, the directed-dyad year design used in this study cannot consider each time period as independent. This problem is partially corrected by clustering the standard errors by directed dyad. However, further problems arise because of the correlation of the error structure when there are multiple levels of data.

In the present analysis, we have data on directed dyads over time, extrapolating to two levels of data. There are some directed-dyad specific traits (level-2), for example contiguity, and some directed-dyad year characteristics (level-1). Most analyses do not differentiate between the levels, estimating:

$$Y_t = B_0 + B_1 X_1 + B_2 X_2 + r,$$

where Y_t is an outcome variable measured at time t (in this case, conflict-cooperation), B_0 is the intercept, X_1 a matrix of variables at the first level, B_1 the level-1 coefficients, X_2 the level-2 variables, and B_2 the level-2 coefficients. Finally, r is the residual. If OLS is applied to this equation in a cross-sectional time-series design, the observations are assumed to be independent, and the variables are assumed to predict the cross-national variance perfectly.

To see this process, imagine a different and more complex model.

---

with the dyad duration variable. These variables were insignificant in all analyses of rivalry escalation (without controlling for selection).

Table 5

Description of control variables

	Mean	Std. Dev.	Min.	Max.	Description
Democracy	-2.92	6.74	-10.000	10.000	Actor's democracy score minus autocracy score[a]
Capability Ratio	3.29	9.44	0.004	235.052	Actor's capability/target's capability
Contiguity	0.26	0.44	0.000	1.000	Contiguous by land[b]

$N = 2798$

Note: Data from EUGene (Bennett and Stam 2000)

[a] Data from Polity III (Jaggers and Gurr 1995)

[b] 1 = yes; 0 = no

Begin with a model that predicts an outcome just for one directed dyad, at a specific time, ignoring the cross-sectional component:

$$Y_t = B_0 + B_1 X_1 + r, \tag{1}$$

where again Y_t is the outcome, B_0 is the intercept, and B_1 and X_1 refer to the level-1 coefficients and variables. Now, note that we might think that other variables explain the cross-national variance in rivalry interactions. For example, we might expect contiguous rivals to have a higher level of conflict than noncontiguous rivals. To account for the level-2 variables, we can make the level-1 coefficients outcome variables for the level-2 equations:

$$B_{0i} = g_1 + B_2 X_2 + u_1, \tag{2}$$
$$B_{1i} = g_2 + u_2, \tag{3}$$

where g_1 and g_2 are intercepts, B_2 and X_2 represent the level-2 coefficients and variables, and u_1 and u_2 are random error terms. The subscript *i* refers to each of the cross-sections. This framework improves upon the previous example in several ways. Most obviously, the inclusion of u_1 allows for random cross-sectional variation, relaxing the assumption that the included variables measure the difference between nations perfectly. Second, adding u_2 to the B_1 equation relaxes the assumption that all of the level-1 variables perfectly mirror the data-generation process. Most important, this method, known as hierarchical linear modeling (HLM), mixed effects, or random-coefficient models, is sensitive to the nonindependence of the observations. Thirty years of data for 120 directed dyads are not treated as 3,600 independent observations, but instead as "nested" data, where the thirty observations within the directed dyad are all related to each other. Even a fixed-effects model that includes dummy variables for each cross-sectional unit fails to account for this nonindependence if the coefficients vary cross-nationally. Substituting equation 2 and 3 into 1, yields:

$$Y_t = g_1 + B_2 X_2 + u_1 + g_2 X_1 + u_2 X_1 + r. \tag{4}$$

The model is sometimes referred to as a mixed-effects model because it allows the researcher to specify some random components (hence the error terms), and some "fixed" components (the variables included in the model). This functional form cannot be estimated with ordinary least squares or maximum likelihood alone. Instead, empirical Bayesian estimates are computed and then augmented with maximum likelihood methods. I compute the HLM estimates by including conflict and cooperation as the dependent variable, and the behavior received, past behavior, and the selection probability (inverse-mills ratio from the censor-correction model discussed above) as level-1 variables. Level-2 variables include the mean level of democracy, capability ratio, the presence of contiguity or an alliance, and dynamic two-level pressures.

In addition, the HLM techniques allow for an even more sophisticated test of dynamic two-level pressures. In a separate analysis, I include the duration of the rivalry as a level-1 variable, and test the interaction between dynamic two-level pressures and rivalry duration. I expect that states with positive expectations of the future and high outbidding environments should illustrate different rivalry dynamics over time. For example, as time goes on, the rivalries with high dynamic two-level pressures should be increasingly bellicose, while rivalries that have low dynamic two-level pressures should remain relatively stable or even be able to slowly increase cooperation.

Findings

Conflict/Cooperation Event Data

The results for predicting escalation and de-escalation, using the conflict/cooperation event data, strongly support the two-level dynamic logic.[5] As hypothesized, expectations of high future costs alone are not a significant predictor of conflict/cooperation (see model 1 of table 6). More dramatically, as shown in model 2 (table 6), the dynamic two-level index, measuring the interaction between high expected future costs and information centralization mechanisms, is significant and in the predicted direction ($t = 2.04$, $p \leq 0.05$, for a one-tailed test). The greater the

---

5. These results used the first difference of the data to remove the unit-specific effects as well as a deterministic trend. A random effect for each directed dyad is included in the analysis and is significant at the .01 level. Additionally, a Hausman test comparing the random effect to a fixed-effect model for the difference data was insignificant, reassuring us that the unit specific effects were removed by the differencing process (see Hsiao 1986, 86–95).

information-centralization mechanisms, in the presence of expected high costs, the greater the escalation and conflict directed to a rival, all else equal. Specifically, increasing the dynamic two-level pressure index from 0 to 3 leads to a 0.14 increase in conflict and decrease in cooperation on the WEIS scale, ceteris paribus. Further supporting the logic of dynamic two-level pressures is the fact that the expectations coefficient switches signs (as compared to model 1). In models 2–5 (table 6), the expectations coefficient represents the effect of high future costs when information centralization mechanisms are absent or unchanging. As predicted, expectations of high costs leads to a 0.06 increase in cooperation when information asymmetries are low.[6]

When using a GLS procedure to control for possible residual correlation, in model 3 (table 6), the interaction between information-centralization mechanisms and future expected costs continues to be a significant predictor of escalation and de-escalation ($t = 2.21$, $p < 0.05$, for a one-tailed test). The selection coefficient shows a negative but insignificant correlation between conflict and the probability of being in a rivalry. This suggests that the same unmeasured factors that affect the presence of rivalry may have the opposite effect on rivalry interactions. Similar results are reported for models 4 and 5 (table 6), which account for the endogenous nature of past behavior, and possible autocorrelation. Neither the significance levels nor the substantive impact of dynamic two-level pressures is compromised by using simultaneous equation estimators or a generalized estimating equation approach.[7]

The event data model also supports the importance of looking at past behavior, reciprocity, and threat environments. It was hypothesized that past conflict (cooperation) should engender greater levels of conflict (cooperation) in the future as leaders feel pressure to continue their specific courses of action. Similarly, it was suggested that the behavior received from the rival would be positively related to escalation and de-escalation.

---

6. Because the models are dynamic (include lagged endogenous variables), the coefficients must be transformed into interpretable figures. The substantive changes reported here are the rise or fall in equilibrium conflict or cooperation given the dynamic system. Unless otherwise noted, the specific figures are calculated using model 2.

7. The GEE approach in model 5 (table 6) is robust to autocorrelation and heteroskedasticity (see Zorn 2001).

Table 6
Regression results for dynamic two-level pressures and conflict-cooperation scale

	FD—Model 1		FD—Model 2		GLS—Model 3		2SLS—Model 4		GEE—Model 5	
	Coefficient	SE	Coefficient	SE	Coefficient	SE	Coefficient	SE	Coefficient	SE
Expectations	-0.046	0.044	0.099	0.074*	0.103	0.069*	0.102	0.075*	0.094	0.071*
D2LP			-0.074	0.036**	-0.075	0.034**	-0.076	0.037**	-0.073	0.031***
Past Behavior	-0.489	0.023***	-0.496	0.025***	-0.574	0.024***	-0.497	0.026***	-0.415	0.035***
Received	0.086	0.028***	0.074	0.029**	0.074	0.028***	0.073	0.029***	0.067	0.041**
Shared Threat	0.087	0.043**	0.109	0.043**	0.103	0.041***	0.109	0.043***	0.117	0.051**
Democracy	-0.005	0.005	-0.003	0.005	-0.001	0.005	-0.003	0.005	-0.005	0.004
Capability Ratio	0.059	0.037*	0.076	0.037**	0.075	0.034**	0.075	0.037**	0.076	0.029***
Contiguity	0.323	0.507	0.335	0.491	0.189	0.492	0.366	0.493	0.438	0.592
Selection	-0.135	0.267	-0.135	0.268	-0.042	0.261	-0.163	0.263	-0.188	0.388
Constant	0.045	0.022**	0.036	0.022*	0.039	0.027	0.037	0.022	0.031	0.011***
N	1666		1536		1536		1525		1532	
Wald test	498.88(8)		439.82(9)		439.82(9)		436.06(9)		287.17(9)	
Rho					0.225				0.289	

Notes: All tests are two-tailed, except for those on expectations, D2LP, and shared threat, which are one-tailed. FD represent the first difference estimator and includes a random effect. GLS represents the Baltagi and Wu (1999) model, where rho is the estimated autocorrelation coefficient. 2SLS represents the two-stage least square estimate where past behavior is considered endogenous and its past value plus all other variables are used as instruments. Finally, the GEE model is a population averaged generalized estimating equation that controls for first order autocorrelation.

*p < .10 **p < .05 ***p < .001

The greater the conflict received from a rival, the less likely is cooperation and de-escalation. Both of the relationships are supported in all three models. Each coefficient is significant at the 0.001 level for a two-tailed test.[8]

Also, the greater the shared threat faced by two rivals the less likely is escalation, and the greater the likelihood of de-escalation. Specifically, if the rivals face a growing external threat (from being even to doubling their own capabilities) the equilibrium cooperation level is expected to increase by 0.134 on the WEIS scale. The effect of this shared threat is significant in all three models at the 0.05 level for a one-tailed test.

Militarized Interstate Disputes

When we turn to an analysis of MIDs in table 7, the support for the dynamic two-level model continues. The dynamic two-level pressure index was significant in each case, and in the predicted direction. An increase in information centralization mechanisms from 0 to 3 in the face of high expected costs increases the odds of initiating a militarized dispute with a rival by a factor of 1.67, holding all other variables constant ($p < 0.01$ for a one-tailed test). The relationship remains significant (at the 0.01 level) when a Weibull model (model 3, table 7) is estimated.[9] Paralleling the results for the conflict/cooperation scale, fewer information-centralization mechanisms and high expected future costs significantly decrease the risk of escalation.

Other results also support the previous findings. The greater the shared threat between two states the less likely is escalation. A doubling of a shared threat faced by a state in a rivalry reduces the risk of initiating a militarized dispute by a factor of 2.01, holding all other variables constant.

---

8. The past behavior coefficient in each of the models is negative because the first differenced data is utilized. When we transform the conflict/cooperation scores into levels algebraically, a one unit increase in past conflict leads to an increase of 0.667 in conflict above the status quo equilibrium conflict level (see Mills 1990). Intuitively, the negative coefficient on the "change" data represents that each successive change, after the initial "shock," is smaller and in a different direction than the previous change. At its limit, these changes converge to a new equilibrium.

9. I also estimated an exponential model with similar results.

Table 7

Hazard results for dynamic two-level pressures and conflict/MIDs

	Cox—Model 1		Cox—Model 2		Weibull—Model 3	
	HR	SE	HR	SE	HR	SE
Expectations	0.823	0.149	0.470	0.125***	0.623	0.092***
D2LP			1.478	0.204***	1.226	0.098***
Shared Threat	0.886	0.076*	0.893	0.071*	0.926	0.070
Democracy	1.006	0.021	1.014	0.022	1.021	0.015
Capability Ratio	1.240	0.197	1.232	0.190	1.046	0.132
Contiguity	1.168	0.457	1.390	0.480	0.986	0.209
Selection	0.825	0.228	0.797	0.192	0.899	0.139
One Prev. Disp.					2.760	3.419[1]
Two Prev. Disp.					1.132	1.843[1]
Three+ Prev. Disp.					3.332	3.410[1]
N	1934		1934		1934	
Wald test	6.76(6)		15.34(7)		22.93(10)	

Notes: All tests are two-tailed, except for those on expectations, D2LP, and shared threat, which are one-tailed. Cox represents the Cox proportional hazard model. Weibull represents the Weibull parametric hazard model. In all of the models the coefficients are reported in hazard ratio (HR) form. All results stratified by the number of previous disputes.
[1]These variables do have significantly different shape parameters, meaning that the relationship between time and escalation is contingent on past conflict. Therefore, one should not conclude that past sequences do not influence escalation propensities.
*p < .10 **p < .05 ***p < .001

As in the event-data model, the censored hazard models show limited signs of selection effects. The probability of selection is negatively related to the outbreak of a MID, but the relationship is not statistically significant. The data provide only weak evidence for the presence of unmeasured heterogeneity that makes selection less (more) likely, and also makes militarized interstate disputes more (less) probable. One possible explanation, if future research were to confirm this relationship, is that an asymmetric dyad will not get involved in rivalry, but if it had, escalation would become more likely, as the stronger state would attack. For example, Djibouti bowed to pressure from a stronger Ethiopia in the 1970s concerning railroad and trade routes, rather than pressing the issues (see Laitan and Samatar 1987).

Control Variables

Of the control variables, few had consistent and significant effects on escalation and de-escalation. Only capability ratios remained significant in both sets of analyses. However, the substantive conclusions from the conflict/cooperation models and the MID initiation models were contradictory. Capability dominance was predicted to increase cooperation but also the risk of a militarized dispute. These results call for future research and more complex specifications when predicting rivalry behavior. Colaresi and Thompson (2002) have shown that the frame of rivalry can change the relationship between many independent variables and conflict propensities, and this may be the case with the present inconsistent results.[10]

Rivalry Dynamics over Time

As explained above, the theory suggests that rivalries facing dynamic two-level pressures should follow a different course from other rivalry types. I test this expectation by estimating the trend in rivalry conflict and cooperation over time, contingent on dynamic two-level pressures and random inter-dyad variation. Table 8 lists the results of this mixed-effects model. It is apparent that the interaction between time and dynamic two-level pressures is significant at the 0.05 level (for a one-tailed test), and that the relationship is negative. Rivalries with low dynamic two-level pressures tend to increase cooperation slightly over the course of a rivalry. Conversely, the opposite trend is shown in high dynamic two-level pressure rivalries, where conflict increases as the rivalry endures, supporting the "dynamic" nature of the hypothesized relationships.

10. Substantively similar results for all variables were estimated when conflict was aggregated quarterly and when the conflict and cooperation scores were separated.

Table 8

Mixed-effects interaction between rivalry duration and dynamic two-level pressures (conflict-cooperation scale)

	Mixed-Effects (HLM)	
	Coef	*SE*
Past Behavior[a]	0.602	0.027***
Target Behavior[a]	0.021	0.032
Shared Threat	0.041	0.024*
Democracy	-0.018	0.010*
Capabilty Ratio	0.048	0.097
Alliance	0.072	0.045
Contiguity	-0.036	0.055
Constant	-0.042	0.107
Rivalry Duration[a]	0.006	0.002**
Rivalry Duration * D2-LP	-0.004	0.001***
Selection[a]	-0.024	0.049
Variance Components		
Intercept(RE)		0.175***
Past Behavior(RE)		0.029***
Target Behavior(RE)		0.034***
Rivalry Duration(RE)		0.003***
Level-1 Variance		0.369

RE: Random effect
[a]Level-1 variables; all others level-2 variables
*$p < .10$ **$p .05$ ***$p < .001$

Conclusion

The results of the present analysis support the observable implications of the dynamic two-level pressure model. Information-centralization mechanisms interact with high future expected costs of rivalry to make escalation in the form of more conflict and a greater probability of initiating a militarized dispute more likely. Conversely, fewer information-centralization institutions and a pessimistic future outlook make de-escalation and cooperation between rivals more likely. These results are significant even when unit-specific effects are included, possible selection bias is corrected, and the complex correlation structure of the data is modeled (the mixed effects).

Additionally, the conflict/cooperation analysis shows that past behavior, as well as actions received from an adversary, were important predictors of escalation and de-escalation. Past conflict makes future conflict more likely, while conflictual behavior from a rival elicits a like response. Finally, the importance of a rival's threat environment is highlighted by the findings relating de-escalation and shared threat. If both states have a common enemy, the probability of escalating a dispute or increasing conflictual actions decreases. This finding was robust to estimation technique also.

8 Conclusion

THE DYNAMICS of international rivalry and war evolve out of the interaction between international and domestic policy arenas. Neither level of analysis dominates this political system. International actions and reactions or pure power calculations explain little of rivalry behavior in isolation. Egyptian forces did not perceive a capability advantage in 1968 but still pressed the war of attrition. Somalia was actually in a stronger international position in 1974 than in 1977, yet waited three years before launching the Ogaden offensive. China and the United States surely reacted to each other's international behaviors, but what is left unexplained is the significant deviations such as the Korean War, the Taiwan Strait crises, and Nixon's trip to Beijing.

These deviations are explained by rivalry outbidding, future expectations, and opportunities for escalation. External threats from a rival reinforce and spur domestic bellicosity. For example, Nasser viewed starting a war of attrition with Israel as politically more beneficial than cooperating with Israel. As long as Barre's continued rule relied on perpetuating claims on the Ogaden, he committed scarce funds into competing with Ethiopia. Yet the publicly perceived level of threat depends on what information is released. Therefore, we saw the domestic benefits of open debate and contestation in early Somali, Israeli, and U.S. rivalry policy. In general, a higher level of external threat and pressure was needed to generate support for conflict in these cases. Although outbidders were intermittently successful in democracies, their political appeal was limited. The greater scope of information-centralization mechanisms in Barre's Somalia, Egypt, and China opened perverse opportunities and incentives for threat

231

inflation. In many of these cases, the leaders themselves became powerful outbidders.

Changes in the international environment and shifting alliances played a role in all three rivalries analyzed in the previous case studies. Barre was shocked when the Soviet Union chose to back Ethiopia in 1977. The fear of superpower intervention at various times constrained both Egyptian and Israeli actions. The Camp David Accords may not have been possible without U.S. security guarantees. The Chinese alliance with Russia helped perpetuate the Sino-American rivalry in the 1950s, while Chinese-Soviet rivalry in the late 1960s served as motivation for cooperation between Beijing and Washington in the early 1970s. It is the intersection of high and low politics, rather than merely the international or domestic alone, that imbues the sheep and bear peregrinations discussed in the introduction with their escalatory potential.

Domesticating International Relations

Recently, Bueno de Mesquita (2002) has argued that scholars should analyze international politics as part and parcel of domestic politics. He notes that international outcomes are "chosen" by leaders who are situated in domestic institutions, and that these institutions profoundly influence the foreign policy calculations. I have spent a good part of this book analyzing and arguing for the importance of domestic variables. The MOD clan in Somalia influenced Barre's decisions to pursue the Ogaden and rivalry with Ethiopia to the detriment of the country's economy and other international objections. But it is hasty, at best, to view international "policy" just as another domestic policy arena, like welfare, taxes, land reform, or the like.

There are several important and distinct differences between international and domestic policy decisions that make a replication of public policy models in international politics research inefficient and ineffectual. First, in democracies, the citizenry plays a role in monitoring and sometimes post hoc punishing decision-making elites. Yet this punishment and monitoring presupposes information on which to make decisions. It is not just that people tend to care less about international affairs (though they do) than domestic policy, but that the flow of immediate information to citizens is controlled to a unique degree by the very elites being held accountable for their decisions.

If people were merely apathetic but could learn what they wanted, international politics would be similar to other low-salience issues such as subsidies for apple growers in Washington. However the control of information for "national security" purposes, as well as the perverse incentives elites may have to misinform or fail to inform the citizenry or other competing elites, makes international politics distinct. Minimally, the effect of information-centralization mechanisms like executive privilege and classified information suggest divergent international and domestic policy dynamics in the short term.

Another basic difference between domestic and international theories of politics is that the international realm has no ultimate arbiter of last resort. In domestic politics, there is usually an institutional body that has a monopoly on the use of legitimate force, usually a government. No such player exists in international interactions. Both the United Nations and the International Court of Justice rely on states themselves to provide the policing power. The lack of an arbiter of last resort, short of war, makes pure legislative bargaining models inappropriate for the direct study of USSR-U.S. relations during the Cuban missile crisis and the like.

Domestic politics plays an important role in international outcomes. Leaders want to stay in office. Institutions affect the number and standing of those making the decisions. Armies must be mobilized to fight. Taxes must be levied to support an army. However, none of these things happen in isolation from other international factors.

Most important, a focus purely on domestic politics misses the dynamic interaction between international actions and national reactions. Democracies may indeed be more pacific than other types of dyads; however, strong external threats can both decrease democracy levels within a state (Colaresi and Thompson 2003) and increase the probability of public support for escalation in the near future. In Somalia, a newborn democracy turned toward dictatorship in 1969 as Mogadishu's high threat burden persisted. In Korea, U.S. intervention was domestically popular at least in part because of the public perception of intense communist threats in the region. Additionally, democracy did not prevent Israel or the United States from perpetuating conflicts with a number of adversaries throughout the middle to late twentieth century. The de-escalatory value of democracy depends on the presence or absence of other international factors. For example, strong parallel threats emanating from Moscow lead to Nixon's visit to China. Security decrees from the United States helped alleviate Israeli (and Egyptian) insecurity at Camp David. Democracies and autocracies have equally strong motivations to avoid being caught unaware, attacked, and conquered.

What are needed, and what this book has attempted to identify, are clear linkages between the levels of analysis. Domestic and international theories of conflict and war need to be subsumed and integrated. Current theory highlights a litany of variables, from asymmetric capability ratios to zero growth rates. Yet these variables interact and suppress each other in complex ways. The interconnections need further exploration.

Toward this end, dynamic two-level pressure theory can be applied to a number of related questions. For example, one might expect the duration of wars to be related to expectations about the future as well as domestic constraints. Also, the confluence of dynamic two-level pressures in a rivalry may greatly enhance the probability of rivalry termination. Alternatively, some other forces in addition to these pressures may be necessary to move a rivalry from de-escalation to termination.

Multilevel pressures could also provide important intervening variables for existing theories. Considerable emphasis has been given to the constraints that democratic institutions place on leaders. While this attention has spawned important insights into the behavior of some states, other related processes have received less attention. One of the constraints on elites in democracies is the empowerment of the citizenry. Through education, open contestation, press freedoms, and the decentralization of information, foreign policy decision makers are robbed of propaganda tools.

Pressure from the outside world, as well as the internal workings of states, affects the probability of war. A focus on the interaction between democracy, press freedoms, and external threat may provide a more thorough explanation of not just conflict propensities, but also the growing trend toward democratization in the world (see Van Belle 2000a and Finel and Lord 2000). In addition, the initiation and volatility of arms races may be exacerbated by dual and overlapping domestic and international pressures. While Diehl and Crescenzi (1998) found that rivalry mediates arms racing, high dynamic two-level pressures make an arms race more likely.

Moreover, arms racing could be framed as an attempt by one rival to pry open an opportunity for escalation. In this case, a pessimistic future outlook, a mobilized domestic arena, and a lack of opportunity might start an arms race, as one country attempts to create an opportunity while the other continues to deter. Finally, it is possible that dynamic two-level pressures could play a similar role within civil war situations. The closer the civil combatants approximate states in military capacity and leadership selection, the greater the applicability of the theory.

Sequences, Dynamics, and Expectations

Other questions relating to the dynamics and sequences of interactions over time arise as a result of merging domestic and international rivalry theories. Quantitative research in international relations has controlled for "time dependence" and complex autoregressive processes. The reasons those dynamics are present have received considerably less attention. Why is there persistence in international interaction? Does it matter if a dispute or war occurs early in a dyad's history as opposed to late? This analysis has paid particular attention to the dynamics and sequences of events over time.

When a leader decides to court domestic opinion for bellicose rivalry policies, future decisions will be constrained by this choice. For example, Barre's decision to base his rule on the claims to the Ogaden made reconciliation with Ethiopia in 1975 unlikely, even in the face of droughts, famine, and poverty. The previous inflation of Ethiopian threats to Somalia's national pride and territory reduced Barre's choices in 1977 and eventually helped bring about the Ogaden war. Similarly, Nasser's hands were tied by his own domestic and inter-Arab outbidding. In Asia, Mao found it useful to trumpet the "imperialism" of the United States throughout the 1950s and 1960s. Eventually, it took a tectonic shift in superpower rivalries to alter the competitive momentum in the Sino-American rivalry.

These mobilized domestic arenas changed the course of future events. Had Barre decided not to pursue the Ogaden and disbanded the MOD coalition, it is more likely that the famines and droughts of the 1970s and early 1980s would have been met by decreased rather than increased arms expenditures. Parallel, although not identical, changes may have diminished conflict between the United States and China.

Not only has the past influenced future decisions, but expectations of the future provide powerful motivations for change and continuity in rivalry interactions. There are numerous formal models that highlight the effect of the "shadow of the future" on international interactions. However, few case studies and theories have carefully analyzed the role expectations play in international politics. Work by McGinnis and Williams (2001) as well as Li and Sacko (2002) point to important ways of further exploring decision makers' projections.

By using the past as a guide to identifying expectations, the new and surprising can be isolated and tested. Specifically, events that are surprising and unexpected can serve as intervention points for pre–post testing. This testing can be done statistically or through case-study methodology. The past informs the present and future. There is likely to be further meaningful analytical leverage gained from treating international politics as dynamic.

An Agenda for Future Research

An emphasis on dynamics, sequences, and the interaction between domestic and international politics calls for new measures, data, and historical research that capture these concepts. Most obviously, the lack of a large-scale database on cooperative events to juxtapose with militarized interstate disputes impedes theory testing. A simple-conflict or no-conflict measure collapses the processes of maintenance and de-escalation, ignoring some potentially significant differences. A string of zeros preceded by one dispute could mean either maintenance or de-escalation. If a researcher wants to understand the sequence of conflict, cooperation, and maintenance in rivalry, the presence or absence of crises are only one pixel within the picture. The puzzle cannot be solved before the pieces are taken out of the box or, in this case, manufactured.

Preexisting libraries of international conflict need to be cross-referenced with information on domestic outbidding and expectations of the future. The interaction between domestic and international politics calls for better public opinion data on foreign threats. Even the most complete data sources on the cold war do not offer consistent questions and answers over long periods of time. A standard and long running opinion poll, measuring, for example, Indian and Pakistani perceptions of their rivalry, would be very helpful in understanding the dynamic of conflict there. Does public opinion lead or follow threats made by elites? Does the rally-'round-the-flag effect differ cross-sectionally? Only when data collection efforts can supply the necessary information will these types of dynamic and multilevel questions be answered.

Data on outbidding could be collected through standardized public opinion polls conducted regularly in hot spots around the globe, for example the Gallup series of questions on U.S.-Soviet relations that contains only intermittent information for 1945–90 (see Page and Shapiro 1992). This information could be augmented with content analysis of political speeches from the foreign policy leadership and potential outbidders. When the distribution of distrust and conflict among the populace, as well as the elites, is measured, the dangerous ebbs and flows in rivalry outbidding can be studied in depth.

Finally, more information on trends in economic and security situations, rather than mere static year-by-year analyses, has the potential to aid in the identification of changing expectations within strategic rivalries. The construction of a library of dynamic two-level pressures for ongoing and past rivalries will allow for both increased testing of the interaction between domestic and international variables on conflict/cooperation and more opportunities to build early warning conflict systems to monitor existing conflicts.

Minimizing War

Unlike many other theories of war and peace, the dynamic two-level pressure theory does not promise an end to war or conflict. Several centuries ago, Immanuel Kant (1949) spelled out a program to create perpetual peace. Building on Kant, the democratic peace research program suggests that a world populated only by democracies can potentially relegate wars to the dustbin of history (Russett 1993). More broadly, Mueller (1989) has suggested that war has become subrationally unthinkable. Although the obsolescence of war is relegated to major powers at present, the future could hold the possibility for global peace.

On the other hand, the argument presented in this book suggests that the causes of war (a mobilized domestic constituency, a pessimistic future outlook, and a military opportunity to change the status quo) are likely to continue operating well into the future. Real goal incompatibilities exist in the international realm and feed domestic fear and insecurity. Even the most democratic of governments are designed to maintain, at least temporarily, the foreign policy information asymmetries that make threat inflation and outbidding possible. Similarly, economic depressions and inhospitable international climates are unlikely to disappear around the world. Even in a progressive world with rising global development and decreasing great-power war, short-term pessimism is possible and probably inevitable. Even the rising East Asian tigers of the 1980s suffered a deep financial crisis and descending fortunes. The outlook in the United States turned pessimistic after the events of September 11, 2001. Natural disasters and the uneven pattern of military and political innovation around the globe further ensure the immortality of pessimism (see Thompson and Modelski 1999).

Yet this story is not entirely devoid of a happy ending. Although states may always desire to alter the status quo, an understanding of multilevel rivalry pressures suggests several strategies for minimizing the chances that this policy change will involve escalation and war. First and foremost, domestic foreign policy institutions can be designed to reverse political outbidding incentives. Although a competent foreign policy may not be possible without some information-centralization mechanism (Colaresi 2005), both the ability and the payoffs for expanding information asymmetries can be institutionally limited. Government-sponsored information-leveling mechanisms can take the form of legal protections for opposition movements, free speech and press, and whistleblowers. In addition, institutional checks on the executive, including judicial and legislative oversight, can provide the public with independent sources of foreign policy information.

The routine release of foreign policy information can undercut outbidding behavior. For example, freedom of information laws can ensure that, while the executive has control of foreign policy information for some set period of time, eventually the public will learn what that information was and whether the leader was acting in the sincere national interest. Competitive elections and political parties allow informed citizens to punish leaders or their parties for threat inflation. In many ways, this suggests a republican antidote to the endemic problem of outbidding and threat inflation (Colaresi 2005).

These republican institutional forms will not eradicate war, or even suffocate all threat inflation. Yet republican mechanisms, when compared to their autocratic counterparts (punishment of opposition, control of press, lack of routine information release, high leadership turnover costs) provide incentives for leaders to report threat assessments sincerely. If all wars are not unavoidable, some may be. Democratic governments, with their greater diffusion of information, decrease the incentives for escalation and conflict when de-escalation and peace are viable alternatives. Although sheep will wander, snow will fall, and bears will climb, one can hope that an understanding of the pressures that drive these situations from the mundane toward the malign can empower both citizens and leaders to avoid unnecessary death and destruction.

WORKS CITED

INDEX

Works Cited

Accinelli, Robert. 1996. *Crisis and Commitment: United States Policy Toward Taiwan, 1950–1955*. Chapel Hill: Univ. of North Carolina Press.

Achen, Chistopher. 1986. *The Statistical Analysis of Quasi-Experiments*. Berkeley: Univ. of California Press.

Africa Research Bulletin. 1977. Exeter, U.K.: Africa Research Ltd. Mar. 15.

Albrecht-Carrié, R. 1958. *A Diplomatic History of Europe: Since the Congress of Vienna*. New York: Harper.

Allison, Graham, and Philip Zelikow. 1999. *Essence of Decision: Explaining the Cuban Missile Crisis*. 2d ed. New York: Longman.

Avi-Hai, A. 1974. *Ben-Gurion, State Builder: Principles and Pragmatism, 1948–1963*. New York: Halsted Press.

Azar, Edward E. 1993. "Conflict and Peace Data Bank (COPDAB), 1948–1978." Computer file. Ann Arbor, Mich.: Inter-university Consortium for Political and Social Research.

Azar, Edward E., and Thomas N. Havener. 1976. "Discontinuities in the Symbolic Environment: A Problem in Scaling." *International Interactions* 2, no. 4:231–46.

Azar, Edward E., and Thomas J. Sloan. 1975. "Dimensions of Interaction: A Source Book for the Study of the Behavior of 31 Nations from 1948 Through 1973." Paper presented at the International Studies Association meeting, Pittsburgh, Pa.

Baldwin, David, ed. 1993. *Neorealism and Neoliberalism: The Contemporary Debate*. New York: Columbia Univ. Press.

Baltagi, Badi H., and Ping X. Wu. 1999. "Unequally Spaced Panel Data Regressions with AR(1) Disturbances." *Econometric Theory* 15, no. 6:814–23.

Banks, Arthur S. 2000. *Cross National Time Series Data Archive*. Binghamton: SUNY Binghamton. Dataset.

Bar-Siman-Tov, Yaacov. 1987. *Israel, the Superpowers, and the War in the Middle East*. New York: Praeger.

Bennett, D. Scott. 1997. "Measuring Rivalry Termination, 1816–1992." *Journal of Conflict Resolution* 41:227–54.

———. 1998. "Integrating and Testing Models of Rivalry Termination." *American Journal of Political Science* 42:1200–32.

Bennett, D. Scott, and Allan Stam. 2000. "EUGene: A Conceptual Manual." *International Interactions* 26 no. 1: 179–204.

———. 2003. *The Behavioral Origins of War.* Ann Arbor: Univ. of Michigan Press.

Bennett, D. Scott, and Timothy Nordstrom. 2000. "Foreign Policy Substitutability and Internal Economic Problems in Enduring Rivalries." *Journal of Conflict Resolution* 44:33–52.

Berend, Ivan T. 1998. *Decades of Crisis: Central and Eastern Europe Before World War II.* Berkeley: Univ. of California Press.

Bergmeier, Horst J. P., and Rainer E. Lotz, eds. 1997. *Hitler's Airwaves: The Inside Story of Nazi Radio Broadcasting and Propaganda Swing.* New Haven: Yale Univ. Press.

Bollen, Kenneth A. 2001. "Cross-National Indicators of Liberal Democracy, 1950–1990." Computer file. Ann Arbor, Mich.: Inter-university Consortium for Political and Social Research.

Box-Steffensmeier, Janet M., and Christopher J. W. Zorn. 2000. "Duration Models with Repeated Events." Unpublished manuscript.

Brecher, Michael. 1972. *The Foreign Policy System of Israel.* New Haven, Conn.: Yale Univ. Press.

———. 1974. *Decisions in Israel's Foreign Policy.* London: Oxford Univ. Press.

Brecher, Michael, with Benjamin Geist. 1980. *Decisions in Crisis: Israel 1967 and 1973.* Berkeley: Univ. of California Press.

Brecher, Michael, and Jonathan Wilkenfeld. 1997. *A Study of Crisis.* Ann Arbor: Univ. of Michigan.

Bremer, Stuart A. 1993. "Advancing the Scientific Study of War." In *The Process of War,* edited by Stuart A. Bremer and Thomas Cusack, 1–33. Philadelphia: Gordon and Breach.

Brockner, Joel, and Jeffrey Z. Rubin. 1985. *Entrapment in Escalating Conflicts: A Social Psychological Analysis.* New York: Springer-Verlag.

Brown, Seyom. 1968. *The Faces of Power: Constancy and Change in United States Foreign Policy from Truman to Johnson.* New York: Columbia Univ. Press.

Brzoska, Michael, and Frederic S. Pearson. 1994. *Arms and Warfare: Escalation, De-escalation, Negotiation.* Columbia: Univ. of South Carolina Press.

Bueno de Mesquita, Bruce. 2002. "Domestic Politics and International Relations." *International Studies Quarterly* 46, no. 1:1–9.

Burns, E. L. M. 1969. *Between Arab and Israeli.* Beirut: Institute of Palestinian Studies.

Butow, R. J. C. 1961. *Tojo and the Coming War.* Princeton, N.J.: Princeton Univ. Press.

Campbell, Charles Soutter. 1980. *The Anglo-American Understanding.* Westport, Conn.: Greenwood Press.

Chan, Steve. 1997. "In Search of Democratic Peace: Problems and Promise." *Mershon International Studies Review* 41, no. 1:59–91.

Chang, Gordon H. 1988. "JFK, China, and the Bomb." *Journal of American History* 74, no. 4:1287–310.

———. 1990. *Friends and Enemies: The United States, China, and the Soviet Union.* Stanford, Calif.: Stanford Univ. Press.

Chang, Gordon H., and He Di. 1993. "The Absence of War in the U.S.-China Confrontation over Quemoy and Matsu in 1954–1955: Contingency, Luck, or Deterrence." *American Historical Review* 98:1500–24.

Chen Jiang. 1994. *China's Road to the Korean War, 1950–1953.* New York: Columbia Univ. Press.

———. 2001. *Mao's China and the Cold War.* Chapel Hill: Univ. of North Carolina Press.

Christensen, Thomas. 1996. *Useful Adversaries: Grand Strategy, Domestic Mobilization, and Sino-American Conflict, 1947–1958.* Princeton, N.J.: Princeton Univ. Press.

Cioffi-Revilla, Claudio. 1998. "The Political Uncertainty of Interstate Rivalries: A Punctuated Equilibrium Model." In *The Dynamics of Enduring Rivalries,* edited by Paul Diehl, 64–97. Ann Arbor: Univ. of Michigan Press.

Colaresi, Michael P. 2000. "Shocks to the System: Great Power Rivalries and the Leadership Long Cycle." Paper presented at the Annual Midwestern Political Science Association meeting, Chicago, Ill.

———. 2001. "As Time Goes By: A Dynamic Analysis of the Level, Trend, and Variance of Rivalry Interactions." Paper presented at the Annual Midwestern Political Science Association meeting Chicago, Ill.

———. 2004. "When Doves Cry: Leadership Tenure and Unreciprocated Cooperation." *American Journal of Political Science* 48, no. 3:555–70.

———. 2005. "The Secrecy Dilemma in World Politics: Information, Institutions and Foreign Policy." Unpublished manuscript, Michigan State Univ.

Colaresi, Michael, and William R. Thompson. 2000. "Strategic Rivals, Protracted Conflict, and Crisis Behavior." Unpublished manuscript.

———. 2001. "The Economic Development–Democratization Relationship: Does the Outside World Matter?" Unpublished manuscript.

———. 2002. "Hot Spots or Hot Hands?: Serial Crises, Escalating Risks, and Strategic Rivalry." *Journal of Politics* 64, no. 4:1175–98.

———. 2003. "The Democracy–Economic Development Nexus: Does the Outside World Matter?" *Comparative Political Studies* 36, no. 4:381–403.

Cold War International History Project Bulletin. 1995. Washington, D.C.: Woodrow Wilson International Center for Scholars. Issue 6/7, 5.

Conroy, Hillary. 1955. "Japanese Nationalism and Expansionism." *American Historical Review* 60, no. 4: 818–29.

Conroy, Hillary, and H. Wray. 1990. *Pearl Harbor Reexamined: Prologue to the Pacific War.* Honolulu: Univ. of Hawaii Press.

Copeland, Dale. 2000. *The Origins of Major Wars.* Ithaca, N.Y.: Cornell Univ. Press.

Cumings, Bruce, ed. 1983. *Child of Conflict: The Korean-American Relationship, 1943–1953.* Seattle: Univ. of Washington Press.

———. 1997. "Feeding the North Korea Myths." *Nation,* Sept. 29.

Davis, Darren W., and Brian D. Silver. 2004. "Civil Liberties vs. Security in the Context of the Terrorist Attacks on America." *American Journal of Political Science* 48, no. 1:28–46.

Dawisha, Adeed. 1976. *Egypt in the Arab World: The Elements of Foreign Policy.* London: Macmillan.

Dayan, M. 1966. *Diary of the Sinai Campaign.* Jerusalem: Steimatzky's.

Deac, Wil. 1996. "The Rise of Militaristic Nationalism Led Japan Down the Road to Pearl Harbor and World War II." *World War II* 11, no. 4:20–24.

Diehl, Paul, and Mark Crescenzi. 1998. "Reconfiguring the Arms Race-War Debate." *Journal of Peace Research* 35, no. 1:111–18.

Diehl, Paul, and Gary Goertz. 2000. *War and Peace in International Rivalry.* Ann Arbor: Univ. of Michigan Press.

Dixon, William J. 1994. "Democracy and the Peaceful Settlement of International Conflict." *American Political Science Review* 88, no. 1:14–32.

Doran, Charles F. 2000. "Confronting the Principles of the Power Cycle: Changing System Structure, Expectations, and War." In *Handbook of War Studies II,* edited by Manus I. Midlarsky, 332–70. Ann Arbor: Univ. of Michigan Press.

Eastman, Lloyd. 1974. *The Abortive Revolution: China under Nationalist Rule, 1927–1937.* Cambridge, Mass.: Harvard Univ. Press.

Eban, Abba. 1979. "Camp David: The Unfinished Business." *Foreign Affairs* 57, no. 2.

Eisenberg, Laura, and Neil Caplan. 1998. *Negotiating Arab-Israeli Peace: Patterns, Problems, and Possibilities.* Bloomington: Indiana Univ. Press.

Eisenhower, Dwight D. 1963. *Mandate for Change, 1953–1956.* Vol. 1 of *The White House Years.* New York: Doubleday.

Elbedour, Salman, and David T. Bastien. 1997. "Identity Formation in the Shadow of Conflict." *Journal of Peace Research* 34, no. 2:217–32.

El-Gamasy, Mohamed Abdel Ghani. 1993. *The October War: Memoirs of Field Marshal El-Gamasy of Egypt.* Trans. Gillian Potter, Nadra Morcos, and Rosetee Frances. Cairo: American Univ. of Cairo Press.

Esherick, Joseph. 1995. "Ten Theses on the Chinese Revolution." *Modern China* 21, no. 1:45–76.

Esman, Milton J. 1994. *Ethnic Politics*. Ithaca: Cornell Univ. Press.

Farer, Tom. 1976. *War Clouds on the Horn of Africa: The Widening Storm*. 2d. ed. New York: Carnegie Endowment.

Fearon, James D. 1994. "Domestic Political Audiences and the Escalation of International Disputes." *American Political Science Review* 88, no. 3:577–93.

Feis, H. 1950. *The Road to Pearl Harbor*. Princeton, N.J.: Princeton Univ. Press.

Festinger, Leon. 1957. *A Theory of Cognitive Dissonance*. Evanston, Ill.: Row, Peterson.

Finel, Bernard L., and Kristin M. Lord. 2000. "The Surprising Logic of Transparency." In *Power and Conflict in the Age of Transparency,* edited by Bernard L. Finel and Kristin M. Lord, 137–80. Houndsmills, England: Palgrave.

Fiske, Susan T., and Shelley E. Taylor. 1991. *Social Cognition*. New York: McGraw-Hill.

Gaddis, John Lewis. 1998. *We Now Know: Rethinking Cold War History*. New York: Oxford Univ. Press.

Gazit, Shlomo. 1995. *The Carrot and the Stick: Israel's Policy in Judea and Samaria, 1967–68*. Translated by Duevek Danielli; edited by Patrick R. Denker. Washington, D.C.: B'nai B'rith Books.

Gelpi, Christopher. 1997. "Democratic Diversions." *Journal of Conflict Resolution* 41, no. 2:255–83.

George, Alexander. 1979. "Case Studies and Theory Development: The Method of Structured, Focused Comparison." In *Diplomacy: New Approaches in History, Theory and Policy,* edited by Paul G. Lauren, 43–68. New York: Free Press.

Gershoni, Israel. 1981. *The Emergence of Pan-Arabism in Egypt*. Tel Aviv: Shiloah Center for Middle Eastern and African Studies.

Gibbs, David N. 1995. "Secrecy and International Relations." *Journal of Peace Research* 32, no. 2:213–26.

Goertz, Gary, and Paul F. Diehl. 1993. "Enduring Rivalries: Theoretical Constructs and Empirical Patterns." *International Security Quarterly* 37:147–71.

———. 1995. "The Initiation and Termination of Enduring Rivalries: The Impact of Political Shocks." *American Journal of Political Science* 39:30–52.

Goldstein, J. 1992. "A Conflict-Cooperation Scale for WEIS Event Data." *Journal of Conflict Resolution* 36, no. 2:369–85.

Goldstein, J., and J. R. Freeman. 1990. *Three-Way Street: Strategic Reciprocity and World Politics*. Chicago, Ill.: Univ. of Chicago Press.

Goncharov, Sergei N., John W. Lewis, and Xue Litai. 1993. *Uncertain Partners: Stalin, Mao, and the Korean War*. Stanford, Calif.: Stanford Univ. Press.

Gorman, Robert F. 1991. *Political Conflict on the Horn of Africa*. New York: Praeger.

Green, Donald P., Soo Yeon Kim, and David H. Yoon. 2001. "Dirty Pool." *International Organization* 55, no. 2:441–70.

Greenfield, Richard. 1994. "Towards an Understanding of the Somali Factor." In *Conflict and Peace in the Horn of Africa: Federalism and Alternatives,* edited by Peter Woodward and Murray Forsyth, 103–13. Brookfield, Vt.: Dartmouth.

Gross Stein, Janice. 1985. "Calculation, Miscalculation and Conventional Deterrence: The View from Cairo." In *Psychology and Deterrence,* edited by Robert Jervis, Richard Ned Lebow, and Janice Gross Stein, 93–111. Baltimore: Johns Hopkins Univ. Press.

———. 1998. "Image, Identity, and Conflict Resolution." In *Managing Global Chaos: Sources of and Responses to International Conflict,* edited by Chester A. Crocker and Fen Osler Hampson, with Pamala Aall, 93–111. Washington, D.C.: United States Institute of Peace.

Hasou, Tawfig Y. 1985. *The Struggle for the Arab World: Egypt's Nasser and the Arab League.* London: Routledge Press.

Heckman, James. 1976. "The Common Structure of Statistical Models of Truncation, Sample Selection and Limited Dependent Variables, and a Simple Estimator for Such Models." *Annals of Economic and Social Measurement* 5, no. 2:475–92.

Heikal, Mohamed H. 1973. *The Cairo Documents: The Inside Story of Nasser and His Relationship with World Leaders, Rebels, and Statesmen.* New York: Doubleday.

———. 1975. *The Road to Ramadan.* New York: Quadrangle.

———. 1986. *Cutting the Lion's Tail.* London: Andre Deutsch.

Hensel, Paul. 1994. "One Thing Leads to Another: Recurrent Militarized Disputes in Latin America, 1816–1986." *Journal of Peace Research* 31:281–98.

Hensel, Paul R., Gary Goertz, and Paul F. Diehl. 2000. "The Democratic Peace and Rivalries." *Journal of Politics* 62, no. 4:1173–88.

Hermann, Margaret G., and Charles W. Kegley. 1995. "Rethinking Democracy and International Peace." *International Studies Quarterly* 39, no. 4:511–34.

Hermann, Richard K., and Michael P. Fischerkeller. 1995. "Beyond the Enemy Image and Spiral Model: Cognitive-Strategic Research after the Cold War." *International Organization* 49, no. 3: 415–51.

Holcomb, Bonnie K., and Sisai Ibssa. 1990. *The Invention of Ethiopia: The Making of a Dependent Colonial State in Northeast Africa.* Trenton, N.J.: Red Sea Press.

Holsti, Ole. 1996. *Public Opinion and American Foreign Policy.* Ann Arbor: Univ. of Michigan Press.

Hooglund, Eric. 1993. "Government and Politics." In *Somalia: A Country Study* edited by Helen Chapin Metz, 151–78. Washington, D.C.: Library of Congress.

Horowitz, Donald. 1985. *Ethnic Groups in Conflict.* Berkeley: Univ. of California Press.

Hourani, Albert. 1991. *A History of the Arab Peoples*. Cambridge, Mass.: Belknap Press.

Hsiao, Cheng. 1986. *Analysis of Panel Data*. Cambridge: Cambridge Univ. Press.

Huntington, Samuel. 2000. "Try Again: A Reply to Russett, Oneal, and Cox." *Journal of Peace Research* 37, no. 5:609–11.

Huth, Paul K. 1998. *Standing Your Ground: Territorial Disputes and International Conflict*. Ann Arbor: Univ. of Michigan Press.

Ike, N. 1967. *Japan's Decision for War: Records of the 1941 Policy Conferences*. Stanford: Stanford Univ. Press.

Israeli Department of Information. 1960. *Israel's Struggle for Peace*. New York: St. Martin's Press.

Jaggers, Keith, and Ted Robert Gurr. 1995. "Transitions to Democracy: Tracking Democracy's Third Wave with the POLITY III Data." *Journal of Peace Research* 32, no. 6:469–82.

Janis, Irving. 1982. *Groupthink: Psychological Studies of Policy Decisions and Fiascos*. Boston: Houghton Mifflin.

Jervis, Robert. 1976. *Perception and Misperception in International Politics*. Princeton, N.J.: Princeton Univ. Press.

Jervis, Robert, Richard Ned Lebow, and Janice Gross Stein, eds. 1985. *Psychology and Deterrence*. Baltimore, Md.: Johns Hopkins Univ. Press.

Jones, Daniel M., Stuart A. Bremer, and J. David Singer. 1996. "Militarized Interstate Disputes, 1816–1992: Rationale, Coding Rules, and Empirical Patterns." *Conflict Management and Peace Science* 15, no. 2:163–213.

Kant, Immanuel. 1949. "Perpetual Peace." In *The Philosophy of Kant: Immanuel Kant's Moral and Political Writings,* edited by Carl J. Friedrich, 430–76. New York: Random House.

Kaufman, Chaim. 2004. "Threat Inflation and the Failure of the Marketplace of Ideas: The Selling of the Iraq War." *International Security* 29 (summer): 5–48.

Keller, Edmond. 1993. "Government and Politics." In *Ethiopia: A Country Study,* edited by Tom Ofcansky, 189–234. Washington, D.C.: Library of Congress.

Keohane, Robert. 1986. "Realism, Neorealism and the Study of World Politics." In *Neorealism and Its Critics,* edited by Robert Keohane. New York: Columbia Univ. Press.

Kerry, John. 2004. Speech at Temple Univ. Sept. 24. Available at www.vote-smart.org/index.

Khong, Yuen. 1992. *Analogies at War*. Princeton, N.J.: Princeton Univ. Press.

Kim, Kwan Ha. 1975. *China and the U.S.: 1964–72*. Facts on File, New York.

King, Gary. 2001. "Proper Nouns and Methodological Propriety: Pooling Dyads in International Relations Data." *International Organization* 55, no. 2:497–509.

King, Gary, Robert Keohane, and Sidney Verba. 1994. *Designing Social Inquiry.* Princeton, N.J.: Princeton Univ. Press.

Kissinger, Henry A. 1982. *Years of Upheaval.* Boston: Little, Brown.

Kriesberg, Louis. 1992. *International Conflict Resolution: The U.S.-USSR and Middle East Cases.* New Haven, Conn.: Yale Univ. Press.

———. 1998. *Constructive Conflicts: From Escalation to Resolution.* Lanham, Md.: Rowman and Littlefield.

Kusnitz, Leonard A. 1984. *Public Opinion and Foreign Policy: America's China Policy, 1949–1979.* Westport, Conn.: Greenwood Press.

Kydd, Andrew. 1997. "Game Theory and the Spiral Model." *World Politics* 49, no. 3:371–401.

Laitan, David D. 1993. "The Economy." In *Somalia: A Country Study,* edited by Helen Chapin Metz, 119–50. Washington, D.C.: Library of Congress.

Laitin, David D., and Said S. Samatar. 1987. *Somalia: Nation in Search of a State.* Boulder, Colo.: Westview Press.

Lake, David A., and Robert Powell, eds. 1999. *Strategic Choice and International Relations.* Princeton, N.J.: Princeton Univ. Press.

Lake, David A., and Donald Rothchild. 1998. *The International Spread of Ethnic Conflict.* Princeton, N.J.: Princeton Univ. Press.

Laqueur, Walter Zeev. 1968. *The Road to War, 1967: The Origins of the Arab-Israel Conflict.* London: Weidenfeld and Nicolson.

Lebow, Richard Ned. 1981. *Between Peace and War: The Nature of International Crisis.* Baltimore, Md.: Johns Hopkins Univ. Press.

Lebow, Richard Ned, and Janice Gross Stein. 1995. *We All Lost the Cold War.* Princeton, N.J.: Princeton Univ. Press.

Leeds, Brett Ashley. 1999. "Domestic Political Institutions, Credible Commitments, and International Cooperation." *American Journal of Political Science* 43, no. 2:979–1002.

Lefebvre, Jeffrey A. 1991. *Arms for the Horn: U.S. Security Policy in Ethiopia and Somalia, 1953–1991.* Pittsburgh, Pa.: Univ. of Pittsburgh Press.

Lemke, Douglas, and William Reed. 2001. "War and Rivarly among Great Powers." *American Journal of Political Science* 45, no. 2:457–69.

Leng, Russell. 1983. "When Will They Ever Learn: Coercive Bargaining in Recurrent Crises." *Journal of Conflict Resolution* 27:379–419.

———. 1984. "Reagan and the Russians: Crisis Bargaining Beliefs and the Historical Record." *American Political Science Review* 78:338–55.

———. 2000. *Bargaining and Learning in Recurring Crises: The Soviet-American, Egyptian-Isreali, and Indo-Pakistani Rivalries.* Ann Arbor: Univ. of Michigan Press.

Levi, Ariel S., and Glen Whyte. 1997. "A Cross-Cultural Exploration of the Reference Dependence of Crucial Group Decisions under Risk." *Journal of Conflict Resolution* 41, no. 6:792–814.

Levy, Jack S. 1989. "The Diversionary Theory of War: A Critique." In *Handbook of War Studies,* edited by Manus I. Midlarsky, 259–88. London: Unwin-Hyman.

Lewis, I. M. 1991. "The Ogaden and the Fragility of Somali Segmentary Nationalism." In *Conflict in the Horn of Africa,* edited by Georges Nzongola-Ntalaja, 89–96. Atlanta: African Studies Press.

Lewis, Mark A. 1990. "Historical Setting." In *Israel: A Country Study,* edited by Helen Chapin Metz, 1–80. Washington, D.C.: Library of Congress.

Li, Q., and D. H. Sacko. 2002. "The (Ir)Relevance of Militarized Interstate Disputes for International Trade." *International Studies Quarterly* 46, no. 1:11–43.

Long, J. Scott. 1997. *Regression Models for Categorical and Limited Dependent Variables.* Thousand Oaks, Calif.: Sage.

Lorenz, Joseph P. 1990. *Egypt and the Arabs: Foreign Policy and the Search for National Identity.* Boulder, Colo.: Westview Press.

Lowe, Peter. 1986. *The Origins of the Korean War.* London: Longman Press.

Lustick, Ian. 1996. "History, Historiography, and Political Science: Multiple Historical Records and the Problem of Selection Bias." *American Political Science Review* 90, no. 3:605–18.

Mansfield, Edward D., and Jack Snyder. 1995. "Democratization and the Danger of War." *International Security* 20, no. 1:5–39.

Maoz, Zeev. 1984. "Peace by Empire?: Conflict Outcomes and International Stability, 1816–1976." *Journal of Peace Research* 21:227–41.

———. 1996. *Domestic Sources of Global Change.* Ann Arbor: Univ. of Michigan Press.

Maoz, Zeev, and Ben D. Mor. 2002. *Bound By Struggle.* Ann Arbor: Univ. of Michigan Press.

Marcus, Harold G. 1995. *The Politics of Empire: Ethiopia, Great Britain, and the United States, 1941–1974.* Lawrenceville, N.J.: Red Sea Press.

Maxwell, Neville. 1972. *India's China War.* Garden City, N.Y.: Anchor.

May, Ernest. 1973. *Lessons from the Past: The Use and Misuse of History.* New York: Oxford Univ. Press.

———. 1993. *American Cold War Strategy: Interpreting NSC 68.* New York: Bedford/St. Martin's Press.

McClelland, Charles. 1999. "World Event Interaction Survey (WEIS) Project." Computer file. Ann Arbor, Mich.: Inter-university Consortium for Political and Social Research.

McGinnis, Michael D., and John T. Williams. 2001. *Compound Dilemmas: Democracy, Collective Action, and Superpower Rivalry.* Ann Arbor: Univ. of Michigan Press.

Meir, Golda. 1973. *A Land of Our Own: Golda Meir Speaks Out*. London: Weidenfeld and Nicolson.

Meital, Yoram. 1997. *Egypt's Struggle for Peace: Continuity and Change, 1967–1977*. Gainesville: Univ. Press of Florida.

Mills, Terence C. 1990. *Time Series Techniques for Economists*. Cambridge: Cambridge Univ. Press.

Miwa, K. 1975. "Japanese Images of War with the United States." In *Mutual Images: Essays in American-Japanese Relations,* edited by A. Iriye, 115–37. Cambridge, Mass.: Harvard Univ. Press.

Moore, John Norton, ed. 1974. *The Arab-Israeli Conflict*. Vol. 3. Princeton, N.J.: Princeton Univ. Press.

Mor, B. D. 1993. *Decision and Interaction in Crisis: A Model of International Crisis Behavior.* Westport, Conn.: Praeger.

Mueller, John E. 1973. *War, Presidents, and Public Opinion*. New York: Wiley.

Mueller, John E. 1989. *Retreat from Doomsday: The Obsolescence of Major War.* New York: Basic Books.

Neustadt, Richard, and Ernest May. 1986. *Thinking in Time: The Uses of History for Decision Makers*. New York: Free Press.

Nincic, Miroslav. 1989. *Anatomy of Hostility: The U.S.-Soviet Rivalry in Perspective.* San Diego, Calif.: Harcourt Brace Jovanovich.

Nixon, Richard. 1967. "Asia after Vietnam." *Foreign Affairs* 46 (Oct.): 111–25.

Nutting, Anthony. 1972. *Nasser.* New York: Dutton.

Ofcansky, Tom. 1993a. "National Security." In *Ethiopia: A Country Study,* edited by Tom Ofcansky, 235–90. Washington, D.C.: Library of Congress.

———. 1993b. "National Security." In *Somalia: A Country Study,* edited by Helen Chapin Metz, 179–226. Washington, D.C.: Library of Congress.

Ogata, Sadaka. 1964. *Defiance in Manchuria.* Berkeley: Univ. of California Press.

Ostermann, Christian F. 1994/95. "East German Documents on the Sino-Soviet Border Conflict, 1969." *Cold War International History Project Bulletin.* Washington, D.C.: Woodrow Wilson International Center for Scholars.

Ottosen, Rune. 1995. "Enemy Images and the Journalistic Process." *Journal of Peace Research* 32, no. 1:97–113.

Page, Benjamin, and Ian Shapiro. 1992. *The Rational Public: Fifty Years of Trends in Americans' Policy Preferences*. Chicago, Ill.: Univ. of Chicago Press.

Page, Benjamin I., and Robert Y. Shapiro. 1992. *The Rational Public.* Chicago, Ill.: Univ. of Chicago Press.

Peres, Shimon. 1995. *Battling for Peace: Memoirs.* London: Weidenfeld and Nicolson.

Prentice, R. L., B. J. Williams, and A. V. Peterson. 1981. "On the Regression Analysis of Multivariate Failure Time Data." *Biometrika* 68, no. 2:373–79.

Project Solarium Reports. 1953. Box 39, National Security Council Papers 1948–1961, Disaster File Series. Dwight D. Eisenhower Library, Abilene, Kans.

Prozumenschikov, M. Y. 1996. "The Sino-Indian Conflict, the Cuban Missile Crisis, and the Sino-Soviet Split, October 1962: New Evidence from the Russian Archives." *Cold War International History Project Bulletin.* Washington, D.C.: Woodrow Wilson International Center for Scholars.

Przeworski, Adam. 1991. *Democracy and the Market: Political and Economic Reforms in Eastern Europe and Latin America.* Cambridge: Cambridge Univ. Press.

Putnam, R. D. 1988. "Diplomacy and Domestic Politics: The Logic of Two-Level Games. *International Organization* 42:427–60.

Quandt, William B. 1993. *The Peace Process: American Diplomacy and the Arab-Israeli Conflict since 1967.* Washington, D.C.: Brookings Institution.

Rabinovich, Itamar. 1991. *The Road Not Taken: Early Arab-Israeli Negotiations.* New York: Oxford Univ. Press.

Rabushka, A., and K. A. Shepsle. 1972. *Politics in Plural Societies: A Theory of Democratic Instability.* Columbus, Ohio: Merrill.

Rafael, Gideon. 1981. *Destination Peace: Three Decades of Israeli Foreign Policy.* New York: Stein and Day.

Reed, William. 2000. "A Unified Statistical Model of Conflict Onset and Escalation." *American Journal of Political Science* 44, no. 1:84–93.

Reuveny, Rafael, and Heejoon Kang. 1996. "International Trade, Political Conflict/Cooperation, and Granger Causality." *American Journal of Political Science* 40, no. 3:943–70.

Ridgway, Matthew B. 1956. *Soldier: The Memoirs of Matthew B. Ridgway, as Told to Harold H. Martin.* New York: Harper.

Roberts, Geoffrey. 1995. *The Soviet Union and the Origins of the Second World War: Russo-German Relations and the Road to War, 1933–1941.* London: Macmillan.

Rock, S. 1989. *Why Peace Breaks Out: Great Power Rapprochement in Historical Perspective.* Chapel Hill: Univ. of North Carolina Press.

Ross, Marc Howard. 1993. *The Culture of Conflict.* New Haven, Conn.: Yale Univ. Press.

Ross, Robert S. 1995. *Negotiating Cooperation: The United States and China, 1969–1989.* Stanford, Calif.: Stanford Univ. Press.

Rubin, Jeffrey Z., Dean G. Pruitt, and Sung Hee Kim. 1994. *Social Conflict: Escalation, Stalemate and Settlement.* New York: McGraw Hill.

Russett, Bruce M. 1967. "Pearl Harbor: Deterrence Theory and Decision Theory." *Journal of Peace Research* 4:89–106.

———. 1993. *Grasping the Democratic Peace.* Princeton, N.J.: Princeton Univ. Press.

Russett, Bruce M., John R. Oneal, and Michaelene Cox. 2000. "Clash of Civilizations, or Realism and Liberalism Deja Vu? Some Evidence." *Journal of Peace Research* 37, no. 5:583–609.

Russett, Bruce M., and Harvey Starr. 2000. "From Democratic Peace to Kantian Peace: Democracy and Conflict in the International System." In *Handbook of War II Studies,* edited by Manus I. Midlarsky, 93–128. Ann Arbor: Univ. of Michigan Press.

Sachar, Howard M. 1981. *Egypt and Israel.* New York: Richard Marek Publishers.

Sagan, Scott D. 1993. *The Limits of Safety: Organizations, Accidents, and Nuclear Weapons.* Princeton, N.J.: Princeton Univ. Press.

Samatar, Said S. 1993. "The Society and Its Environment." In *Somalia: A Country Study,* edited by Helen Chapin Metz, 55–118. Washington, D.C.: Library of Congress.

Schwab, Peter. 1985. *Ethiopia: Politics, Economics, and Society.* Boulder, Colo.: Lynne Rienner.

Schweller, R. L. 1992. "Domestic Structure and Preventive War." *World Politics* 44, no. 2:235–71.

Shlaim, Avi. 2001. *The Iron Wall: Israel and the Arab World.* New York: Norton.

Shlaim, Avi, and Raymond Tanter. 1978. "Decision Process, Choice, and Consequences: Israel's Deep-Penetration Bombing in Egypt, 1970." *World Politics* 30, no. 4:483–516.

Simmel, George. 1955. *Conflict.* Translated by Kurt F. Wolff. New York: Free Press.

Singer, J. David. 1987. "Reconstructing the Correlates of War Dataset on Material Capabilities of States, 1816–1985." *International Interactions* 14, no. 1:115–32.

Snyder, Jack L. 1989. "International Leverage on Soviet Domestic Change." *World Politics* 42:1–30.

———. 1991. *Myths of Empire: Domestic Politics and International Ambition.* Ithaca: Cornell Univ. Press.

Stoessinger, John. 1993. *Why Nations Go to War.* New York: St. Martin's Press.

Summers, Robert, and Alan Heston. 1991. "The Penn World Table (Mark 5): An Expanded Set of International Comparisons, 1950–1988." *Quarterly Journal of Economics* 106, no. 2:327–68.

Swartz, Marvin. 1985. *The Politics of British Foreign Policy in the Era of Disraeli and Gladstone.* New York: St. Martin's Press.

Telhami, Shibley. 1992. *Power and Leadership in International Bargaining: The Path to the Camp David Accords.* New York: Columbia Univ. Press.

Tetlock, Philip. 1998. "Close-Call Counterfactuals and Belief-System Defenses: I Was Not Almost Wrong But I Was Almost Right." *Journal of Personality and Social Psychology* 75, no. 3:639–53.

Thompson, William R. 1995. "Principal Rivalries." *Journal of Conflict Resolution* 39:195–223.

———. 2001. "Identifying Rivals in World Politics." *International Studies Quarterly* 45, no. 2:557–86.

Thompson, William R., and George Modelski. 1999. *Leading Sectors and World Power: The Coevolution of Global Politics and Economics.* Columbia: Univ. of South Carolina Press.

Thompson, William R., and Richard Tucker. 1998. "A Tale of Two Democratic Peace Critiques." *Journal of Conflict Resolution* 41, no. 3:428–55.

Thorton, Thomas Perry. 1999. "Pakistan: Fifty Years of Insecurity." In *India and Pakistan: The First Fifty Years,* edited by Selig S. Harrison, Paul H. Kreisberg, and Dennis Kux, 170–88. Cambridge: Cambridge Univ. Press.

Tiruneh, Andargachew. 1993. *The Ethiopian Revolution: 1947–1987.* Cambridge: Cambridge Univ. Press.

Tomlinson, Rodney G. 1993. "World Event Interaction Survey (WEIS) Update." Computer file. Annapolis, Md.: United States Naval Academy.

Tsebelis, George. 1991. *Nested Games: Rational Choice in Comparative Politics.* Berkeley: Univ. of California Press.

Turner, John. 1993. "Historical Setting." In *Ethiopia: A Country Study,* edited by Tom Ofcansky, 1–56. Washington, D.C.: Library of Congress.

Tyler, Patrick. 2000. *The Great Wall: Six Presidents and China, an Investigative History.* New York: Century Foundation.

U.S. Defense Dept. 1963. "Harriman Trip to Moscow—Briefing Book, Vol 2." June 20, 1963. Tab D, ACDA, Disarmament Box 265, National Security files 1961–1963, Kennedy Papers. Boston, Mass.: John F. Kennedy Presidential Library.

Van Belle, Douglas A. 2000a. *Press Freedom and Global Politics.* London: Praeger.

Van Belle, Douglas A. 2000b. "Press Freedom and Peace." In *Power and Conflict in the Age of Transparency,* edited by Bernard L. Finel and Kristin M. Lord, 115–35. Houndsmills, England: Palgrave.

Vasquez, John A. 1993. *The War Puzzle.* New York: Cambridge Univ. Press.

———. 1996. "Distinguishing Rivals That Go to War from Those That Do Not: A Quantitative Comparative Case Study of the Two Paths to War." *International Studies Quarterly* 40:531–58.

Vincent, Jack E. 1983. "WEIS vs. COPDAB Correspondence Problems." *International Studies Quarterly* 27, no. 2:160–68.

Walt, Stephen. 1987. *The Origins of Alliances.* Ithaca: Cornell Univ. Press.

Ward, Michael D. 1982. "Cooperation and Conflict in Foreign Policy Behavior." *International Studies Quarterly* 26:87–126.

Weart, Spencer. 1998. *Never at War: Why Democracies Will Not Fight Each Other.* New Haven, Conn.: Yale Univ. Press.

Weathersby 1995/96. "New Russian Documents on the Korean War." In *The Cold*

War in Asia, edited by Chen Jian, 30–40. Washington, D.C.: Woodrow Wilson International Center for Scholars.

Westad, Odd Arne. 1993. *Cold War and Revolution: Soviet-American Rivalry and the Origins of the Chinese Civil War.* New York: Columbia Univ. Press.

———. 1995/96. "Mao on Sino-Soviet Relations." In *The Cold War in Asia,* edited by Chen Jian, 156–69. Washington, D.C.: Woodrow Wilson International Center for Scholars.

———, ed. 1998. "77 Conversations Between Chinese and Foreign Leaders on the Wars in Indochina, 1964–1977." CWIHP working paper no. 22. Washington, D.C.: Woodrow Wilson International Center for Scholars.

Whaley, Barton. 1973. *Codeword Barbarossa.* Cambridge, Mass.: MIT Press.

Whetten, Lawrence L. 1974. *The Canal War: Four-Power Conflict in the Middle East.* Cambridge, Mass.: MIT Press.

Whiting, Allen S. 1960. *China Crosses the Yalu: The Decisions to Enter the Korean War.* New York: Macmillan.

Woodward, Peter. 1996. *The Horn of Africa: State Politics and International Relations.* London: Tauris.

Yaar, Ephraim, and Tamar Hermann. 2000. "The Peace Index." October. Tel Aviv: The Tami Steinmetz Center for Peace Research.

———. 2004. "The Peace Index" October. Tel Aviv: The Tami Steinmetz Center for Peace Research.

Young, Kenneth T. 1968. *Negotiating with the Chinese Communists: The United States Experience, 1953–1967.* New York: McGraw-Hill.

Young, Peyton. 1998. *Individual Strategy and Social Structure: An Evolutionary Theory of Institutions.* Princeton, N.J.: Princeton Univ. Press.

Zagoria, Donald S. 1962. *The Sino-Soviet Conflict, 1956–1961.* Princeton, N.J.: Princeton Univ. Press.

Zhang, Shu Guang. 1992. *Deterrence and Strategic Culture: Chinese-American Confrontations, 1949–1958.* Ithaca: Cornell Univ. Press.

Zorn, Christopher J. W. 2001. "Generalized Estimating Equation Models for Correlated Data: A Review with Applications." *American Journal of Political Science* 45:470–90.

Zubok, Vladislav, and Constantine Pleshakov. 1996. *Inside the Kremlin's Cold War: From Stalin to Khrushchev.* Cambridge, Mass.: Harvard Univ. Press.

Index